Heavy Burdens
on Small Shoulders

Heavy Burdens on Small Shoulders

THE LABOUR OF PIONEER CHILDREN
ON THE CANADIAN PRAIRIES

Sandra Rollings-Magnusson

 THE UNIVERSITY
of ALBERTA PRESS

Published by
The University of Alberta Press
Ring House 2
Edmonton, Alberta, Canada T6G 2E1

Copyright © 2009
Sandra Rollings-Magnusson

LIBRARY AND ARCHIVES CANADA
CATALOGUING IN PUBLICATION

Rollings-Magnusson, Sandra, 1960–
Heavy burdens on small shoulders : the
labour of pioneer children on the
Canadian Prairies / Sandra Rollings-
Magnusson.

Includes bibliographical
references and index.
ISBN 978–0–88864–509–8

1. Pioneer children—Employment
   —Prairie Provinces.
2. Pioneer children—Prairie
   Provinces—Social conditions.
3. Rural families—Prairie
   Provinces—Social conditions.
4. Child labour—Prairie Provinces
   —History.
5. Farm life—Prairie Provinces.
6. Child labour—Prairie Provinces
   —History.
7. Prairie Provinces—Rural
   conditions.
1. Title.

HD6250.C32R64 2008
331.3'18   C2008–903761–8

All rights reserved.
First edition, first printing, 2009.
Printed and bound in Canada by
   Houghton Boston Printers, Saskatoon,
   Saskatchewan.
Copyediting by Leslie Robertson.
Proofreading by Mary Williams.
Indexing by Elizabeth Macfie.

The University of Alberta Press is
committed to protecting our natural
environment. As part of our efforts,
this book is printed on Enviro Paper: it
contains 100% post-consumer recycled
fibres and is acid- and chlorine-free.

The University of Alberta Press
gratefully acknowledges the support
received for its publishing program
from The Canada Council for the Arts.
The University of Alberta Press also
gratefully acknowledges the financial
support of the Government of Canada
through the Book Publishing Industry
Development Program (BPIDP) and from
the Alberta Foundation for the Arts for
its publishing activities.

Canada   Canada Council   Conseil des Arts   Alberta Foundation
          for the Arts   du Canada   for the Arts

"For those who wish to live in idleness, or expect to get rich in some uncertain way without work, the North-West is no place."

—*The North West Farmer* (CPR, 1891, p. 10)

[CONTENTS]

Preface

THIS BOOK DETAILS THE FINDINGS of a study into the role that children's work played in the operation of family farms in the western Canadian prairie region during the period of settlement between 1871 and 1913. I have analyzed the labour performed by children in isolation from other facets of pioneer life and, by intent, have made no effort to provide the complete story of the lives lived by these children of the prairies. Their social interactions, schooling, cultural activities, religious devotions, and forms of entertainment are subjects for another day. However, unlike other texts, here a concentrated effort has been made to take what may be seen as an endless chain of interchangeable and entwined chores and expected duties and to analyze these activities to determine what, if any, contribution such expected and seemingly unremarkable work made to the successful development of the family farming economy in western Canada. This is not to say that a child milking a cow consciously recognized that he or she was contributing to family earnings or to physical survival, or that parents assigned milking duties to a child with the thought that enough time might thereby be freed up to enable ploughing an extra acre of land that year. Digging beneath the surface appearance of actions taken by rote, or as a result of unspoken expectations as a matter of common sense, allows for a greater understanding of the role children played. Analyzing tasks in light of the context in which they were performed and the outcomes generated provides a means of assessing the importance of child labour that is not otherwise available given the lack of any independent data by which such understanding might be reached.

The data used in the study were obtained from writings prepared by pioneer children during or in relation to the study period, such as diaries, memoirs, letters, and poems, together with official records such as census reports. This information expands our knowledge of the child labour involved in farming an undeveloped region where settlers had to overcome numerous geographic, climatic, and financial obstacles if they wished to succeed. Many settlers managed to endure and prosper despite the obstacles that existed, but it is evident that success was dependent on the availability of labour. The technology of the day determined that operations were labour-intensive rather than mechanized and thus created a situation in which children's work could provide value and necessary assistance to the family farm.

Using a sociological approach, this study reveals that children contributed to the operation of family farms in the prairie region for a variety of reasons, not least of which were family and social expectations and their own personal survival. A typology of the work performed by children allows for an analysis of the nature of the contributions made, and divisions by gender and age are discussed for purpose of quantitative analysis. I also note that the economic importance of children's efforts often went unrecognized, as was women's labour on family farms. Given the similar positions of women and children within the economic and power relations of farm families, I argue that the theories developed to explain the role of women as economically invisible farmers can be extended to include farm children within their explanatory reach. In short, the role played by men, and more recently by women, has been noted, but a full understanding of how families survived and how the wheat economy was developed requires that burdens carried on the shoulders of the smallest farm labourers also be taken into consideration.

Acknowledgements

Often, people will ask me why I study the homesteading era and, in particular, the life of prairie farmers. My response is that even though I was born and raised in an urban setting, I grew up with family stories about how my German great-grandparents, Emil and Bertha Kroening, left their home in White Russia at the turn of the century. They were a young married couple who left friends and family behind in the mother country in order to begin a life of opportunity in western Canada. The prospect of being able to own their own land, to live in freedom, free of political and religious purges, and to provide their own children with a positive future motivated them to adapt quickly to their new environment. Emil and Bertha had twenty-one children, all of whom worked on the family farm as soon as they were able to. Their lives were not without hardship. All family members were expected to work hard over the course of the year. As succinctly stated to me by my grandfather, "I was born to be a worker on the farm."

Stories relating to the Rollings's side of the family were also passed down to me. My grandfather, Guy Rollings (born in Prince Edward Island), made the long trek west to Saskatchewan to claim his homestead land. Unfortunate circumstances, such as choosing land located in the Palliser Triangle, produced an inevitable outcome. He was forced to give up his land due to drought.

These family stories had a great effect on me while I was growing up. I remember always wondering what would drive people to leave all of their friends and family members behind knowing that they were unlikely ever to see them again. How could they part from their parents and sisters and brothers? And when they arrived on their homestead land, how did they survive before a house was built? How did they break the land? How did they deal with all of the problems associated with acquiring water, food, clothing, and other necessities that were so urgently needed? And how did they manage to buy seed and stock so that land production could begin?

Most importantly, how much and what kind of labour did each family member have to do? I know from family stories that the children received little education because the work on the farm was more important. So I often wondered what it would have been like to have to work on a homestead each and every day, dealing with the sun-up-to-sun-down labour during seeding and harvesting times. How did the children manage? Did they lead happy lives?

My family history has also had a great influence on my academic career. During my time at the University of Regina (for my BA high honours and master's degrees), I became interested in pursuing archival research into the pioneer period. In fact, it was Dr. Robert Stirling, my advisor from the Department of Sociology and Social Studies, who introduced me to the archives and over the years constantly encouraged my passion for socio-historical study. I would like to thank Dr. Stirling for this encouragement as I have now been researching the pioneer period for over fifteen years and have enjoyed every stage in the process.

This academic interest followed me when I entered the University of Alberta for my PhD program. Under the guidance of Dr. Susan McDaniel, I furthered my research into the pioneer labour of family members, particularly the work of children. It is on this research that this book is based. Without the input of Dr. McDaniel, this book would not exist.

There have also been many other individuals (friends, colleagues, and advisors) who have helped me throughout the years, such as Eileen (Woo) Tsui, John Conway, Murray Knuttila, Paul Gingrich, Laureen Gatin, Sharon Abu-Laban, and Judith Golec. I would also like to thank all of my good friends associated with the Society for Socialist Studies and with Grant MacEwan College. I deeply appreciate their input, positive feedback, support, and assistance.

I would also like to offer my thanks to the Social Sciences and Humanities Research Council for funding this project and to the Canadian Federation for the Humanities and Social Sciences Aid to Scholarly Publications Program. I am indebted to the ASPP's anonymous reviewers for their helpful suggestions. Heartfelt thanks are also offered to Nadine Charabin (chief archivist at the Saskatchewan Archives Board) and to the Saskatchewan Archives staff, and to the staff of the Alberta and Manitoba Provincial Archives. I would also like to extend my appreciation to Linda Cameron, Peter Midgley, and the staff at the University of Alberta Press.

As a final note, I would like to offer a personal thank you to my mother, Mary Etta Rollings, for her continuous support, and a special thank you to Christina, my daughter, who has been with me every step of the way.

ONE

The Division of Labour in the Family Farming Economy

THE ROMANTICIZED VIEW OF PIONEERING on the Canadian prairies envisioned happy young families leaving their homes to grasp the freedom and opportunities abounding in the newly opened region. If the beautiful drawings that adorned the covers of advertising brochures were to be believed, these men and women would enter the region, claim their free land, and settle down to growing crops, raising cattle, and building a log house from the supplies of timber that were readily available, all with little apparent effort. This imaginary scene graces the cover of the pamphlet issued by the North-West Canada Company, Limited (1880), while material published by the Minister of the Interior (Canada, 1905) highlights a bountiful Mother Nature pouring kernels of wheat out of a horn of plenty for the deserving settlers. Similarly, a booklet published by the Minister of Immigration and Colonization (Canada, 1894) depicts what could be taken for a typical prairie farm with large fields of ripened wheat, a herd of cattle, well-built and attractive buildings, and a stream running through the property to supply ample fresh water for drinking, washing, and cooking. If needed, the stream would also be a ready source of water for the family's livestock and poultry as well as the garden, whose soil was so fertile that it would eventually be filled with fast-growing, large, and delicious fruits and vegetables. After cutting through the protective layer of sod on the fields and casting seed onto the rich soil beneath, the family could relax until the fall, when their fields of golden wheat would mature in the warm prairie sunshine. Standing arm in arm, listening to their happy children playing, and watching the sun set over grain that grew as far as the eye could see, the couple would bask in a feeling of satisfaction, knowing that once the harvesting chores were complete and the profits banked, their future and that of their children would be well on its way.

Unfortunately, real life in the prairie region did not match this fantasy. For the hundreds of thousands of men, women, and children (see Table 1) who came to "The Last Best West" (Canada, 1906),[1] the pioneer era

TABLE I

Population of the Prairie Provinces and North-West
Territories by Sex and Child or Adult Status: 1881–1911

PROVINCE/STATUS	1881			1891		
	Total	Male	Female	Total	Male	Female
MANITOBA						
Adult	36,434	21,910	14,524	89,598	52,224	37,374
Child	16,294	8,548	7,746	39,442	20,273	19,169
NWT						
Adult	6,212	3,693	2,519	33,850	21,484	12,366
Child	3,294	1,705	1,589	12,945	6,636	6,309
SASKATCHEWAN						
Adult	*	*	*	*	*	*
Child	*	*	*	*	*	*
ALBERTA						
Adult	*	*	*	*	*	*
Child	*	*	*	*	*	*
Total						
Adult	42,646	25,603	17,043	123,448	73,708	49,740
Child	19,588	10,253	9,335	52,387	26,909	25,478

Source: *Sixth Census of Canada, 1921, Volume 1; Table 4*
   * *Included with the North-West Territories*
   An "adult" is defined as an individual over the age of 14.
   A "child" is defined as an individual between the ages of 4 to 14 inclusive.

was filled with misunderstandings, disappointments, and back-breaking labour for which many were ill-prepared. According to Morton (1938, p. 82), the migrant and immigrant population that surged onto the plains to participate in the rush for free land was "entirely unaware of the difficulties which settlement in the Northwest was experiencing"; he believed that they would have had a difficult time surviving the prairie conditions.

This lack of understanding was a likely result of the quantity of false information that was provided to potential settlers by the federal government and the Canadian Pacific Railway Company (the CPR). Clifford Sifton and Frank Oliver, successive Ministers of the Interior in the federal government, believed that the only way to convince millions of people to enter a strange land was to use hard-sell techniques. Thus, numerous brochures and pamphlets filled with exaggerations and misleading information were distributed by the government, the CPR, and land settlement companies. They alleged that the climate was ideal for farming and the winters were

PROVINCE/STATUS	1901			1911		
	Total	Male	Female	Total	Male	Female
MANITOBA						
Adult	157,537	89,104	68,433	298,667	169,945	128,722
Child	68,991	35,093	33,898	107,622	54,436	53,186
NWT						
Adult	3,825	1,744	2,081	2,916	1,473	1,443
Child	1,842	935	907	1,425	747	648
SASKATCHEWAN						
Adult	52,319	29,682	22,637	320,178	202,674	117,504
Child	24,386	12,394	11,992	109,305	55,724	53,581
ALBERTA						
Adult	43,981	26,031	17,950	248,959	158,250	90,709
Child	19,978	10,076	9,702	81,023	41,537	39,486
Total						
Adult	**257,662**	**146,561**	**111,101**	**870,720**	**532,342**	**338,378**
Child	**114,997**	**58,498**	**56,499**	**299,375**	**152,444**	**146,931**

Between 1881 and 1911, there was a 20-fold increase in the number of men, a 19-fold increase in the number of women, and a 15-fold increase in the number of children on the prairies.

reasonable, fuel was abundant, crop yields were phenomenal, and it was virtually certain that settlers would become wealthy. Even prairie fires were presented as advantageous events rather than as dangerous experiences that could result in animal and human deaths since, it was explained, the ash would be an efficient fertilizer for new growth (Canada, 1905; 1906; 1909; CPR, 1884; The North-West Canada Company, Limited, 1880; The Saskatchewan Land and Homestead Company, Limited, 1884).

Such advertising was discounted by researchers of the time. For example, while Henry Youle Hind (a geologist and co-leader of a Dominion of Canada expedition to the western prairie region in 1857) believed that conditions in the area were suitable to settlement if necessary precautions were taken, he was concerned with what he believed were lies about temperature (Friesen, 1987). He wrote directly to the Governor General, advising him that settlers were being attracted by dangerous misinformation, and stated that every death on the prairie which can be traced to immigration under the lure of false information is veiled manslaughter. Every pound taken from the Immigrants by similar information is veiled robbery. Every share consciously sold by a promoter or agent in companies formed under the glozing pictures embodied in the official 'Information for Intending Immigrants,' is a cruel swindle. Finally, every conscious inveigler of poor, uninstructed and *unprepared* immigrants to settle without foreknowledge, on free grant prairie farms under the aggregated attractions scattered throughout England by Sir Alexander Galt, is a man fit for the dock [emphasis in original]. (Hind, 1883, pp. 24–25)

In addition, the pessimistic attitude of some was not surprising given that the land was completely undeveloped and settlers had to begin their stay on the prairies by creating the means to satisfy their most basic needs. Shelter was a necessity, but building a home meant back-breaking work for an extended period while trees were located, felled, trimmed, hauled to the site, notched, and stacked into walls. All of this labour had to be done by hand, including the digging of a deep cellar under the house to store root crops. If a soddie was being built in one of the many areas where few trees grew, the work would be just as difficult. Thousands of heavy sod blocks had to be cut out of the ground, hauled, and stacked like bricks to form walls, and more had to be carried to build the roof.

In terms of productive labour, acres of sod had to be broken, or trees and brush felled and the roots destroyed, in order to prepare the land for the planting of crops. Neither task was easy since thick mats of roots and dirt yielded stubbornly and rocks that might damage machinery had to be removed from the fields. The lack of mechanized ploughs made the task difficult and labour-intensive. Once the sod was broken, additional labour had to be invested in the fields since the land had to be harrowed to grind the dirt into a finer mix that would support wheat seed. Seeding by hand or mechanical seeder would follow. In addition to the volume of labour directed at crop production, having livestock or poultry on the farm also increased the family labour requirements since animals had to be fed and watered, their stables, pens, and coops cleaned, eggs collected, cows milked, cream separated, and butter churned.

With the late summer would come the need to divert labour to harvesting tasks. Wild fruits would have to be collected for making jams, and garden produce had to be picked or dug up, and then stored or canned for consumption over the winter. Animals had to be slaughtered and the meat preserved; hay had to be cut, gathered, and stacked to feed the remaining animals over the winter; and market crops had to be harvested. The harvest season was extremely hectic and all available labour was needed to cut the wheat, tie the sheaves, and stook them until threshing was complete.

In addition to all of the work that had to be done out of doors, domestic labour was also necessary if the family wished to eat decent meals, live in a comfortable environment, and wear clean clothing that was kept in good repair. All of these needs meant many hours of labour each day, year-round, to perform all of the necessary tasks. Wood or buffalo chips had to be chopped or found and hauled to the stove for burning, and fresh water (purified when necessary) had to be put into storage for use during the day.[2] Bread, cakes, and pies had to be prepared and baked, vegetables cleaned, milk and butter chilled, meals cooked, and the table set. Dishes had to be washed and put away, floors swept or scrubbed, shelves dusted, clothes washed and ironed, beds made, and clothes sewn or mended. Child care would be an additional burden.

Even though the list of jobs set out above does not cover every individual task that had to be performed on the farm each day, week, month, and year, it is clear that no single person would have had the energy, skills, or time to handle all of them completely and competently on a consistent basis. The working capacity of each individual was finite and, as such, could only be applied to the completion of a certain number of hours of labour each day (and to fewer hours if the tasks were physically wearing) before it had to be restored with food, water, and rest. However, as seen above, even arranging for essential subsistence required the use of the settler's labour, because the land was undeveloped and without conveniences. Literally every aspect of life, from obtaining subsistence to producing marketable commodities, relied upon the settler's labour assets.

Given that homestead regulations allowed settlers only three years to prove the farm functional—that is, homesteaders had to prove their farming ability by building a home and breaking ten acres to crop each year if they wished to obtain free title to their 160 acres (see Figure 1 for more detail on the land divisions used in the homesteading system)—long-term success for the family thus meant organizing the homestead to generate the maximum possible output at the lowest possible cost (Dawson and Younge, 1940; *Dominion Lands Act*, 1872).

Typically, labour was divided between family members for efficiency and along gender lines due to cultural imperatives, with men handling the tasks related to financial survival such as caring for crops and livestock, while women's contributions were focussed on providing family subsistence and handling the domestic sphere (Scott and Tilly, 1980; Sachs, 1983; Cohen,

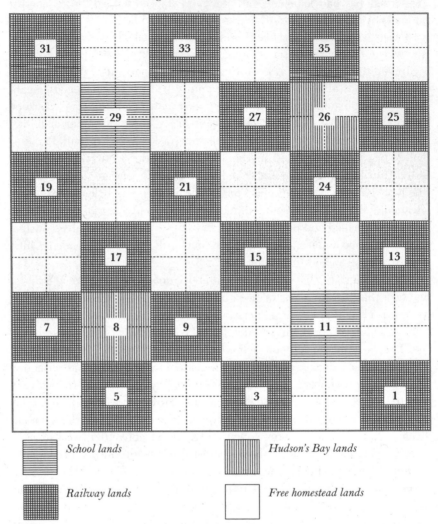

School lands

Hudson's Bay lands

Railway lands

Free homestead lands

Plan of township showing: (a) school lands (sections 11 and 29), (b) Hudson's Bay lands (section 8 and three-quarters of section 26; the whole of 26 in every fifth township), (c) free homestead lands (even-numbered sections, except 8 and 26), (d) railway lands (odd-numbered sections reserved for selection as railway land grants). Each section is bounded on three sides by road allowances (66 feet).

1988).[3] However, a woman's ties to the home were sometimes broken at the husband's request when her labour was needed for the cash crop during busy times, particularly during the harvesting season (Kohl, 1976; Sachs, 1983; Ursel, 1992; Rollings-Magnusson, 2000). As noted by Silverman,

The Jacob Lowenberger family, 1910. [SAB, R-A12139]

wives on the Alberta frontier at the turn of the nineteenth century did not live the lives of leisure in the home that their city cousins may have hoped to enjoy. Rather, they "worked with the same intensity as men through the day," and in the evenings did the housework "traditionally assigned women" (1984, p. 95). These pioneer women worked side by side with their husbands, and their efforts were necessary to the success of the farm.

The intensity of this effort on the part of men and women is confirmed by Davisson, who states that "I have seen these free-born men and women of the prairies work harder and more incessantly than men can be driven in penal settlements. I have seen their lanterns glimmer around the barns before daylight, and after it" (1927, p. 14). In short, every waking moment of the homesteader's life and his family's was devoted to working to ensure title to their farms and to guarantee their continuing success.

In addition to the amount of work that had to be devoted simply to the creation and operation of prairie farms, settlers had further burdens to face in order to maintain their farms. Retailers, banks, and machinery dealers were able to charge virtually any price they wished for most items and services, given that the settlers were in a captive market situation (Conway, 1984; Fowke, 1957; Innis, 1954). Such gouging was made worse by government-imposed tariffs that increased the price of necessary goods by 25 per cent for agricultural machinery, 35 per cent for hardware items such as nails and screws, 20 per cent for lumber and shingles, and 25 per cent for glass (Mackintosh, 1939; Easterbrook and Aitken, 1963). The CPR added to the problem by charging excessive shipping rates (Naylor, 1975), while grain companies fixed the prices farmers could receive for their crops. Cheating was rampant as elevator agents underweighed deliveries, assigned lower grades to the wheat to cut the price paid, and colluded with other agents to restrict competition (Fairbairn, 1984; Gleave, 1991; Wilson, 1978; Knuttila, 1994). The combined result of the numerous financial manipulations by these entities imposed massive financial burdens on prairie settlers that were difficult to overcome. In fact, the situation eventually became so bad, and farmers so exploited, that they rebelled. They fought for new laws to control the unethical activities of the CPR and grain companies, established co-operative grain associations, took part in the "Siege on Ottawa" in 1910, and established political parties to represent their views (Gleave, 1991; Knuttila, 1994; Wilson, 1978).

While men's work on prairie homesteads has been noted in the historical record, the economic importance of women's work was not recognized until studied by feminist researchers in the 1980s. At that time, many asserted that women's work was of extraordinary value. For example, Sachs (1983) and Scott and Tilly (1980) argue that women's subsistence labour kept families from starving, while Cohen (1988) takes this idea one step further and argues that the free provision of subsistence by a wife translated into either greater capital accumulation for the farm or greater profits for commercial capitalists who could extract funds from the operation. Others such as Kohl (1976) and Strong-Boag (1985) have investigated women's unpaid work, argued for recognition of its importance to family survival and economic development, and thus have made women's economic contributions part of the public record. Similar themes have also been emphasized by Ghorayshi (1989), Fox (1991), and Ursel (1992), who, like Sachs (1983), note that despite its value, the work of women was never credited or visible outside of the family.

While such research into women's work has clarified the composition of the farm labour system, other theorists have argued that the work of children was just as vital as the work of women. For example, Fontaine and Schlumbohm (2000) and Wallace, Dunkerley, Cheal, and Warren (1994) indicate that the work performed by children was a necessary element of family survival strategies. Others report children as being adaptable and capable of assuming more difficult roles as they gained experience and physical ability (Light, Hertsgaard, and Martin, 1985; Neth, 1995) and as valuable components of the family labour pool (Tilly and Scott, 1987).

In fact, researchers have found that children actually increased a family's level of market production by handling domestic and subsistence requirements, thereby freeing adults to apply more time to productive activity (Kohl, 1976; Stansell, 1976); enhanced family subsistence by gardening, hunting, and caring for animals (Horn, 1994; Neth, 1995); and helped to reduce the amounts spent on external goods or services (Reimer, 1986). Performing tasks that would otherwise have to be hired out was particularly useful since children could provide inexpensive labour and also become more skilled over time. Where land was available (particularly free land), children could represent a double value to parents since they might also eventually acquire homesteads of their own and thereby increase the wider family's fortunes (Levy, 1985; Sharif, 1993; Gjerde and McCants, 1995). Taking off-farm work and returning wages to the family (Symes and Appleton, 1986; Neth, 1995) or earning funds through entrepreneurial initiatives could also improve the chances of farm survival by providing the money necessary to pay for goods the family could not produce on its own. However, it should also be noted that children were not just of economic worth. As indicated by Espenshade (1977), the value of children lay in both the emotional and economic spheres since children provided a sense of immortality, group ties, adulthood, fun, power, accomplishment, prestige, and morality through self-sacrifice at the same time as they added to the financial well-being of the family.

Other theorists have also examined the work of children but from a different perspective. These investigations have attempted to explain why, if children were not paid for their labour contributions, they continued to perform work for the family. Engelmeyer (1995) and Ursel (1992), for example, attribute children's work to the historically produced patriarchal power possessed by men within the family structure, while in a similar vein Folbre (1982) notes that as head of the household, the male controlled all property and other assets. In either case, the father's power enabled him to issue orders as to the functions that other family members carried out on pain of physical punishment or economic sanction. Fraad (1995) equates women and children to serfs who owed absolute obedience and support to the lord of the home who, once again, controlled all family assets.

Others view the relationship between parent and child in less exploitive terms. For example, Symes and Appleton (1986), Mendelievich (1979), and Nett (1988) argue that parental control over child labour is better explained as an aspect of the parents' duty to socialize their children. The parents' duty included ensuring that their children accepted the norms and conditions of their society, obtained necessary formal knowledge, were exposed to social customs, and received training in the practical skills essential for survival. Assigning work to children thus fulfilled parental duty and supported the family, but given that children's efforts for the family, and family support for their children, seem to have been voluntary rather than directed, researchers such as Finch (1989) and Horn (1994) focus on mutual familial obligations as an explanation for children's work. In a sense, the provision of labour by children repaid the care and support that parents provided as the children grew toward competence, transforming the relationship into one of mutual dependence. Hendrick (1997) argues that this sense of mutual obligation was in evidence prior to the twentieth century but that it shifted as the century progressed. The socially accepted ideal that children would assist their families eventually converted to an acknowledgement of childhood as a period of learning and enjoyment in which work was seen as undesirable.

It may be noted that the socialization and obligation approaches to the issue of children's labour both correspond to the social expectations of the study period. Historically, children had been seen as little different from adults once they reached an age at which they could undertake helpful work. Children were thus expected to contribute to their own and their family's welfare in whatever way they could. At various times, this attitude has been explained as a matter of religious compliance (Aries, 1970; Cunningham, 1995; Pollock, 1983), a philosophical position (Sommerville, 1982), or simply a matter of necessity (Cunningham, 1995; Sommerville, 1982). These views have differed across cultures and time, but in terms of the Canadian farming situation, the socially accepted position among the English-speaking majority was that children's labour would contribute to their morality, productivity, and work ethic (Sutherland, 2000).

With respect to the use to which children's labour might have been put, all farming and domestic activities required labour of some sort. Whether the labour was used for picking rocks, caring for livestock, growing fruits and vegetables for consumption, or running the home, every input was valuable in the struggle to overcome the harsh conditions of prairie life. Seeking out paid employment, increasing production of smaller items such as butter or eggs that could be sold to raise cash, or undertaking fur trapping in the winter could add to the family coffers.

Intensified labour directed at subsistence activities could also prove profitable in the sense of saving valuable cash reserves for necessary items. Growing additional foods, undertaking extra expeditions into the bush to hunt for fruit and table game, or spending additional time chopping wood to save on the purchase of coal could all reduce the need to buy products in the market. Similarly, activities such as sewing could save the family money. Skill with a needle and thread meant spending less on manufactured clothing since bolts of cloth could be converted to clothing at a fraction of the cost. In addition, clothing could be repaired rather than replaced when feasible, thus effecting a further cost saving or at least delaying the inevitable expenditure until items were too damaged to salvage. Taking care of younger brothers and sisters was also a valuable use of children's labour since it allowed parents to undertake other farm chores.[4]

Based on the foregoing, I argue in this book that although farm children (those aged between four and sixteen) did not receive payment or documented recognition for their economic contributions, boys and girls expected, and were expected, to work and did in fact perform essential duties and necessary tasks that contributed to the success of farms and family survival. In this way, children were in a position similar to that of women in that they worked hard to assist in achieving success, but were treated as economically invisible labour on the farm. It is this extension of feminist theory to the analysis of children's work, the revelation of an apparently gendered and aged division of labour that existed between the boys and girls, and the development of a system of classification (a typology) that organizes the labour contributions of pioneer children for analysis that set this study apart from others.

In arriving at this position, the research concentrated on the following issues and questions:

1. Did the prairie farming culture of the settlement period accept the view that childhood was a special period during which children were in need of care and time to relax, or did it see children as capable of handling work responsibilities like adults?

2. Were children socialized to work? Did children feel obligated to work? Were children forced to work under a patriarchal system? Why did children work?

3. Did children contribute their labour to the ongoing operation of family farms? If so, what type of work did they do?

4. Were there gender- or age-based differences in the types of work performed?

5. Was the labour performed necessary and of importance to the farming venture? Were children paid or otherwise rewarded for their labour?

6. Can feminist theory regarding women's work be used to explain the labour of children? That is, were children unpaid, economically invisible labourers on pioneer farms?

Research Method: A Sociological Analysis of Historical Data

The term "socio-historical analysis" will be used throughout this book to convey the fact that while this study was designed to accumulate previously untapped historical data respecting the child labour on pioneer family farms, the sociological interpretation of this raw data was the ultimate goal. The reports made by 260 children of both genders and various ages concerning dozens of types of tasks that they performed had to be quantitatively organized before a more detailed analysis of factors that may have influenced child labour could be undertaken in a systematic fashion. Tables 2 and 3 set out the gender, residence, and age breakdowns of the study population in detail.

TABLE 2

Number of Boys and Girls by Province*

SEX	ALBERTA	SASKATCHEWAN	MANITOBA	TOTAL
Boys	26	35	71	132
Girls	20	27	50	97
Total	46	62	121	229

> * Twenty-four individuals did not indicate their place of residence and seven failed to note their gender. If these individuals were included, the total number of subjects would be 260.

TABLE 3

Age by the Number of Boys and Girls*

AGE	BOYS	GIRLS	TOTAL
4–5	3	0	3
6–8	7	9	16
9–11	40	32	72
12–14	53	60	113
> 14	12	7	19
Total	115	108	223

> * Thirty subjects did not mention their age and an additional seven did not identify their sex. If these individuals were included, the total number of subjects would be 260.

My pursuit of information focussed largely on documents prepared by individuals personally involved in the settlement process; these documents are located at the main prairie archives in Regina and Saskatoon, Saskatchewan; Edmonton, Calgary, and Lethbridge, Alberta; and Winnipeg, Manitoba. The documents are of diverse types including lengthy personal writings such as diaries and memoirs, autobiographies, family histories, poems, and stories, plus shorter writings such as letters submitted by children and others to prairie newspapers and sent to relatives.[5] Ultimately, the materials collected and reviewed consisted of over 289 letters, memoirs, interview transcripts, diaries, autobiographies, and family histories plus eleven items that were published in book form. Of the published books, three were self-published by the authors (Murray, 1982; Pratt, 1996; Stewart, 1962), four were autobiographies produced by publishing firms (Caswell, 1968; Hiemstra, 1997; Merriken, 1999; Minifie, 1972), and two were diaries included in a collection of Ukrainian memoirs (Adamowska, 1978; Farion, 1978). The final two books were prepared by sons of the women involved, namely Nellie Hislop (Nuffield, 1987) and Sarah Roberts (Roberts, 1971), based on diaries left by these women. Many of these documents contain highly detailed accounts of the work that children performed on the farm, but a number also provide information on the lives and attitudes of farming families and revelations about the effects of gender on work roles.

These materials were subjected to analysis by means of individual scrutiny to locate and isolate the quantitatively relevant information respecting children's work that was intermingled with qualitative data in the form of personal memories of life on pioneer farms. Each document was also studied for the identity of the writer, birth date, farm location, information on family goals, details of family structure, and the types of crops and animals being grown or raised. In addition, references to the type and amount of work the child was involved in, the types of work handled by siblings, the tools and implements used, indications of parental working behaviour, and information on the family's history were all pursued in the hope of obtaining a more detailed picture of settler life.[6]

Beyond the documents prepared by pioneer children, materials (primarily letters) written by adult residents of the prairies that were published in newspapers available to farmers were also of assistance. They provide background information respecting the beliefs and attitudes about work with which children were imbued, particularly as to whether they should work at all and what were the appropriate types of work for boys and girls. The settlers did not operate in a vacuum and create totally new rules of behaviour as they went along; rather, they imported certain attitudes and beliefs with them and interacted, even if only to read or hear about the views of others, with the broader society. Clearly, these documents identify limits on acceptable behaviour as to child labour and gender or age roles, or shifts in attitude within the developing prairie culture.

A Typology of Children's Labour
Contributions to the Operation of Prairie Farms

While the work performed by children within the family economy may have been a function of family and social expectations, and the work itself may have flowed seamlessly from task to task as an ordinary and expected aspect of day-to-day living, some means of identifying and, if possible, quantifying the different aspects of children's labour was necessary if the goals of this study were to be achieved. A research tool, a typology of labour contributions, was designed for this purpose. When reviewing the historical documents for data on the work performed by children, I paid particular attention to identifying not only the work tasks performed by children but also the context in which these tasks were carried out. Understanding the intended outcome of the task allowed children's work to be classified in the typology based on the nature of the labour. Four categories were established in terms of whether labour was productive (directed at producing commodities for the market),[7] entrepreneurial (devoted to raising funds for the family),[8] subsistence (used to produce goods directly for family consumption), or domestic (directed at family lifestyle, carrying on day-to-day household tasks, and the conversion of subsistence items into consumable form). This typology was, in turn, used to organize further analysis of the data to determine, for example, whether gender or age differences could be identified in the types of contribution children made or in the specific types of work performed.

As may be seen in the child labour typology set out below, various subcategories of specific work tasks were combined to establish the labour outcome category. However, several tasks overlap and thus may be found in different labour categories depending upon the intended outcome of the work. For example, livestock production (productive labour), raising animals for sale by the individual (entrepreneurial labour), and obtaining animal products to consume (subsistence labour) all involve children working with and raising animals. The context revealed by a given document determined the appropriate labour outcome category, but where a writer was not clear in stating that he or she was, for example, collecting eggs from the family flock for sale to the local grocer, reasonable assumptions were used to make this determination.

If the child referred to a large number of animals (more than ten) or handling large volumes of milk, cream, butter, eggs, or fleece (drawn from ten animals or twenty-five fowl), these numbers were used to separate animals destined for the market from those kept for personal consumption. The decision to use ten animals as a cut-off point is somewhat arbitrary. The writings of most children are inconclusive as to the destiny of larger ʒrds of cattle or other stock, but it is unlikely that farmers would hold m re than ten animals for personal use. They would require feed, water, anć care for several years even if only three were slaughtered each year. Calvɔ (or lambs or piglets or chicks) would maintain the supply, and holding th ʒ many animals would also provide a cushion for losses to predators, the weɑ her, or disease. The poultry limit was set at twenty-five birds as their sizɛ nakes them single-meal animals and the need for a regular supply of eggɔ for eating meant a higher number might conceivably be kept on the farm strictly for family consumption.

Entrepreneꞇurial activity also required a reference to sale (but with the animal identified as belonging to the child), and subsistence labour was identified by references to family consumption of the animal or its products, or references to smaller numbers of animals for family use. Where other such overlaps occurred, similar distinctions based on references to items as being for sale, hunted for a bounty, or used for personal, family, or stock subsistence were used to categorize the tasks referred to by the children. The primary assumption in all cases was that in the absence of an alternative context, labour was expended for the general benefit of the family productive operations.

Child Labour Typology

PRODUCTIVE LABOUR: includes field work, livestock production, working with horses, doing stable chores, transporting crops, clearing fields, performing chores, running errands, and generally helping out with farm work.

ENTREPRENEURIAL LABOUR: includes paid employment, working as a field hand for others, raising animals or fowl for sale, selling milk, butter, eggs, fruit, or other produce, taking part in gopher bounties, and trapping and selling furs.

SUBSISTENCE LABOUR: includes hauling water, digging wells, obtaining fuel (i.e., chopping down trees, collecting coal, or gathering buffalo chips), feeding and watering animals and cleaning stalls or pens, milking, churning butter, gathering eggs to eat, slaughtering chickens, turkeys,

and/or ducks, skinning rabbits, hunting for family consumption, gardening, foraging for berries, and helping to
protect the family from insects, wild animals, and prairie
fires.

DOMESTIC LABOUR: includes preparing food, washing clothes
and making beds, cleaning the home and its contents,
sewing, knitting, and crocheting, and caring for children.

Using this methodology, the initial calculations derived from the data
collected in this study suggest that boys' labour tended to focus on productive activities, with 66 per cent of them reporting such work, while girls
were more likely to perform domestic tasks (73 per cent). Both worked
for subsistence (40 per cent and 51 per cent respectively) and entrepreneurial outcomes as well (37 per cent and 27 per cent respectively), but
their primary labour functions in the family are quite clear (see Table
4). Table 5 makes it evident that for most children, contributions to the
family economy began early (between six and eight years) and continued
throughout their years with the family. (More detailed analyses by type of
work performed, gender, and age are discussed in Chapters 3 to 6.)

TABLE 4

*Type of Labour by Gender**

TYPE OF LABOUR	BOYS	%	GIRLS	%
Productive	87	66	39	32
Entrepreneurial	48	37	33	27
Subsistence	53	40	62	51
Domestic	17	13	89	73
Total Number of Boys and Girls in the Study Population by Gender Group	131		122	

* *Children could report participating in multiple jobs. As such, totals
compiled from this data would not be representative of the total number of
children working. Note also that seven subjects did not mention their sex.*

TABLE 5

Type of Labour by Age*

TYPE OF LABOUR	AGE (YEARS)				
	4–5	6–8	9–11	12–14	>14
Productive	1	13	40	77	·14
Entrepreneurial	1	6	30	36	10
Subsistence	-	11	45	77	12
Domestic	-	13	44	48	9
Total Number of Children in the Study Population by Age Group	3	17	75	116	19

* *Children could report participating in multiple jobs. As such, totals compiled from this data would not be representative of the total number of children working. Also, thirty subjects did not mention their age.*

Outline of the Book

Analysis of the results begins in Chapter 2 with a review of the need for, and attitudes toward, children's labour contributions on the prairies. This chapter also highlights the use of children's labour power in pre-production work, namely the construction of farm buildings and other necessary infrastructure. Chapters 3, 4, 5, and 6 detail the findings of the study in terms of the types of work that children performed in support of the operation of prairie farms. The chapters are divided by the nature of the work reported, with Chapter 3 detailing productive work in growing crops and raising livestock. Entrepreneurial activity to earn money for the farm is discussed in Chapter 4, while Chapter 5 deals with subsistence labour, the creation of the means of physical survival for the family. Chapter 6 highlights domestic labour directed at the comfort and well-being of the family. The book concludes with Chapter 7, which provides a summary of the study and its results. It discusses the possibility that age and gender divisions of labour existed historically among farm children and provides an expanded explanation for the success of family farming in the prairie region. Further, since the revelations made by these children fit well with the feminist approaches dealing with the importance and invisibility of women's work, extending these theories to explain the role of children seems justified.

TWO

Attitudes toward Child Labour and Children's Assistance in Pre-production Work

THE NATURE OF THE TASK UNDERTAKEN by prairie pioneers, to settle a new frontier and adapt it for low-technology farming use, was a labour-intensive one. This chapter makes it clear that the social attitudes of the time not only supported but called for the use of children's labour in this process. The statements of both farming and non-farming residents of the prairies enthusiastically endorsed farm work as a positive force in children's lives that would be advantageous to them in their future endeavours. Such attitudes were translated into reality for children on the plains, initially in the form of assisting in the construction of homes and necessary farm buildings and support structures. Whether the family found itself using trees, sod, mud, or clay plaster to build shelters, the work was difficult and exhausting, and having children involved allowed a division of the work among more hands and an easing of the burden on each individual. Children were thus involved in some of the more physically demanding and dangerous aspects of pioneer farming and were co-workers, not merely apprentices performing light duties.

The Labour Needs of the Pioneer Family Farm

Given that settlers brave or strong-willed enough to enter the prairie region faced the prospect of having literally to build their enterprise from the ground up, the need for labour power, both human and animal, was extreme since the implements settlers had to rely on were all muscle-powered.[1] Wagons, stoneboats, walking ploughs, harrows, and seeders were all drawn by horses or oxen, while hand tools such as scythes, pitchforks, axes, hoes, and rakes all relied upon the power of the settler wielding them.[2] Thus, every aspect of the development process and all phases of operating a farm as an ongoing business were labour-intensive and depending upon muscle power to develop and then operate a farm meant that leisure was virtually non-existent and progress was slow. In other words, life on the frontier was difficult and filled with hard work.

Given the need to comply with government regulations respecting the breaking of land and the building of a home and the survival imperative of locating sources of water, food, and fuel, the first season on the homestead could be particularly intense. Following the establishment of the farm, the need for labour continued as buildings, fences, fields, and the home had to be maintained, and the natural assets of the homestead had to be converted to marketable crops, livestock, food, and ultimately cash resources each year. However, the margin between success and failure in frontier farming was so slim that one farm management specialist, G.F. Warren, defined success as "raising each summer a little more than enough food and clothing for the winter" (1917, p. 4). Thus, in his view, labour-intensive farming would not make settlers rich quickly, but if sufficient effort was invested in the operation, it could support the farming family on a year-to-year basis. Only by increasing the available labour power could more rapid progress be made, and for settlers with limited funds, this meant increasing the size of their families.

As mentioned earlier, in order to utilize the available family labour efficiently, a gendered division of labour existed for adult men and women in farming situations (Cohen, 1988; Ursel, 1992). Men generally handled work activities relating to the performance of heavy labour such as felling trees and hauling rocks, but also took on the production of cash crops and livestock, thereby maintaining control over the financial affairs of the farm. Women performed subsistence labour and domestic tasks suited to their supposedly natural ability to care for others by taking charge of the home and seeing to the washing and ironing of clothes, cooking, sewing, and cleaning (Rasmussen et al., 1976). However, the division of labour was not inflexible since women could be called upon to assist their husbands with the field work at any point when needed, despite the fact that men seldom reciprocated with household chores (Bennett, Kohl, and Binion, 1982; Cohen, 1988; Kohl, 1977; Sachs, 1983). This facet of the division of labour between men and women was clearly recognized by farmers, as evidenced by a letter published in a July 1900 issue of *The Nor'-West Farmer*. The writer, J.L. Tipping of Waghorn, Alberta, is clearly sympathetic to the plight of women and makes a point of addressing the issue with humour. Tipping writes that while men often expected their wives to "help them with their outdoor work," few men would reciprocate (1900, p. 563). As the writer sizes up the situation, "I wonder what the average man would say, if his wife said to him some morning, 'Abijah, dear, I have a big washing on hand to-day, also bread to bake, etc., I wish you would darn Kitchener's stockings before he goes to school, and after that is done help me prepare the dinner for the hired men'" (Tipping, 1900, p. 563).

Regardless of the inequity of the division of work between adults, the benefits of working together for the farm were clear and obvious. With two adults available, the amount of work that could be performed would be increased in comparison to the capacity of a single settler attempting to balance all of the tasks necessary to establish the farm and ensure personal survival on his or her own.[3] The importance of the distribution of work among family members is clearly noted by Cherwinski (1985, pp. 117–118) who indicates that

> It presented the potential for growth of the labor force within the family, it created the possibility of diversification into poultry and livestock, it promised an improved standard of living which went with a more pleasant environment, and it solved the problem of isolation.

In short, having the assistance of one or more family members made farm life more bearable and at the same time enhanced the chances of success.

The difficulty of dealing with all of the demands on a single settler's time is discussed by Herbert Stringer (1888), who farmed near Edmonton, Alberta, in the late 1800s. Herbert had never married and therefore lived through the deprivation and hardships that were an individual's companions on the prairies. Constant work improving the farm meant ignoring personal needs such as decent food, clean and repaired clothing, and the maintenance of reasonable conditions within the home.[4] Too much attention to the niceties of living could mean a failure to accomplish all of the tasks needed to produce crops or complete other necessary projects on time. Having help on hand could solve such concerns and at the same time hold the loneliness of a single life in a shack on the empty prairies at bay. Stringer (1888, p. 2) clearly recognized how he had ruined his own life in the prairie region and thus wrote to advise others before they were caught in the same trap:

> By all means…young fellows should come out here (anything over 15's old enough) but they ought to get married or arrange with some girl to come out to them as soon as they are fixed. I neglected this [and] have payed [sic] for it ever since. Baching is *universally* allowed to be one of the curses of the American west [emphasis in original].

From Singer's perspective, having a woman's labour available to create and maintain a pleasant living environment might have made his life a pleasure rather than a constant state of weary drudgery, but this leaves unanswered the question of what his wife's life would have been.

While women had a necessary part to play in the performance of tasks on the farm, their importance extended beyond that of subsidiary workers performing physical labour in the home, garden, or field. Their significance in a farming situation could also be found in their role as mothers since they were responsible for creating a labour advantage over the long term (Neth, 1995; Sachs, 1983; Tilly and Scott, 1987). Each birth temporarily reduced the woman's physical labour potential since a portion of her time would be devoted to nurturing the child, but the more children she bore, and the older they grew, the greater their compensating labour input would be (Sharif, 1993). As mothers, women were at least as important to the operation of a farm over the long term as were men.

As noted above, the usefulness of children on a settler farm depended to some degree on their age. The physical strength, natural abilities, and skills of the child would all increase with time and training (Kohl, 1976; Light, Hertsgaard, and Martin, 1985; Stansell, 1976), but the additional labour power provided by any child would increase the likelihood of succeeding at creating and operating a family farm. The argument that even young children could provide benefits for the family with their work was widely accepted in the prairie region during the settlement period, as shown by the written comments of numerous individuals. For example, an anonymous contributor to the "Household" column of *The Nor'-West Farmer* (p. 817) in 1899 scoffed at those who felt that a child could not contribute to the farming process:

> If any say a small child cannot earn his keep let those who
> are blest with such help send the child away for a month into
> some family where they are not in possession of such help,
> and two families will have learned something to the advan-
> tage of humanity.

Similarly, a number of women residing on the prairies indicated in their responses to a questionnaire sent out by the *Montreal Herald* in 1885 that settlers would be wise to have their children on the farm from the outset. These women, answering the question "Would you recommend an emigrant to bring his wife and family with him, or leave them behind till he has a home ready for them?" (*Montreal Herald*, 1886, p. 1), were most enthusiastic about bringing the family along to share in the farm labour or earn income for it.

For example, the response of Mrs. Helen Bell indicates that she was in favour of bringing her children west to help with the farm. The sincerity of her statement is unquestionable since she had moved all eight of her children to the prairies without waiting for her husband to complete all of the work necessary to establish a comfortable home for them all (*Montreal Herald*, 1886, p. 5). While Helen Bell does not expressly mention the advantages that could be gained if children were brought to the West, these benefits are noted by several other women who responded to the survey, including Mrs. J.D. Hanson. She suggests that financial gains were possible since "[if] a son and daughter came with the father, they could go and work out [take on a paid job]," but for Mrs. A.G. McDonald, the advantage lay in the fact that "a man cannot farm alone very well," implying that children would be of most assistance by helping with the work of the farm (*Montreal Herald*, 1886, pp. 4–5). A very strong positive opinion is also expressed by Mrs. G.M. Yeoman, who indicates that settlers should bring along "every chick and child, unless there is some strong reason for not doing so; they will all help to pull through; and feel all the better for having done so, even if it is a severe tug. I speak from experience" (*Montreal Herald*, 1886, p. 4).

However, three women do sound a cautionary note concerning children. Mrs. G. Butcher (*Montreal Herald*, 1886, p. 4), while indicating that families should be brought west to establish the homesteads, argues that only healthy wives and good-sized children could be of assistance in the heavy work needed to set up a farm. Mrs. J. Sutherland (*Montreal Herald*, 1886, p. 5) mentions that only strong families "willing to work" were needed, and the same sort of qualifier appears in the answer of Mrs. George Cheasley, who says that "if the family is small, leave them [at home until the initial work is complete]; if grown up, bring them. There will be lots of work for them" (*Montreal Herald*, 1886, p. 5).

Thus, in the opinion of many prairie residents, children could provide an advantage for their families with their work. In other words, the extra labour power provided by children increased the family's capacity for work, opening up the possibility for more produce to be grown, for expansion of the family's holdings, and for improvements in living conditions.[5] Aside from the potential work-related benefits associated with having children, relying on family members for support also made practical financial sense. With a wife and children resident on the farm, a constantly available source of labour could be maintained at little cost. Unlike hired hands, family members did not have to be paid a wage, and scarce cash resources

Ukrainian immigrants, Quebec City, 1911. [LAC, C-004745]

did not have to be depleted when additional labour was required for a particular project. Further, because of their reliance on the farm's output for their own survival and the emotional ties of the family bond, family members would be more likely to remain loyal and hard-working and not accept alternative offers of employment if their labour power was needed by the family (Easterlin, 1976; Neth, 1995; Webb, 1989). Working with one's own offspring had the additional advantage of fulfilling the settler's social duty to teach children the customs and values of their lifestyle and communities.

Published statements indicating approval of children's work reflected the beliefs of many farmers. One example of such acceptance of child labour is found in the letter of an anonymous reader who contributed to the discussion in a women's section of the 1909 *Grain Growers' Guide*:

> [Children] should be made to know that they also must do their part and that they may have to make sacrifices to contribute to the welfare of the family as a whole, for the home and family as a whole must come before the individual, unless in case of sickness or misfortune, when natural affection will usually set the pace for all. (p. 24)

While child labour clearly benefited the family and the farming operation, the reasons underlying the approval of the practice were not altogether selfish and mercenary. Many strongly believed that farm work was highly beneficial for the children themselves. For example, the editor of a farmer-oriented American newspaper, *The Judd Farmer* (Editor, 1898, p. 116), wrote an opinion column suggesting that the hard work performed on the farm provided country children with a definite advantage over the "city-bred," who suffered from a weaker constitution, poor morals, poor health, and a lack of character because of their upbringing. The "smart air" displayed by city children as a result of their book learning is also discounted by the editor. He argues that the foundation of practical knowledge obtained by a farm child through work and "Nature's school" placed him or her ahead of those who did not have such advantages growing up. All of these factors led the author to conclude that "[the] farm is the place to rear a family."

Comparable sentiments are also expressed by other residents of the prairies, for example, Mrs. F.A. Sanford (1898) of Virden, Manitoba, who wrote of the benefits children enjoyed as a result of their busy farm up-bringing; having the children close by every day allowed the farm family to protect them from the evil influences of decadent city life while ensuring their health and decent development through a program of hard work, healthy food, and clean air. The advantages presented by an active life in the clean countryside are also raised by Mrs. Anna Rees in a column written for *The Nor'-West Farmer* (1901, p. 148). In her view, the country was an idyllic place to raise children since "[our] children, like our calves and colts, thrive better on good wholesome food and plenty of sunshine and fresh air."

On the same topic and perhaps justifying the faith that Mrs. Sanford and Mrs. Rees had in the value of life in the country, Dr. S.J. Evans wrote a letter outlining her medical opinion of the benefits of work for children to the "Household" column in an 1898 edition of *The Nor'-West Farmer*. The letter suggests that children would benefit from

> a patch of ground to cultivate, rabbits to feed, chickens to take care of, house-birds to attend regularly, or a little detail of cooking or housekeeping for the girls, and an out-door "chore" for the boys, [since they are] excellent outlets for early energy. There is nothing more hurtful to young children than the "purring" [soft tones and attitudes] of well-meaning people. (p. 521)

Doctor Evans thus appears to be suggesting that children would lead happier lives if they could work, particularly out of doors, and that the worst thing parents could do was to provide their offspring with a comfortable, relaxing lifestyle or to coddle them.[6] This medical vindication of what might otherwise appear to have been a selfish decision to use children for their labour power makes it clear that a positive attitude toward children's work was not held only by farmers. Further, it seems clear that settler families had reason truly to believe that work and a life close to nature would produce healthy and contented children attuned to the farming life.

Initial Demands on Children's Labour: Establishing Prairie Farms

The belief that work and country living were beneficial to children was sometimes put into practice immediately upon arrival in the prairie region. Several diaries and memoirs speak to the use of child labour in some of the most dangerous and physically challenging labour projects that ever took place on the farm. This pre-production work involved the construction of the family home; while this study focusses on the labour of children in the operation of pioneer farms, the story would not be complete if such initial work practices went unremarked.

For those in the Fertile Crescent[7] or near bodies of water, trees were plentiful and buildings made from logs would have been common. However, few large trees that could provide thick insulating walls existed in most of the prairie region, and importing lumber was inconvenient, expensive, and somewhat impractical since lumber was so thin that it provided almost no insulation from the climate (Taggart, 1958). One example of the poor suitability of lumber homes in prairie conditions was provided by the Hillson family, who had built a sixteen-foot by twenty-foot home with one room, an attic, and no insulation (Taggart, 1958). The house could not be kept warm in the winter, so the family decided to build a sod house with thick walls so that they could be comfortable during the next winter. Mary Waddell (n.d., p. 5) also notes the problems with heating lumber shacks in her memoir and indicates that "[many] a morning there would be ice in the kettle on the stove & ice on the water pail." Similar complaints were made by other pioneer children, including Ellenor Merriken (1999, p. 61), who notes that their kettle was given a "roly poly" bottom by water that froze overnight so that it "would rock, roll, jib and whistle at the same time when it got hot," and John Watson, who believed that he should not have been able to see "out through the roof" and added that he didn't "know how we could stand the cold them days, gosh the mornings our blankets and our beds would be froze, the blankets would be all froze around your head" (1975, p. 5). Leddie Wilson, a young woman whose family was home-steading at Circus Coulee, Alberta, wrote to her sister Dottie in 1902 and described the same sorts of problems with her log house. Wind and snow entered through cracks between the logs, leaving the house so cold that "when all my work was done I opened the oven door and shoved my feet in as far as I could get and even then I shivered" (Wilson, 1902, pp. 1–2). However, Dorthea Calverley (1985) experienced the consequences of poor insulation for wooden structures at a far more personal level. Describing the process of bathing in such a cold shack, Dorthea indicates that the family stove was the primary source of heat for the whole operation. Water had to be boiled to keep things cozy, and in her case, the tub was also placed under the open door to the stove so that the heat circulated around her. Standing in the tub and bending over to grab the soap, Dorthea managed to touch her backside to the door, leaving herself with an identifying brand that few would see.

The only widely available raw material on the plains was the natural grass that grew almost everywhere; by cutting thick sod blocks from the natural turf, settlers could create functional homes (known as soddies) literally out of the ground.[8] The sod hut was thus the shelter of choice in all but the forested areas of the prairies and the extremely arid south, where the sod did not grow thick enough to be used for building (Anderson, n.d.). Little choice existed in that area, and a tent or a cave dug into the side of a hill would have to suffice if the family lacked the skill to build an adobe home with mud or clay plaster. This variety of possible options also led to a number of different tasks that could be assigned to children under different conditions.

In every case, however, the one overriding consistent factor in every family's decision on the type of home to build and whether to use child labour in its construction was time. Construction had to proceed with all possible speed, or the family might be left exposed to uncomfortable or dangerous weather conditions (Dawson and Younge, 1940). Since the weather in the prairie region tended to extremes of heat, cold, dryness, and rain, depending on the area in question, death could strike anyone who was unprepared (Hind, 1883). A well-built shelter could prevent such incidents and protect settlers from the rain, snow, wind,[9] and sun, but only if the necessary labour was invested in building shelter quickly and properly. Even in those areas of southern Alberta and Saskatchewan that benefited from the warming effects of chinook winds,[10] the only reliable shield from the storms and cold was a house.

While the process of building a soddie was simple, the amount of hard work required was enormous. An initial search for the best sod would be required since, while any mature sod could be used for building, the best material that would not break down in the rain or as a result of freezing was deep-rooted sod taken from dried slough areas (McLeod, 1977). A strong, if not clean and comfortable, home could then be built using locally available resources and muscle power supplied by the settler family.

One of the clearest descriptions of the process followed in building a soddie, and of the role that children might play in the process, is provided by Evelyn McLeod in her 1977 memoir. She was only six years old in 1909 when her family immigrated from North Dakota and thus did not have the strength to lift the blocks of sod that her father sliced out of the ground, but she was observant and remembered the details almost seventy years later. The first step in the building program, after her father used the family breaking plough to obtain long strips of sod sixteen inches wide and four inches thick, was to cut the material into rectangular blocks approximately thirty-two inches long (McLeod, 1977, p. 6).

In building the home, the sod bricks were stacked so that the resulting wall would be thirty-two inches thick to provide the maximum amount of insulation. This meant that, after the necessary overlap of each piece of sod was considered, only eight inches of wall length, at the most, could be achieved with each brick. A twelve-foot by twenty-foot house would thus require sixty-four linear feet of sod bricks or ninety-six bricks in each layer to achieve the needed perimeter, and the layers then had to be piled to the height necessary for comfort and convenience. It would thus take over 2,304 bricks to achieve an eight-foot ceiling height, even if none of the four-inch thickness of each brick was lost to compression as the weight of each layer pressed down on those below. (The number of sod bricks is calculated as ninety-six bricks per layer, multiplied by three stacked layers per foot of height of the wall, multiplied by an eight-foot height of the wall [$96 \times 3 \times 8 = 2,304$].) Given that the roof of such sod structures could be enclosed either with hay or straw thatch or with sod bricks laid over a criss-crossed framework of long wooden poles (thin trees) bridging the space between the sod walls, hundreds of additional bricks might be needed to complete the structure (McLeod, 1977).

However, McLeod notes, before the walls were begun or room partitions planned, a cellar for the preservation of food had to be dug. Her family used a seven-foot-wide by ten-foot-long design for their storage space. The cellar had to be dug deep enough under the house to be partly below the freezing depth of the soil so that the warmth of the ground and whatever heat filtered through the trap door to the cellar would prevent the temperature from dropping to the freezing point and spoiling the stored produce (McLeod, 1977). Builders also had to keep in mind the fact that

The Louis Orge homestead (sod house and barn), 1907. [SAB, S-B 7539]

the cellar had to remain dry, and in the absence of a naturally draining sandy soil, a drainage system had to be considered while the cellar was under construction. A trench two feet deeper than the cellar had to be dug around the cellar and filled with gravel. This trench then had to be extended to a spot away and downhill from the house so that water would drain away through the gravel rather than collect in the less porous cellar itself (Anonymous, 1908, p. 43).

All in all, building a soddie required that tons of sod be gathered, hauled to the building site, and stacked to a height above the heads of the settlers, and that thousands of pounds of soil be dug out of the cellar area and hauled away. The individual tasks were arduous, and even with the assistance of every family member capable of helping in some way, the construction of a home was clearly a difficult job that absorbed a great deal of labour power. In most cases, only the strongest children could be called upon to stack sod or dig cellars, but younger boys and girls could cut the blocks to size. While most families studied did not report requiring their children to assist with the more strenuous aspects of construction work, the Smith family was, to a degree, an exception to the rule. Kathleen Smith (n.d., p. 6) indicates that every member of her family, including her six siblings, all under eleven years of age, helped to dig a "small cellar, about eight by eight by six feet deep" under their home. They then helped to lay the lower layers of sod bricks to make walls, and later her father and a younger brother drove a wagon to a nearby valley and cut "two big loads of poplar poles" to use as rafters for the sod roof (Smith, n.d., p. 6). The children also helped to peel the bark off the poles and sort out the straight shafts to be used in the building.

A more common task for children who helped with the construction process, one that even the smallest children could perform, was finishing the walls by chinking the inevitable cracks.[11] For example, Mildred Hyndman (1979) talks about the process of building with sod in her memoir of life on a homestead near Morse, Saskatchewan. Her family had arrived at the farm in 1910 and in their first year put up several buildings. Although she was only ten and her brother was just turning seven, they were called upon to assist with the work, but she indicates that it "was fun to us, chinking the cracks with mud, and watching the walls get higher every day" (Hyndman, 1979, p. 2). As small hands were able to fit into tighter spots, children might actually perform the finishing tasks more efficiently than could adults.

Children could also help with decorating the interior once construction was complete, since a mud layer to seal the interior walls was needed. In Evelyn McLeod's case (1977), her mother put cheesecloth and wallpaper over the mud to complete the illusion that the house was made with flat walls rather than with layers of sod. The children helped her with this lighter labour since it called more for patience and skill than for muscular strength. The family of Sue Harrigan (1980) took a similar approach to finishing their home. All family members chinked the walls of the soddie so that leaks would not occur and maintenance work could be avoided. Mud was pressed into crevices on both the exterior and the interior of their house to seal leaks, but they went on to improve the arrangement even further. After they smoothed the interior walls with a mud plaster, cotton cloth was pasted to the mud, and wallpaper was then glued over the cotton to complete the sealing of the structure. The extra precautions must have worked since no report of maintenance work for the walls appears in Sue's memoir.

For those with access to the necessary materials, it was possible to enhance the interior of the soddie to a higher level than was achieved by either the McLeod or the Harrigan families. This finishing technique is reported by Kathleen Smith (n.d.), whose family had access to a white mud clay found in a local coulee near their homestead in the Weyburn, Saskatchewan, area. Her mother was from a poor farming family in Ireland that had also been required to make the most of their farm's resources and thus was aware that suitably prepared clay could be used as wall plaster. If properly applied, the clay coating gave the rough sod walls a professionally finished look. However, this experiment in decorating took a great deal of effort on the part of Kathleen, her siblings, and their mother. Clay had to be excavated and moved to the farmyard, a trench had to be dug near the house to use as a mixing tub for the clay slurry, and water had to be hauled in barrels from a nearby lake to mix with the raw clay. Before it could be applied to create a flat finished surface, the clay had to be smooth and soft, and the necessary consistency could only be achieved if the water and clay in the trench were stirred constantly, a tiring job for children, and one that required both muscle and endurance.

Inside the house, hatchets were used to smooth out bumps in the walls, and once all of the preparation was complete, the clay had to be pressed onto the walls to seal the dirt and form a flat surface. Kathleen noted that the clay "did not stick by just trying to put it on with a trowel, so [they] all helped by throwing it against the sod and then it was evened out with a board covered with a piece of carpet dipped in water" (Smith, n.d., p. 6). The clay cracked as it dried, but by monitoring the walls closely, the children were able to locate and fill the cracks and then smooth the repaired section until a stable surface was achieved. At that point a thin paste of clay was made and used to "paint" the walls with a final conceal- ing coat, with the result being flat, white, washable walls that appeared to be made of plaster. The contrast with the previous uncleanable mud and grass walls presumably boosted morale and thus made the expenditure of labour worthwhile.

Other ideas for improving sod houses included using blankets as room dividers, newspapers as wallpaper to hide the dirt, and rough-cut trees for flooring to keep the family's feet out of the dirt, all of which consumed ei- ther labour power or its equivalent, money. Emptied flour sacks could also make the home more livable if they were bleached to remove the writing, dipped in paraffin wax to make them waterproof, and then fastened into place as windows by someone with enough time and energy remaining to work on "frills" (Kennedy, 1970). A person could not see out of this type of window, but some light could enter the house and improve the ambience. Thus, sod houses could be made somewhat more comfortable to live in, but only if sufficient labour was employed for that purpose.

While soddies were essentially cost free and could be built even by those with little knowledge of construction techniques, they remained a continuous draw on the family's labour power after construction was completed. Beautification programs for the interiors may have improved morale, but simply maintaining the houses took time away from other needs. For example, the damage done by water and wind erosion of the exterior had to be repaired to keep the dwelling secure and to avoid any weakening of the walls.

In addition to regular maintenance, unexpected problems such as dam- age caused by animals or pests could arise and lead to an immediate need for reallocation of labour resources. For example, the experience of the Hillson family of Drinkwater, Saskatchewan, is instructive. The family had built a hybrid soddie dug partially into the side of a hill.[12] Sod walls were built out from the hill to expand the living space, and a sod roof supported by wooden posts extended from the hill to the front wall of the home. The difficulty with the soddie design was that the Hillsons had not provided any form of divider or fence on the hillside to keep animals from walking onto the sod roof. The defect was discovered when a cow walked onto the hill. When it crossed onto the sod roof, the thin poplar trees supporting the sod were not strong enough to hold the weight of the animal, and the cow fell through into the bedroom. The hole in the roof and the damage to the home had to be repaired quickly, forcing the family to expend valuable labour on repairing the damage and making the new roof secure from other unexpected visitors (Taggart, 1958).

Aside from the occasional large animal that caused damage, the homesteaders also had to remain aware that while the building material for their homes was free of charge, it had been taken from what had been, up to the moment of severance, a complex, interdependent grassland ecosystem filled with life. Just as the sod used on the roofs of the soddies did not die,[13] neither did the insects and animals inhabiting the sod. This became evident to Gladys Kennedy when a weakened section of sod fell into the house while she was caring for her sick grandmother. This piece of the roof, along with the family of newborn mice living in the sod, fell onto her grandmother's bed, but rather than panicking, the ever-practical Gladys noted that since one of her other duties was to protect the house from pests, the broken roof saved her some work because it was easy to catch the baby mice. She "soon did away with the little things…[and this] saved catching them in traps later to keep them out of…[the] food" (Kennedy, 1970, pp. 5–6). Of course, the time Gladys saved on pest control would have been lost to the labour required to repair the depredations of their resident mice.

Mice were not the only prairie creatures to find the sod a comfortable place to take up residence. For example, Kathleen Smith (n.d.) reports that garter snakes crawled onto the walls of her family's home; luckily the reptiles appeared to enjoy sleeping in the cracks between layers of sod but did not get into the house at all. Since the snakes were harmless and ate other pests, no harm was done and no extra work was created. However, a story told by Viola Cameron (1975) is quite different. Viola (an orphan from the United States being raised by her maternal grandmother) was under five years old when brought to Canada in 1908 to live on her grandmother's homestead near Bandfurley, Alberta.[14] They became established in a sod house next to a Russian settler who had the misfortune to possess a sod roof on his house. In the winter, the warmth attracted garter snakes to nest in the roof, and unfortunately "it wasn't unusual for a garter snake to stick its head down. I guess looking for food or something" (Cameron, 1975, p. 3). The neighbor would then "blast" the snake with either his .22 rifle or a shotgun, depending on which was closer at hand.

Family labour was also called upon to limit or repair the damage caused to the home by rain, particularly in terms of keeping the roof in a decent state of repair. However, rainwater eventually leaked through thatch or sod roofs to drip into the interior no matter what or how many precautions were taken or how much labour was devoted to seeing that this did not happen. Leaks were inevitable since sod, even if laid in multiple layers, was not waterproof. The water soaked the sod and then trickled through once the sod could hold no additional moisture. Thus, a roof could protect settlers from limited rainfall, but if enough rain fell to saturate the sod, the drips would begin and last until the excess water worked its way through to the interior. Isabel and Betty McNaught describe the protection that sod roofs provided from the rain by indicating that a "flat sod roof doesn't shed any rain, it just starts a little later and lasts longer" (1976, p. 10). In other words, a two-day rain outside might leak through and continue for three days inside.

Gladys Kennedy makes a similar point in her story of the mud and straw roof on her grandmother's home on the family homestead near Mannville, Alberta. She notes that "when it rained hard the roof leaked and dripped for a day or two after, so we had to put buckets etc., to catch the drips, even had to move the beds sometimes" (Kennedy, 1970, p. 5). The same point is made by Harriette Parkinson, who indicates that she slept with her parents in the one corner of the house that stayed dry in a storm. Her mother tried wallpapering the ceiling to solve the problem, but water accumulated on the paper and created a bulge hanging from the roof. As "a helpful nine-year-old," Harriette poked the bulge with a fork to drain the water, but it poured through, tearing the paper and thus ending that experiment (Parkinson, 1978, p. 1). Even adopting different designs for the roofs did not always work, as shown by the experience of Elmer Spackman. Elmer wrote of the house that he and his family lived in after immigrating to Stirling, Alberta, from Utah in 1902 when he was just a boy. Even though the house had a roof made of sawn planks (the bottom layer was laid in place with its bark side down while an overlapping layer was placed on top with its bark side up to shed water), the rain poured through. Spackman (1975, p. 6) explains that "whenever we had a rain storm it rained in the house as well...[and we had to] put pans all over the beds and all over the house" to protect the interior.

The inability to build a roof that remained watertight wasted a great deal of labour power in maintenance, repairing of water damage, and setting out and emptying drip pots when the rain leaked through despite the work done to prevent this. However, given the lack of resources available to the settlers, there was little choice but to live with the situation and expend the necessary labour. There was no means to build a consistently leak-proof roof given the materials and technology of the time.

Of course, the inconvenience and extra work for Gladys and Harriette were quite minor compared to the experience of Delia Crawford (1976) after her family migrated to a homestead near Athabasca, Alberta, in 1912. Nothing could have prepared them for the deluge of water drips that came through their sod roof after fifty-two straight days of rain. Confinement inside the small house was claustrophobic, and the constant dampness, the sound of water splashing inside the house, and irregular sleeping arrangements were devastating to family health and morale. As Delia describes the situation,

> it was raining inside as well as outside. Oh that was really
> something. The only dry place there was was over the one
> bed, the rest of us we all slept on the floor.... It was hard
> times. I remember mom took the oilcloth off the big table we
> had and put it over, nailed it to the roof like. And that's the
> only place it was kind of halfways dry in there. The rest of it
> was soaking wet. (Crawford, 1976, pp. 2–3)[15]

Because of the damage done by wildlife, decay, and the rain, sod roofs had to be replaced every two years at most if serious seepage was to be avoided.[16] However, if necessary repairs were performed on a regular basis, the houses could last many years, as Mabel Hawthorne's family proved by living in their original soddie for fourteen years after arriving at their homestead near Saskatoon, Saskatchewan. Aside from the regular work that it took to maintain the house, Mabel enjoyed living as a settler in a soddie. She noted in her memoir that the thick walls made it quite warm in the winter, cool in the summer, and quiet in all seasons since it blocked out the sound of the wind and prairie thunderstorms that she hated (Hawthorne, n.d.).

Sod was such a versatile building material that in addition to homes, it was also used in the construction of buildings such as barns. For example, in her diaries, Nellie Hislop (Nuffield, 1987) indicates that when her father decided to build a barn from sod to save money on lumber, the children were set to hauling the sod pieces ploughed up by their father earlier in the day. As described by Nellie,

We lifted the sod piece by piece, onto lengths of sacking and dragged it to the building site. Johnnie [her brother] began cutting the pieces of sod into blocks of regular width, and when he had a supply, he showed us how to lay them along the line of poles, packing them carefully to make an air-tight wall. It was much like building a play fort out of blocks of snow, except the sods were considerably heavier. (Nuffield, 1987, p. 58)

Of course, the children were unable to build the walls very high, but they did help as much as they were able to. Even Nellie's father was stymied for a time when he could not lift the sod high enough to finish the barn, but by hiring two brothers from the neighbouring farm, he was able to complete the barn and move on to other projects. Sheds for equipment and shelters for livestock were also built with sod, as was a "cool room" for processing milk, cream, butter, and cheese. The labour of all of the members of the Hislop family went into building these structures, but the one thing they could not build of sod was a pigpen. They discovered that pigs would either rip through a sod wall or burrow under it to escape confinement. For this reason, "a trip to the Big Bush, eight miles east, to fetch a load of logs became necessary. The logs were cut into six foot lengths, then sharpened on one end, and driven into the ground" to make a fence that would hold the pigs (Nuffield, 1987, p. 59). The burrowing and destructive habits of pigs were also known to the English-born Minifie family, but they were not as efficient in their construction techniques. Rather than making a solid wall with its foundation driven into the ground, they attempted to use fence posts with nailed boards as their defence against their pigs running free. "By tea-time, [the pigs] were galloping happily about the prairie" and the boys' next task was to track down their future market products and return them to the pen, which was immediately re inforced (Minifie, 1972, p. 101).

An additional use for sod as a building material was revealed by the Minifies' son James in 1909. He was disappointed that he had not been able to assist with building a soddie because his father had decided to build the family home with lumber. However, he did find a way to follow in the path of the earlier settlers. In his words, "the romantic urge to build was strong enough to set me to erecting a sod house for my dog, from turf turned over in the garden. I shared the kennel and fleas with Tim, the inevitable farm collie, happily enough," but after a few days of living in the doghouse, he came better to appreciate the wooden house his father had built (Minifie, 1972, p. 61).

Felling and hauling logs on a sleigh in the winter, n.d. [PAA, A-3476]

Other experiments with unique building materials and/or techniques are reported by farm children in their stories of life on the frontier. Elmer Spackman (1975), for example, used his ingenuity to handle the task of building a chicken coop without the wood necessary to construct the usual wooden shed. His solution was to build the coop like a root cellar in the side of a coulee near the family home. The chickens were protected from adverse weather by roofing the hole with boards left over from construction of a barn, piling on a layer of straw for warmth, and covering this with dirt to weigh the roof down. Rocks cleared from the fields were also put to good use by innovators such as Ellenor Merriken's family (1999), who used them to build a small smokehouse that could be used to cure ham and other meats for later use.

Unlike many families that homesteaded in the central Alberta area, the DeVore family was able to build a log house on their homestead, but it was due more to luck than to careful planning. The family had lived in southern Oregon (an area that had been settled for approximately 50 years and had access to large supplies of wood) and thus did not like the idea of improvising a home out of sod cut from the unbroken prairie, or a hole dug into the side of a hill. For this reason, Roy DeVore's father was determined to find a suitable parcel of land with sufficient trees for their needs. The family spent a year in Calgary, and during this period, Roy's father took the train to Innisfail twice and walked the land west of the town trying to find an appropriate farming location. He finally gave up the search when he could no longer stand the flies, mosquitoes, dust, and heat of the long walk into the unclaimed lands and settled for a poor piece of hilly property covered in poplar and willow trees. The land had minimal topsoil lying over a thick layer of clay and "boasted seven sloughs" (DeVore, 1970, p. 27).

When the time came to move to the homestead and build a home, only the father and fourteen-year-old Roy went ahead, while the rest of the family waited in Calgary. Luckily, the homestead had access to many spruce trees that were relatively straight and of similar circumference and height. The father also arranged for a supply of cut lumber to be prepared at a local sawmill for use as flooring, doorframes, and gables in the new house. They cut and hauled enough trees to the building site for a log cabin sixteen feet wide by twenty-six feet deep.

Unfortunately for Roy and his father, they had begun construction on the homestead late in the fall of 1906 and had to continue their construction work during what was recorded as the worst winter in prairie history. In fact, Roy's memoir refers to that first winter on the prairies as "THE winter" (DeVore, 1970, p. 33).[17] He recalled that the winter was like no other in his memory. Bitterly cold temperatures (reaching minus sixty-five degrees Fahrenheit) made the three-person construction crew "dance to keep our ill-clad feet from freezing, beat our mittened hands together to maintain circulation, and...rub bridle-bits with bared hands ere putting them in the oxen's mouths lest they stick to tongues, taking the skin off" (DeVore, 1970, p. 33).

Despite the cold that froze the combs off the roosters, the feet off the chickens, and the ears off the cats and calves, they worked outdoors in the dangerous conditions and did not finish the final chinking with swamp moss until January 15, 1907. A more thorough job of filling the cracks was done in the spring, when it became possible to dig up mud and clay to prepare plaster for spreading between the individual logs. Amazingly, the DeVores spent this first winter in a tent while they were working on the construction of their home. As Roy noted, they endured "hardship, sheer privation, and exhausting dawn to dusk labour that left us aged in middle-life" (DeVore, 1970, p. 34).

Boys, of course, were not the only children to take part in the construction of buildings on the pioneer farms. For example, Mary Hiemstra (1997) entered Canada in 1903 as a six-year-old whose family was part of the group of English "Barr Colonists" being led to settle the Lloydminster area on the present Alberta-Saskatchewan border. The area boasted many trees, so the family decided that a log house would be most appropriate for their needs. There was an argument about the size of the proposed home, but it was the height of the available poplar trees that ultimately set the limits on the length and width. Mary and her father headed into the bush to find, cut, trim, and haul the needed logs back to the homesite. In her memoirs, Mary noted that it was not easy to find even two or three trees out of an entire grove that were straight and long enough to serve in the construction of their home:

> To see if a tree would do Dad stood at the foot and squinted up at it from all sides. If it suited, he chopped it down, lopped off the branches and the top, hitched Nelly [their horse] to one end of it, and dragged it out of the bush. (Hiemstra, 1997, p. 159)

They collected eight to ten suitable logs at a time, and then the wagon was brought around. Lifting heavy logs onto a wagon was difficult labour[18] and far beyond the capacities of a six-year-old; Mary wrote that her father "did the loading, but I kept him company and thought I helped" (Hiemstra, 1997, p. 159). She did have to tolerate the heat, dust, scratches from rose thorns and twigs, bruises from falling over roots, and the jolting ride back and forth in an unsprung wagon with rock-hard seats. In fact, the ride was so bumpy that Mary had to sit at the back behind the wheels so that if she was thrown from the wagon by a bump, she would not be run over before the horse could be stopped.

Mary indicates that once the logs were on site, the building process itself was also arduous:

> logs that had looked straight when they were growing in the groves all curved one way or another when cut down, and they had to be turned this way and that so that the walls would be as even as possible, then the logs had to be notched and fitted to one another. When the walls were low the fitting and turning wasn't too hard, but the higher the walls grew the harder the fitting got. (Hiemstra, 1997, p. 161)

Despite the problems, the weight of the logs, and the difficulty of lifting the highest logs to the top of the wall, the family overcame the obstacles together. One final service that Mary performed in the building of her future home was to help her father with notching the logs so that they would lock together rather than falling apart. The logs would, unless anchored in some fashion, roll away from the wall or shift position so that the bends and curves in one log no longer matched those in the one beneath it. Mary and her father solved this problem by sitting on opposite ends of the logs to brace them as her father chopped the notches. The work was not perfect, but by tolerating the strain of sitting on a slipping log while the shock of each axe blow was transmitted through the log and into her legs, arms, and back, the child contributed to the construction of her future home.

As a result of the social conventions of the time, Mary's mother was unable to help with the construction process to any great degree. She was caring for Mary's young brother, and although they sometimes switched jobs so that Mary could rest while playing with the baby, she was wearing a dress and thus could not straddle the logs to balance them. Sitting sidesaddle did not help because she could not grip the logs with her legs to stop them from shifting under her, and thus Mary helped more often. Despite the rough treatment she took, Mary wrote that she was never hurt and that "helping with the house made [her] feel very big and important" (Hiemstra, 1997, p. 160). Of course, not all children could carry so much of the labour load in their families. Molly Sanford, for example, was capable only of helping her father to roof their newly built home, yet when the job was complete, she still had a sense of accomplishment over what she had done and stated with pride that "it seems I can put my hand to almost anything" (Stansell, 1976, p. 95).

Amelia Smith (1975) was another young girl who sought to help with the workload of establishing her family's new homestead near Fort MacLeod, Alberta. Her father handled all of the heaviest labour needs, which included constructing a house, stable, and fence using materials that had to be hauled across twenty miles of prairie. Living in a tent for the first month while building progressed was exciting for Amelia, but once the roof boards were on the house, she added her efforts to the process and assisted her father in shingling the roof. As she describes her contribution,

> I lay the shingles for my father and he nailed them you see. I remember being so careful not to have one crack over another crack. I enjoyed doing that, I thought it was wonderful. We just moved into the house…and the next day the tent was blown down. (Smith, 1975, p. 4)

The luck of completing their move before anyone was hurt by a storm and the feeling of accomplishment for Amelia were both positive outcomes of encouraging children to contribute to handling the workload on the frontier.

In her memoirs dealing with her life as an immigrant on a farm near

Dauphin, Manitoba, in 1897, Anna Farion also describes taking part in constructing the family's first home. Her father, a carpenter by trade, felled the trees and squared off the logs using an axe while Anna, her mother, and several smaller children hauled the logs to the construction site at the top of a hill. This task was conducted using muscle power alone since no animals were available to be hitched to draglines and was thus exhausting for both the children and their mother. Once enough logs were gathered, the walls were built by laying the trees in opposite directions to reduce the degree of unevenness caused by the fact that the trees were thicker at the base than the top. Anna was too small to help build the walls, so her efforts may not have been as extensive as those of Mary Hiemstra, but she and the rest of her siblings did assist in the construction of their own home. Hauling logs was not skilled work, but it was necessary, and Anna notes proudly that "the palms of our hands were covered with calluses" by the time they were done (1978, p. 87).

Sod and log houses were not the only designs in use on the prairies since settlers made do with whatever resources they could locate. As mentioned earlier, reliable sources of trees were not easy to find in the drier southern zone although some homesteaders did live in the river valleys and could find suitable trees. Others had to be more innovative. For example, Aquina Anderson's (n.d.) family moved to Wood Mountain, Saskatchewan, from South Dakota in 1911. They found that they had access to large deposits of clay on their homestead, but not to the thick sod that made soddies possible. Ingeniously, they adopted the construction techniques used in the southwestern United States and built an adobe house using a mix of clay and straw as wall material.

To make this type of house (referred to as a "doby"), Aquina's father and a friend spent several days cutting slim poplars and fine willow trees to use as frames on the new house and additional days peeling off the bark to obtain a solid surface. "The poplars were nailed horizontally to upright poles and were hewn to give them a flat surface, after which the fine willows were nailed diagonally across the face of the walls, both inside and out" (Anderson, n.d., p. 3). Once the frame was in place, clay, water, and hay were mixed in a wagon into a thick mud until the mixture reached the proper consistency to be applied to the walls. At that point, the other family members were able to help spread the clay mixture over both the interior and the exterior surfaces of the wooden frame to provide a double layer of protection on the walls. The clay dried to form a hard waterproof wall and the hay filler helped to prevent cracking. Given the lack of other suitable materials, the house was completed using boards purchased in Moose Jaw, Saskatchewan, for the floor and roof.

Other experimenters adopted hay as a construction material even though it was also valuable as fodder for livestock. For example, Charles Phillips (1967) was twelve years old when his family migrated to the area of Stettler, Alberta, in 1908. In their first year, Charles and his father harvested hay for their livestock, but because they had no storage buildings, they built a pole structure at the homestead and then stacked the hay around the poles. The hay formed walls; Charles refers to their creation as a "hay barn." Christen Christensen also mentions hay barns in his description of homesteading at sixteen. He and his brother were put in charge of setting up the homestead when his father was crippled by rheumatism while working on a house during their first winter (1903) on the prairies. The boys slept in the one-room shanty that they had built, while their father and mother had a bedroom in the hay barn. Unfortunately, the barn was constantly cold, and their mother "had to have mitts on to make the bed in winter...[because] the cows kept eating through the hay walls" (Christensen, 1976, p. 11).

One of the few construction tasks suited to children with minimal adult assistance was fence construction. The required labour was not as heavy as for other tasks so children could readily handle most of the work necessary for the process. As disclosed in Nellie Hislop's (Nuffield, 1987) memoir, her brother Johnnie's turn to assist in the building of a fence came when he was thirteen years old. Their father would spend a day chopping down trees in a wooded area approximately eight miles from their homestead near Prairie Grove, Manitoba, and the next day, he and Johnnie would sharpen the posts with an axe. Fixing the posts in line would begin on the third day, the father and son using a three-step technique to seat the posts in place. In the first step, a one-foot-deep hole was dug at the appropriate spot; water was then poured into the hole to "soak and soften the dry, hard soil" and prepare it for the third step, which occurred once the water had turned the dirt to mud. This involved their father driving the post into the hole with an axe while Johnnie held it in place, both of them getting splattered with mud every time the post sank a little deeper. Wire was then stretched tightly between posts and nailed securely in place.

Bertha Myer (1978), the only girl to indicate that she had worked on building fences, told of the day her father required assistance with the stringing of a wire fence and she was the only one available. She drove the horses pulling the wagon loaded with wire along the fence line as close as possible to the posts themselves to ensure a tight fit for the wire and was amazed that she could do so without running over any posts or tangling the wire. She was only seven years old at the time.

As an alternative to wire fencing with its need for purchased wire and expensive nails to secure the wire to the posts, Norman Stewart (1962) describes a fence that he and his brothers built without the need to purchase any hardware. The construction process began with locating and felling relatively straight poplar trees at least fourteen feet in height and two to four inches in circumference. It could take weeks to gather enough logs, but once stripped of branches and cut to the appropriate length, these fence rails could be stockpiled near the construction location until needed. Willow trees were gathered and sharpened for use as pickets or posts to support the rails, while skinny but long willow branches, still green and with sap, were collected for use as "withes" or ties to secure the rails onto the pickets.

While the materials were different, the building system used to set the pickets was identical to that described above in reference to Johnnie Hislop. A hole was started using one of the pickets, and water was then poured in to soften the ground at that location. This process was repeated until the picket could be pushed sixteen inches into the ground without hammering. Two pickets were set side by side to act as guides for the rails, and the rails themselves were then put into place and secured using the willow branch "withes" to the height needed for an animal to be confined in or kept out of the area (Stewart, 1962).

Summary

While not every labour project undertaken by children was a success, and not every child could participate in all activities, they were encouraged to participate in whatever way they could. Farming children were clearly seen, with social approval, as workers on family farms. Most settlers could have accomplished their tasks without child labour, but the key point to be made is that for those family farms with child labour available, the work could be more widely distributed and, as such, the capacity to move the family's fortunes forward existed if they wished to use it.

THREE

Productive Labour

THE CHILD LABOUR DIRECTED AT CONSTRUCTION was of assistance but, to succeed in farming, the family also had to move forward quickly with productive operations. Once again, children were regarded as a family labour resource, this time to assist in producing agricultural foodstuffs that would generate money for the family coffers. Tables 6 and 7 below detail the application of boys' and girls' labour in the production of crops and livestock.

TABLE 6

Productive Labour:
Boys' Contributions by Age and Type of Work

AGE	Field Work	Livestock Production	Working with Horses	Stable Chores	Transporting Crops	Clearing Fields	Chores/ Running Errands/ Helping
4–5	1	1	0	0	0	1	1
6–8	2	4	0	1	0	0	3
9–11	25	20	14	2	3	4	10
12–14	38	29	10	2	6	6	4
>14	10	8	1	0	0	4	0

TABLE 7
Productive Labour:
Girls' Contributions by Age and Type of Work

AGE	Field Work	Livestock Production	Working with Horses	Stable Chores	Transporting Crops	Clearing Fields	Chores/ Running Errands/ Helping
4–5	0	0	0	0	0	0	0
6–8	0	2	2	0	0	1	1
9–11	2	9	7	0	0	2	6
12–14	5	18	8	1	0	2	11
>14	0	0	1	0	1	0	0

Much of the labour involved in clearing the land, tilling the soil, planting the crops, and harvesting the grain was physically taxing and thus fell to the stronger boys of the family, but several girls did take part. The raising of livestock required a somewhat lower level of strength than hauling rocks and chopping roots out with an axe but, while boys still made up the majority of the child workforce reporting activity in this area, their participation did not outweigh that of girls to as great a degree. Participation in such heavy labour was limited in the younger age groups but intensified with age. The involvement of children in almost every phase of production suggests that they were active members of the family labour pool, not mere assistants.

Field Work

Despite government advertising brochures that suggested it was possible simply to "scratch the rich virgin soil to ensure good results" (Eager, 1953, p. 2), the pioneers soon found that a great deal of heavy physical labour had to be expended in the preparation of their land for seeding. The brochures were accurate to a degree since the soil was extremely rich in nutrients after thousands of years of natural development, but they did not specify that "scratching" the soil would take much slow, back-breaking effort, particularly when dealing with thick vegetation growth. Depending upon the geography of the site and the extent of tree coverage, settlers had to remove trees and destroy the roots so that cultivation could start the following year. Roy DeVore (1970), for instance, reports that his family cleared and broke new land on a continual basis in the first year. By their second year on their Alberta homestead, they had begun work on a portion of their property in a river valley that was

> covered with brush and timber and had to be literally hewed
> out. Land had to be "grubbed" before it could be plowed; fence
> posts had to be cut, hauled, sharpened and driven before the
> land could be enclosed. Sloughs had to be corduroyed with
> timber before being crossed and wells must need be dug since
> there was no money to pay well drillers. (DeVore, 1970, p. 40)

Clearly, the process of breaking the sod was not as simple as unloading a plough from the settler's wagon and getting started with the work. As indicated by another pioneer, Mr. S.G. Hickley of Nipawin, Saskatchewan, the process of clearing was time-consuming since he was only able to break thirteen acres of land over two years, rather than the twenty acres mandated by the *Dominion Lands Act* of 1872 (Turner, 1955). The problems that he faced were similar to those that had plagued DeVore—that is, the need to remove the brush and destroy the offending roots with an axe.

An anonymous young female contributor to Barry Broadfoot's book *The Pioneer Years* (1976, p. 45) comments on her parents' homestead near Edmonton, Alberta, which was covered with bush:

> Bush. That's what we called it then but bush today means
> little trees and willows. [But] I mean big trees. Pine trees
> and cottonwoods, poplars, every kind of tree seemed to grow
> on that homestead up in the bush, and they weren't small. A
> man is five foot eight, right? An axe is three feet long. A day
> is as long as you want it to last but say, say 10 hours. And do
> you know how big 160 acres is? And then look at those trees.
> Some were only six inches through but lots, many, many
> many were a foot through.

Given the nature of this work, few children were strong enough to assist in this preliminary process.[1] However, those who did work in the fields, such as a fifteen-year-old boy from Wellwood, Manitoba, who wrote under the pseudonym "A Roxburghshire Lad" (August, 1902), were fulfilling several important functions. As the "Lad" notes, he was involved with all phases of the clearing and land-preparation process: chopping down small poplar trees, digging out oak trees (of which he felt there were many in Manitoba!), sawing the wood, and breaking the sod (170 acres in total). He explains that, once broken and turned over to dry, the desiccated sod had to be ploughed, disked, or harrowed to shatter large clumps of dirt before planting could begin.

Even in those areas where only prairie grasses grew, the breaking process was not automatic. Simply using the breaking plough to turn the sod so that the roots would be exposed to air and light and begin to decompose was not feasible if rocks were hidden in the grass. Such rocks could break or dull the cutting blade and thus had to be removed before the plough could cut its first furrow, adding to the amount of labour required to start production (Turner, 1955). Turner (1955, p. 45) relates the story of Mr. H.R. Carson of Bladworth, Saskatchewan, who "spent as much time digging stones with a pick as breaking" and then used an ox to haul the stones away from the fields. Even so, he was more fortunate than Mr. F.N. Krischke, a British immigrant whose homestead appeared to be perfect at the outset. Two streams ran across the land, the grass was thick, and there was a treed area within the quarter section. Unfortunately, there were so many rocks in the soil that the land was almost impossible to farm.

Children such as Alfred Jones (1902), a thirteen-year-old boy living near Eden, Manitoba, were called upon to use their labour in clearing fields of obstructions that would prevent the ploughing of the sod. Alfred indicates that he could "pick stones and roots...[and] pick up scrub and burn it," tasks that required strength and endurance (Jones, 1902, p. 741). Another child, ten-year-old Martin Henderson (1902, p. 507) of Alemeda, Saskatchewan, also notes that he could "draw stone off the land," but he was not able to clear brush or trees, given his small size.

Once any obvious rocks were removed from the area and the roots from trees and brush were eliminated, the settlers could proceed to break the land. However, the ploughs, or more accurately the metal blades, were not necessarily strong enough to cut through the sod. If the metal was dulled or bent in cutting a furrow, the plough might bog down since the horses or oxen might not have the power to pull a dull blade through the resisting ground cover. This meant having to stop to sharpen or repair the plough whenever it was damaged.[2] This difficulty in breaking the land is confirmed in the memoirs of Mr. S.T. St. John (1949), an American immigrant who homesteaded at Wilcox, Saskatchewan. He recalled that breaking called for many weeks of hard toil and frustrating delays for the settlers before they could begin to plant their first crop. Since the thick mat of interlaced roots was hard to cut through with only horses or oxen to power the plough, long days that exhausted animals and farmers alike were the norm.

More children note their participation once the process reached the stage at which ploughing could begin. For example, according to eleven-

Clearing brush and breaking the land, n.d. [PAA, B.705]

year-old Charles Phillips (1967), he and his seventeen-year-old brother, Glen, assisted their father in the process of breaking the land. Glen was less enthusiastic about farming than Charles, so when it was time to begin working, Charles "drove the lead team" that ploughed the land while his father "drove the wheelers and held the walking plow" (Phillips, 1967, p. 17). Charles also had the additional chore of sharpening the plough "shear" to ensure that it would cut through the tough sod, a job that required him to beat any dents out of the metal portions of the plough using rocks and to hone the edge with the same stones. Despite the fact that Charles spent more time in the fields than his elder brother, it was Glen who suffered the consequences of the dangers associated with farm labour. The horses Glen was using to pull a seed drill across the farmyard to a storage location bolted, and he was thrown under the drill and dragged for several feet until the equipment came to rest. Neighbours helped stop the bleeding of the deep gash on his leg, but he then had to be transported over fifty miles of rough terrain to a doctor since the cut went to the bone and had to be properly treated if he was to live and regain the use of the limb. He only recovered after a convalescence of several months.

Once the heavy breaking work was complete, only small teams of horses or oxen were required to pull ploughs through the dead and unresisting sod while the driver wrestled with the problem of keeping the furrow straight and the blade in the ground. Much of the work to be done was thus reduced to ploughing the land in the spring to prepare it for a new crop or using harrows to break up clumps and smooth out the seedbed. In either case, the physical strength required to control the plough and animals was reduced, and the task became one that could be taken over by almost any child if the need arose. Aaron Biehn of Humboldt, Saskatchewan, for example, was only eight years old when his labour was called upon to assist in ploughing land on the family homestead. As he describes the job, there was work enough for the entire family of six children and two adults as they "hitched [their] four horses to a gang plow and broke up sod [that was in large pieces and then] disked and harrowed and planted....All summer long everybody were busy preparing ground for the next year" (Biehn, n.d., p. 3). Frederick Hayne-Stephans (1901) was another child called on to work at ploughing the fields. At fifteen years of age, he was well versed in the use of most farm equipment and took on the job of ploughing the entire eighty acres of summerfallow that his father had left bare the previous year. He pointed out that he started the job using three horses on a walking plough but switched over to a quicker method using four horses on a gang plough to speed up his progress.[3]

Other children younger than Frederick also expended their labour on preparing the land. For example, a ten-year-old boy from Burnside, Manitoba, named Gordon Frook (1901) notes that he worked with both walking and gang ploughs, the harrow, and a land roller. An almost identical story is told by another ten-year-old boy named Charlie Arnold (1901) from Indian Head, Saskatchewan. Charlie ploughed, harrowed, and rolled but also indicates that he was learning to seed. Numerous other boys also stated that they had taken part in "working the fields." For example, J. MacDonald (1901), a twelve-year-old boy from Poplar Grove, Saskatchewan, states that he ploughed ten acres of land when he was only nine years old. Another twelve-year-old, Aylmer Whitehead (1902) from Weyburn, Saskatchewan, says that he was able to handle four horses when he disked and harrowed. Arthur Card (1902), a fourteen-year-old boy from Glenboro, Manitoba, reports that beginning at 5 a.m. every day, he either drove four horses on a gang plough or six horses on the harrows, or used four when operating the cultivator, depending on the work to be done. Only one boy had a complaint: fourteen-year-old Jas. McLean (1901, p. 569) from Ellisboro, Saskatchewan. He says that he was involved with harrowing, disking, and cultivating, but that he preferred chores associated with riding since the field work was "tire-some on the legs."

Despite the absence of the need for physical prowess at this stage of the process, only three girls mention taking part in the ploughing or harrowing of the land prior to seeding. For example, Sue Harrigan (1980, p. 8) of

Using a single-blade riding plough to break sod, n.d. [SAB, S-B 6919]

Battleford, Saskatchewan, reports working the walking plough to prepare a field for the planting of oats that would be used to feed livestock. Her only complaint about the exercise was that "it was slow work." Maryanne Caswell (1968) of Clark's Crossing, Saskatchewan, also took part in soil preparation and wrote in a letter to her grandmother that she had assisted in planting the crop by driving the family oxen to harrow a seedbed while her father hand-sowed the crop behind her. Unlike Sue Harrigan, her inexperience led to a minor disaster when she turned a corner too sharply and the oxen went out of control and dragged her until her father restrained the team. Maryanne's mother prepared a homemade remedy for the rope burns on her hands, "Balm of Gilead (black poplar)" to encourage healing (Caswell, 1968, p. 47). The third girl who mentions ploughing, Jennie Johnston of Neilburg, Saskatchewan, notes that it was never easy to work with animal-propelled machinery. Skill was required and sometimes, despite those skills, events could get out of control. For example, she notes that working with oxen was a problem since they were both large and powerful and followed orders only when convenient. At the first sight of a heel fly, the oxen were distracted from their work and took off with the plough at a run to escape the irritating pest. Similarly, on sighting a slough, "that's where they would go and no amount of coaxing or swearing" would get them to return to the field until they were ready (Johnston, 1973, p. 21).

As with most other functions performed by children, crop seeding (whether by hand or by using a "deep" seeder) was simply one skill among many that they developed. Most of those who indicate that they used a plough or harrow or other implement pulled by animals were also capable of handling the seeding task for their family. For example, Willie Moore, a fourteen-year-old boy from Oak Lake, Manitoba, indicates that his labour was almost solely responsible for the year's crop since he had "plowed, harrowed, cultivated and sowed nearly all the crop" on his own in addition to contributing his labour to other projects on the farm (Moore, 1902, p. 506). Similarly, Arthur Hamlen (1902), an eleven-year-old boy from Beresford, Manitoba, reports helping with seeding operations, while a fifteen-year-old from Miniota, Manitoba, named Charles Clyde (1902) operated the family seeder in addition to all of the ploughs and other machinery they had available. Twelve-year-old Wilbert Frew (1902) of Pense, Saskatchewan, was also handy with farm implements: he drove a plough, mower, rake, and binder in addition to the seeder.[4]

As with most agricultural implements, children could also take over driving the earth roller (otherwise known as a land packer) that was used to cover the seed after it had been planted and create a firm soil bed for the plants to grow in. Aaron Biehn was given this task when he was only nine years old. While he had no problem harnessing the four oxen that pulled the land packer or directing them to the appropriate field, he faced a problem similar to the one noted by Jennie Johnston. He mentions in his memoir that he was packing on a hot day and, unfortunately, the field was not far from a slough. There was "quite a bit of water in the slough so the oxen got hot and they went for the water. They took [Aaron] along and the oxen all laid down to cool off. [He] waited with them on the packer. They soon got up and…went back to packing the ground" (Biehn, n.d., p. 3).

Other tasks that could be turned over to children in order to divide the workload included the weeding of the crops. This job was actually better suited to children's natural abilities because it did not involve great physical strength but did require workers who could be trained to distinguish a wheat shoot from a weed and whose fingers were small enough to fit between rows of grain without destroying the growing plants. Thus, children such as Bertha Myer (1978, p. 3) were sent into the fields with the instruction that "no weeds were allowed to thrive undisturbed. [Her] work was to pull all weeds as they appeared amidst the grain." This same job was also performed by a thirteen-year-old boy named Harvey Potter (1901), whose family farm was located near Montgomery, Manitoba. Weeding was a part of his daily routine, which began at five o'clock in the morning and included milking his family's three cows. Jessie Middleton of Elphinstone,

Manitoba, also mentions that it was her job to pick "noxious weeds" out of the field (1902, p. 1020).

With respect to the final step in the crop cycle, the harvest, early farmers in the region used a scythe to cut the grain and then tied the grain into bundled sheaves. These sheaves were in turn stacked in stooks to lessen the damage that rain or cold weather might cause before a threshing crew separated the grain to be cleaned. As farm tools became more available, the grain could be cut using a mower or a binder that also tied the grain into sheaves for stacking. The process was still labour-intensive but not to the same degree, and harvest proceeded more quickly, reducing the chances of damage from unseasonable weather.

During each step in the harvest scenarios set out above (except perhaps for the threshing stage, given that threshing machines and crews were largely independent of the farms they served), the labour of children could be called upon to assist in bringing the crop in before poor weather arrived. Florence Black (1902), for example, reports that in her area near Assiniboia, Saskatchewan, everyone worked hard cutting down the grain, tying it into sheaves, and then attempting to stook the sheaves despite the strong winds that continually knocked down their stooks. Ralph Clench (1901) also writes about helping to stack the crop a year earlier, while Bertha Myer (1978) notes that she helped with lunches for the men who cut and tied the grain but also contributed, along with other girls and women, by stooking while the men ate and rested. Stooking was also the task assigned to fourteen-year-old Gertrude Winstone (1902) and her thirteen-year-old brother while their father handled the cutting function.[5]

Of course, not all children were required to perform the hard work associated with the stooking process; however, many were responsible for other tasks that had to be accomplished at that time of the year. John Dunn (1902) of Russell, Manitoba, was twelve years old when he drove a mower and binder[6] during the harvest season, while his younger brother Henry Dunn (1902) was limited to a hay mower. His parents felt that Henry, at ten years old, had only limited driving experience and was too inexperienced to work with the cash grain crop. The work of others, such as Walter Brown (1902), a nine-year-old from Portage la Prairie, Manitoba, focussed on a different aspect of the harvest process. Rather than being involved in the use of the binder, Walter was in charge of changing the teams of horses on the two binders the family had operating to harvest their grain. By working efficiently, Walter was able to keep both binders active, thereby increasing the speed and chances of success with the harvest.[7]

With respect to harvesting hay (which was made up of the natural "prairie wool" including grass, weeds, wild oats, and other plants), this crop was as vital as the cash crop of wheat because it was used to feed the horses, oxen, and any cattle held over the winter. Given that a cow and calf could eat three tons of hay, and a horse five tons, during a winter season (Stringer, 1888), at least twenty tons of hay would be required if a farmer had only three horses, a milking cow, and a calf. It could take a week or more to harvest and store the necessary twenty tons of feed. Confirmation of these figures is provided by the biography of Nellie Hislop, who estimates that three tons of hay per head was eaten over the winter season and that the family's harvesting speed was two tons per day with her father mowing and three children (and sometimes their mother) raking and coiling the hay into bundles to dry before stacking (Nuffield, 1987). This would mean approximately ten days to harvest twenty tons rather than only one week. Assuming a settler owned a small herd of ten cows and had two horses to pull his wagon and farm machinery, forty tons of hay would be required to feed the animals over the winter months. Thus, almost three weeks of labour power would have to be expended for the sustenance of the farm animals.

It is worth noting that in addition to feeding the family livestock, this crop could also be sold. For example, Elizabeth Turnbull (n.d., p. 2) indicates in her memoirs that aside from the hay they used for their own animals, her father would "sell it to the farmers around Lumsden [Saskatchewan]." The hay made up a large portion of the family income; when a prairie fire destroyed 200 loads of hay that they had harvested in 1907, money became scarce, and the family was forced to live on wild rabbits and potatoes that winter.

For W.E. McElhone, the experience of working to harvest hay for his grandparents' herd of cattle at the turn of the century was somewhat different from that of a homesteader's child assigned to cut hay on the family's land. In an interview conducted in 1975, he explained that his parents had lived in the town of Stettler, Alberta, but his grandparents had a farm located near Red Deer that he visited during his early teen years at every opportunity. However, his visits were not vacations since he was expected to assist in the search for hay and pasture lands. His grandparents did not have sufficient resources to feed their herd on their own land, and thus he was sent to look for unclaimed land where hay could be harvested and hauled back to the farm.

McElhone would ride the prairies for two or three weeks at a time, thereby making a contribution of his time to his grandparents' support. Of course, he had also been trained to use the machinery needed to harvest the hay, and once a supply was located and mowed down, his job was to rake the hay into convenient piles for transport to the farm. McElhone (1975, p. 6) describes this work:

Hauling hay for feed, n.d. [PAA, B.694]

I worked in the hay fields [and] they would give me an old
team of horses that were quiet enough for me to drive and I
would operate a buck rake...when I was hardly big enough
to hold the lines. Putting up hay in those days was always
put up in stacks, there was none of this bailing. Some of the
machinery was too complicated for me but the buck rake was
one thing I could operate, and bring the hay into the stacker
with a buck Rake.

McElhone also told the interviewer that during haying season, the hours
of work were extremely long as he worked from early morning until sun-
down.

Livestock Production

Just as some children worked long hours in the fields, others were involved
with raising livestock for the market. William Rand (1901, p. 598), for example, wrote that when he was twelve years old, he assisted his father with
the wheat they grew on their homestead near Crystal City, Manitoba. He

was proud to proclaim that he was "a great help" to his father, but he also made a point of noting that he cared for a week-old colt destined to be a riding horse plus several baby pigs, a calf, and a two-year-old mare used for work on the farm. He made it clear that animal husbandry was his preference.

While William did not directly mention the amount of work or the number of different tasks that could go into providing proper care for the family animals, clearly the job was a difficult one requiring certain attributes. Children required at least some size so that the livestock would respect them as the master of the situation, strength and agility to avoid being harmed by large animals, endurance since work was required every day, and also riding skill because until fences were built to contain them, livestock had to be tracked across the prairies. A knowledge of edible plants and some information on livestock illnesses were also of assistance.

While the size and power of many farm animals would deter many smaller children from participating, they could still handle the lighter regular tasks that also had to be performed if the family livestock were to be made ready for the market. Milk cows, pigs, chickens, and other farmyard livestock destined for sale or slaughter had to be fed and watered and their living areas had to be cleaned, the cows had to be milked, and equipment had to be kept in repair. Thus, as noted by Doris Thompson (1979, p. 1), a twelve-year-old girl whose family settled in the Saskatoon, Saskatchewan, area, "work was ever present and as children we were permitted to 'help' with feeding the chickens, gathering the eggs, feeding the pigs, bringing in the cows, etc. but as we grew older the novelty wore off [as] the continuous repetition of such jobs became a chore." Mabel McDonald (1902) of Russell, Manitoba, also mentions her responsibilities on the farm. She had to milk eleven cows, feed the calves and several pigs, and help to turn the cream separator. Lena Prout (1902), an eleven-year-old from Rapid City, Manitoba, worked at milking cows and churning butter, while an eleven-year-old from Brandon, Manitoba, named John Fardoe (1902) cleaned stables and bedded down calves. Similarly, a fourteen-year-old girl from Edberg, Alberta, helped to look after forty-two head of cattle, noting that she had "been herding sheep and cattle since [she] was five years old" (Erickson, 1902, p. 507), while seven-year-old Gordon Hamlen (1902) from Beresford, Manitoba, cleaned the henhouse. In his letter, he exclaims over the mess that ninety laying hens could make! Finally, Edna MacPhail (1902), a fourteen-year-old from Belmont, Manitoba, fed and watered several cows and forty-five hens and cleaned their living spaces.

The home of Beatrice Gaudrey; her daughter feeding the flock, n.d. [SAB, R-A17263]

Other children had more arduous duties to perform if they were responsible for the cattle. For example, William Reesor, a six-year-old Saskatchewan boy, was responsible for checking the cattle pens for dead animals. If any were found, he helped to remove them to a waste area and skin them. Although this job was distasteful, it had to be done since dead cows, if not removed, acted as beacons for predators and scavengers, drawing them to the rest of the herd. However, he noted a positive aspect of this process as the "carcasses of course, made a real banquet for many coyotes and [the family] were greeted every evening and morning with their howling" (Reesor, 1977, p. 5).

Aside from tasks associated with feeding and cleaning up after livestock, or other animals and birds, children could also be assigned to look after livestock in the field and ensure that the animals remained at or travelled to the appropriate locations. In such cases, if cattle were too large for a child to handle, he or she could be charged with herding sheep, for which task the relative size difference would not be as large. For example, Horace Ririe (1974) was given the job of herding the family flock of sheep (his older brothers worked with the horses). By the time he was twelve, his father trusted him well enough to leave him with full authority over the entire herd of 3,000 ewes that were close to giving birth.[8] Of course, in a family of fourteen children there were many hands available to share the workload. Even so, and despite his involvement with the flock, Horace also had to take care of one of the family's twelve milk cows (both in the early morning and in the evening), and take his turn churning the cream that was sold as butter to the local store.

Similarly, sixteen-year-old Bill Graham (1974) and his younger brothers were responsible for the family herd. They handled the feeding of the animals, took them to pasture, found them at milking time, and performed the actual milking process as well. They also had to fit regular field work with a team of horses into their daily schedules. Albert Corbett (1902), a thirteen-year-old boy from Rosser, Manitoba, also reports helping with the herd. He worked alongside the family's hired hands to care for the seventy head of cattle they were raising for market and the thirty milk cows that they kept to produce milk and cream for sale. Wellington McMahon (1902) was also assigned to locating and milking twelve cows twice a day. This twelve-year-old boy from Dunara, Manitoba, woke at 6 a.m. each day, traced the cows, herded them to the barn, milked them, separated the cream, and then repeated the process each evening after supper. Similarly, Frederick Arnott (1902), an eleven-year-old from Calf Mountain, Manitoba, was given the job of moving the family's eighteen head of cattle between the home yard and a pasture located one mile away every morning. Each evening, he had to track the cattle down and herd them back to the farm.

Similar duties were imposed on twelve-year-old Anne Weir (1976) after her family migrated to a farm near Olds, Alberta, from Ontario in 1895. The family had 40 milk cows to care for (some owned entirely and some owned in shares with other settlers), and Anne and her younger sister handled most of this responsibility. She also had an older sister, who helped their mother with the housework; an older brother, who tended to work off-farm for wages; and her father, who worked in the fields. As such, she may have obtained control of the animals by default. Problems for Anne were common since there "was no fenced field.…The cows went where they liked and had to be brought up every night" (Weir, 1976, p. 3). She allocated the job of locating the milk cows to her younger sister, allowing herself some free time in which she could check their inventory of milk and milk products and plan their sale. The milk obtained from these cows was separated, churned for butter, and made into cheese; the butter and cheese were sold, along with any remaining milk and cream, to creameries in nearby towns.

Similarly, but on a larger scale, Isabel Perry (née McNaught) and Betty McNaught (1976) describe their joint responsibility for the family cattle. Their father and an uncle had planned to homestead near Edson, Alberta, in 1911, but because Betty had contracted smallpox and scarlet fever, the

Small child with cattle, n.d. [PAA, B.510]

migration was delayed until she had recovered and her mother had re-
gained the strength and stamina she had used up in caring for her daughter. These young sisters and their mother finally arrived on the prairies in
1912. While their father laboured to build a thirty-foot by twenty-eight-
foot log house with a sod roof and their mother dealt with domestic tasks,
Isabel and Betty took on the responsibility of caring for the family cattle.
As explained by Isabel and Betty, they performed some subsistence and
domestic tasks, but in response to a question concerning whether they
were required to help out at home, they told the interviewer that they
primarily "herded cows, hunted cows, rode horseback for cows and did odd
chores but we weren't very useful as far as housework [was] concerned"
(1976, p. 12).

Of course, in those situations that required more strength than the
girls possessed, their father was always on call to assist. For example, on

the evening of the first Halloween they spent on the prairies, a cow went missing, and given the importance of each and every cow to the family's financial situation, Betty and her father mounted a search. The animal was found stranded near the shore of the lake where it had walked out on the ice to find water, broken through the thin ice covering, and gotten stuck in the muddy bottom. Betty was sent back to the farm to hitch up the family oxen and bring them back to the lake, but they did not have a long enough rope to reach the stranded bovine. Trips to nearby farm sites brought extra help and a longer rope, and eventually the cow was rescued.

Not all of the sisters' experiences involved hard work or danger, and there were on occasion moments of levity to lighten the mood. For example, on the wagon trip to the homestead, the girls had been in charge of the eight chickens and single rooster the family brought with them from Ontario. The rooster "was used to travelling" and left camp without the family one morning; the girls gave chase. The escaping rooster took them halfway around a nearby lake. In comparison to the evening of the mud-stuck cow, this event finished with laughter when a neighbor's daughter who came by to watch the rescue effort found that in honour of Halloween, someone had stuck horns on her horse while she was inside having tea after the event (McNaught, 1976, pp. 3, 12).

Care of the family livestock was also turned over to the young girls in the Houston family, but the circumstances were much graver (McLeod, 1977). The family arrived in the Consort area of Alberta in 1912. The head of the family, James Houston, was ill; as a result, two of his daughters, Ethel and Pearl (aged eleven and nine respectively), were made responsible for herding their cattle to the homestead. On the sixty-mile journey from the nearest railhead, they had to handle the cattle on their own since their thirteen-year-old brother, nicknamed Son, was both a backup driver for the four-ox team pulling their main wagon and the primary driver for the smaller supply wagon pulled by two half-wild horses.

For Ethel and Pearl, two girls with no experience in handling large numbers of cattle, taking on responsibility for a cattle drive in their first week in the West was almost too much to handle. Cattle tended to drift away from the wagons; it was up to the girls to track them down and force them back into the procession, a time- and energy-consuming routine that they managed to reduce with some thought. When a calf was placed in the back section of the second wagon, its mother followed faithfully behind. This provided a focus for the rest of the herd so they did not stray as often.

Unfortunately for the Houston family, their father's condition did not improve: he died just two years after entering the region. Thus, the mother, two daughters, and Son were forced to rely on each other even more. After the father's funeral, Son continued to help with outdoor chores and Ethel and Pearl took on full responsibility for the cattle, while the "indomitable widow, clad in her calico blouse and long full black skirt, was a familiar figure riding the plow in her field and driving four horses" (McLeod, 1977, p. 13). In this case the family banded together for mutual protection and support and generated, through their numbers if not their individual strength, sufficient labour to maintain production and enough income to overcome the obstacles in their path.

One of the more important tasks assigned to children in the early homesteading years was maintaining control of the family livestock. Few fences existed to keep animals from wandering at will and thus, as in the case of James Russell, whose family lived near Drumheller, Alberta, locating the cattle and returning them to the homesite was a daily (or twice daily) job (Russell, 1912). The same task was assigned to the two children of Eliza Wilson, a woman of Scottish descent who entered Canada in 1889 with her husband, an officer in the North West Mounted Police. The family farmed near Red Deer, Alberta, and had several milk cows and many cattle. The boys had to ensure that the cattle did not wander too far, but she indicates in her diary that in June 1901 it took an entire day to trace the animals since their tracks were washed out by a rainstorm that had continued for several days (Wilson, 1901). The Wilsons were not the only ones with such difficulties. Fred Wright (1902) of Rose Hill, Manitoba, also faced a very difficult time when tracing cattle. He was thirteen and understood what he had to do, but, unfortunately, the family did not have a horse for him to use, and he therefore had to track cattle by foot and herd them back the same way. He hoped to have a pony during the next year's tracing season.

The problem with animal care was entirely different for twelve-year-old Marie Desgagnie (1902). Her difficulty was in herding the cattle that she had located back to the family land. She became disoriented and lost in the brush of the McDonald Hills in Saskatchewan and by the time she was found, thirty-six hours later, she was hungry, cold, and wet because it had rained the first night and snowed the second.

Cows were not the only animals to wander off the homesteads, as was illustrated in a story told by Grace Carr (n.d.) in her memoir. She was the youngest of three children whose family had moved to a homestead near Wood River, Saskatchewan, and was idling away an afternoon watching the family's new pigs in their pen. After they dug their way under the boards of the pen, Grace watched them run around the yard and then race up the road. Bored, she went into the house and "casually told [her] mother that the pigs were running away" (p. 4). Grace and one brother were left to entertain themselves while their mother and older brother left in the wagon to find the vacationing pigs. They returned in an hour with both animals.

Summary

While not every child had the strength necessary to contribute to productive activities, those who did take part rendered a valuable service for the family. The output of their labour could be exchanged for cash needed to support the operation and acquire necessary supplies that could not be produced by family members. At the least, their labour eliminated or reduced the need to expend family resources to hire additional labour for market production tasks, saving money for use in improving the farm.

FOUR

Entrepreneurial Labour

CHILD LABOUR WAS CLEARLY USED on pioneer farms to carry out a broad range of tasks and, as with productive activities, the nature of the labour performed by children was influenced by gender considerations. Boys were more active in tasks requiring physical strength, but girls were also drafted into these jobs as required. Thus, all family members contributed to building up the farm according to their abilities and each played a role in ensuring that marketable commodities were produced.

Similarly, many family members including children contributed to satisfying the desperate need of most farm families for money to spend. While cash obtained from crop or livestock sales might be reinvested in expanding the ongoing operation, families also had to purchase necessary items that they could not produce on their own. Garden seed, cloth, thread, needles, foodstuffs, spices, clothing, tools, and other items had to be paid for, and family members with sufficient time and skills devoted part of their labour power to money-making activities. Adults set the example by taking on paid work off-farm, but both boys and girls took up the challenge of seeking employment or using other means to raise funds. As set out in Tables 8 and 9, their most popular on-farm pursuits for obtaining money were raising animals, hunting, and gathering fruits and vegetables, all of which could be sold. Paid employment tended to increase with age. In almost all cases, wages and other earnings were turned over to the family.

TABLE 8

Entrepreneurial Labour:
Boys' Contributions by Age and Type of Work

AGE	Paid Employment	Gopher Bounties and Trapping	Raising Animals for Sale	Sales of Fruit and other Produce
4–5	0	0	1	0
6–8	1	1	3	0
9–11	3	6	16	1
12–14	6	5	18	0
>14	5	4	5	1

TABLE 9

Entrepreneurial Labour:
Girls' Contributions by Age and Type of Work

AGE	Paid Employment	Gopher Bounties and Trapping	Raising Animals for Sale	Sales of Fruit and other Produce
4–5	0	0	0	0
6–8	2	1	2	0
9–11	1	1	12	1
12–14	0	0	11	2
>14	5	1	3	2

Paid Employment

The need for the family to raise funds in every way possible was recognized by the federal government. For example, a 1906 brochure concerning the "Last Best West" recommended that any adult settler with less than $500 take on paid labour for "a year until one learns the value of things as well as the method of farming" (Canada, 1906, p. 15). The real fear may have been that those without sufficient assets and those who did not develop a work ethic quickly would not be able to survive financially and would abandon the land, slow the settlement process, and create a negative image for the region.

The government's work recommendation applied to both single and married settlers and to families with and without children. In fact, the government offered a free placement service that found work for those interested in applying. It made the persuasive argument that by working off-farm, a young man could, "from the beginning, earn and save enough each year to make payment on say 160 acres of land, and young women could find employment as domestics earning between six and ten dollars per month" (Canada, 1906, p. 15).

However, even without such advice, the stories of the individuals who settled the prairie region suggest that the need for money was obvious to settlers. For instance, Olive Lockhart (1978, p. 10) notes in her memoir that "no one had any money to buy" goods. She goes on to explain that her father, in a bid to earn needed cash in the first year that the family was on the farm, went to work for the CPR. He used his wages to purchase three sows, one boar, and pig feed to begin a hog operation on their farm. He had reasonable success on the hog side of the operation. Seventeen piglets were produced and fed up to sale weight, but due to a lack of cash resources in the community, he found it hard to sell the animals. The price he finally received was $2 per animal, far less than he had paid for feed for the pigs. Even investing more labour into the project by taking the time to butcher a sow did not raise the price that people could pay for fresh meat. Instead of generating cash for his family's needs, he ended up losing $100 on the venture.

A similar story was related by Grace Carr (n.d.) in her memoir of life as a child immigrant in the Wood River area of Saskatchewan. Her family moved to Wood River in 1910, but she had two aunts who had immigrated there some years before and thus knew the local economy very well. They were certain that money could be made cooking for bachelors, but their plan fell apart when they discovered that the bachelors were as short on cash as everyone else.[1] However, they did arrange a deal in which her aunts supplied the expertise needed to prepare and bake the bread while the bachelors supplied sufficient ingredients to make enough bread for both themselves and the two ladies. Thus, her aunts may not have received cash, but they did obtain their own bread for the cost of their own labour.

Other methods of fundraising that did not rely on paid employment also existed but could not be depended upon as steady sources of income. Success at winning a prize at a local fair, for example, could add an occasional windfall to the family finance pool. Ten-year-old Willie Darwood (1902, p. 507) from Meadow Lea, Manitoba, was a proficient rider and using this skill won first place in a riding contest at a local fair and a cash award of $3. Thirteen-year-old Harvey Potter (1901) from Montgomery,

Saskatchewan, also won prizes, but his achievements were based on his farming expertise since he had the best Holstein milk cow at the fair and also won for the "early rose" potatoes that he had planted. Similarly, Eva Cox (1902), a twelve-year-old from Pincher Creek, Alberta, obtained prizes for both handwriting and sewing a handkerchief. However, even if a person were as lucky (or skilled) as the mother of Harriette Parkinson (1978, p. 3), who won "many prizes, which were cash—a scarce item," prize money could not provide all of the necessities a family required on a regular basis. Working off-farm in a paid position was thus a more practical alternative. Employment could be pursued during those times in the year when no farm-related labour was required or at any time when the necessary tasks could be distributed between family members while one or more family members were employed elsewhere.

For example, Kathleen Smith was not yet eleven when her family immigrated from Ireland to homestead near Weyburn, Saskatchewan. Her family's "only money supply…was what [her father] made out during the fall" when he went to Manitoba to work on a threshing crew and earn the money needed to buy their "year's supply of food" while her mother and siblings stayed on the farm (Smith, n.d., p. 7). Kathleen explains that extra help could be obtained when needed since "farmers exchanged work with each other and helped each other for a number of years in nearly every way," but these exchanges would have been made out of friendship or as a form of barter rather than as cash transactions since "no money was ever spent except for real necessities" (Smith, n.d., p. 13).

Life was not as difficult for Cora Montjoy (1901) from Yellow Grass, Saskatchewan. She was the seventh and youngest child of English immigrants who arrived in south-central Saskatchewan in 1899 and was too young to take on paid work herself. However, her father, mother, and oldest brother all found ways of obtaining funds for the family. The men both worked for the CPR "ten hours a day, six days a week, for $1.25 a day," while her mother earned extra money for their needs by selling bread to local bachelors, charging 25¢ for three large loaves (Montjoy, 1901, p. 13). This bread production went on for three years until the family was more comfortable with its ability to earn sufficient funds from farming operations.

Employment was also seen as a necessity by the family of Sylvia Mitchell. In 1907 her father "worked in the town [Regina] twenty miles away for money to buy their food and walked home sometimes at the weekend and back again on Sunday night" (Mitchell, 1976, p. 1). A similar story is told by Laura Matz of her father's thirty-mile trip to a sawmill in Prince Albert, Saskatchewan, where he worked to raise the funds necessary for the family. Laura emphasized that such off-farm work was important because they were in desperate financial straits. The family was so poverty-stricken that candles were blown out at night and reading was done by the "dim circle of light" from the opened stove door to save money (Matz, 1978, p. 1).

The family of Augustine Koett (n.d.), who had immigrated to a homestead in the Rosthern, Saskatchewan, area in 1903 from the United States, faced the same poverty as described by Mitchell and Matz above. Recognizing that they did not have enough money to survive, the family went to work for the Canadian National Railway Company (CNR) in 1904 to take part in the building of the northern rail route. Her father was a foreman on a construction crew while her mother worked as a crew cook. All six children were taken along, as there was nowhere else to leave them, and they lived in a tent during the construction season. Unfortunately, the situation did not work out well for the family since at the end of the season the company was supposedly bankrupt and refused to pay wages for the seven months of work the family had performed. This created an even more desperate need for cash for the family, so after delivering the family back to the homestead, Augustine's father went to work on bridge construction through the winter months. Unfortunately, without money, the mother and children had to resort to living on wild birds until the father returned with his wages.

This story emphasizes the point that farmers were only a single mistake away from poverty and starvation. The need to undertake both on- and off-farm work and the need to spend only such amounts as were required for the survival and growth of the farm and the family became so ingrained that these thoughts were translated to poetry such as a verse published anonymously in December, 1898 (p. 577):

> A farmer's life is a happy one,
> Though he toils from day to day,
> Saving and frequently denying himself,
> In his efforts to make things pay.
>
> The city bred with their borrowed airs,
> May turn up a dainty nose,
> And scornfully stare at the thrifty farmer,
> And jeer at his old-fashioned clothes.

The author argues that city people did not have the same focus as farmers and thus would not understand how life had to be lived in the country. This view is substantiated by a woman named Bas Macpherson who in April 1910 wrote a letter to a woman named Lily Anna. Bas makes a rude remark about farmers who "dress most outrageously (probably because money is a novelty to them)" (Macpherson, 1910, p. 7). She obviously failed to realize (and did not bother to discover) that, as implied in the poem, farming an unbroken country under a harsh financial system meant that only necessities could be purchased. To have the best chance at survival, money could not be wasted on fashionable outfits when the following month might see an equipment failure or an illness requiring expensive medicine. In essence, what the poem suggests is that farmers as a group were prepared to work as many hours as necessary, whether on- or off-farm, and to deny themselves comfort and luxuries to establish their farms and keep them running.

The example set by the parents made the need for work clear to their children; many families expected that their children would obtain paid employment and send their wages back to the family. This might mean working for neighbours in the field or in the home if a domestic servant was sought, or employment with one of the small companies operating in the region. In the case of Roy DeVore (1970), for example, work at a variety of paid positions began as soon as his family arrived in Calgary from the United States. Even though Roy was only a teenager, he took on work at a dairy farm (until the haying season was complete), a brick-yard (but had to quit since the labour required more strength than he possessed), and the Calgary Brewery before the family moved to their homestead. Balancing the heavy labour of establishing the farm with the need for money to pay for equipment, food, and other needs, he continued to take on jobs during the winters when the farming operation slowed. At various times, Roy worked in a lumber camp (catching pneumonia and being off work for several weeks), a meat-packing plant, a cement plant, and a sawmill, as well as with a stoking and threshing crew and a lumber company floating timber down the Red Deer River. For his pains over the years, Roy managed to provide funds for the family to buy food, clothing, and two oxen and, between them, he and his father acquired a wagon and a team of horses.[2]

For Charles Phillips (1967), the experience of paid work and labour-ing to help in the development of the homestead was the same, but the circumstances were more dire. His father died when Charles was thirteen years old, two years after arriving at the homestead. Since he, his mother, and his crippled brother, Glen, had no other option, Charles continued to help with the farm but also took on odd jobs for neighbours for little pay. He managed to obtain a position as a ranch hand that paid $1 a day in wages, enough to support the family's needs, and unlike Roy DeVore, managed to hold on to the same position for several years. Similarly, John

Watson (1975) was also lucky enough to hold down the same job for over ten years. His specialty before his family immigrated from Scotland was raising sheep, and he found employment easily once his skills were known. From the time he was ten years old and taking home 50¢ a day to his mother, to the age of twenty when his wage had increased to $1 per day ($35 per month if he also assisted with harvesting hay for winter feed), he continued to work with sheep.

For some farm families, particularly those beginning the process of developing a homestead, circumstances were such that difficult decisions had to be made about priorities for the use of available labour. Balancing the many needs to break the land, plant a crop, grow a garden, build a house, obtain money, and work on any one of hundreds of other important projects could be difficult, but having children to share the burden could reduce the problems. For example, the Roberts family homesteading near Talbot in southern Alberta had the opportunity to send the two older sons off-farm to work for badly needed money. This left fourteen-year-old Brockway, his father, and his mother to work the farm. There was a great deal of work to be done, but the family needed the $100 the two older sons could earn between them for goods that had to be purchased. In turn, those who remained at the farm intensified their work efforts as much as possible to make up for the absent teenagers (Roberts, 1971).

Similar circumstances led to the employment of the three young Hislop children as potato diggers and pickers. The family was short on the cash that it needed to purchase "such diverse things as coal oil, school books and writing materials, matches, salt, and barbed wire," so when their neighbour approached Mrs. Hislop about hiring her three children, she had to consider the request carefully. She had been earning money herself by baking bread for a nearby bachelor at a rate of 50¢ for four two-pound loaves, but her effort to sell fresh and canned vegetables in Winnipeg had failed. Money was not being earned fast enough to pay the expenses, so she had little choice but to rent the three children to the neighbour. He was prepared to pay 50¢ per child per day for three days, plus meals. Although she was "loath to hire out her own children," she was "willing to help out the kindly old man" and the $4.50 could prove valuable for the family, so permission was granted (Nuffield, 1987, p. 48).[3]

While many boys went off-farm to work for wages for their families, two boys, John and Bill Wood, report that they were able to earn wages at home. Their family homestead was located on the trail to Edmonton and travellers frequently spent the night in the family barn. John and Bill earned money by looking after horses for pay and, despite their father's policy that no one would be turned away from a place to rest, refused to make room for a non-paying guest by taking horses from the barn. Instead, they told the gentleman to leave if he wouldn't sleep in the shed instead of the barn but did not bother to advise him that the next closest rest stop was twenty-five miles away. Unfortunately for the brothers, their father was staying at the next rest stop when the weary man arrived the next morning after driving his team all night. Hearing about the lack of hospitality at his farm, the father expressed his displeasure over the greeting the traveller had received and "the boys found out when he arrived home" (Wood, 1976, p. 3).

Boys were not the only children to find themselves in a position where employment off the farm was of greater importance to the family than the labour contribution they could make to direct farming operations. Anne Weir (1976), a child involved in the production of dairy goods for sale, is a case in point. Although she was performing a valuable role in ensuring the viability of the family farm, Anne's position was assumed by one of her older sisters when this sister arrived from Ontario. Anne suddenly had no farm-related work to perform. Thus, it was determined by her family that earning money by working off-farm as a domestic servant would prove a better use of her labour power. Accordingly, Anne went to work for a young family with two children when she was seventeen. She cooked and cleaned and looked after the children, but as a dutiful daughter, she ensured that all of her wages, except for the amount needed to pay for clothing and some personal items, went to her family. Even though she had little money of her own, she enjoyed her independence and "didn't think of being poor…had enough to eat…had enough clothing…[and everyone was] pretty much in the same boat" (Weir, 1976, p. 6).

With respect to the wages that could be expected for domestic labour, Anna Farion (1978) indicates that she obtained a job in 1897 assisting a farm wife with washing clothes, scrubbing the floor, and hauling water for $1 per month. Once the family determined that she was a hard-working girl, the wage was increased to $2.50 per month with a promise of a further raise to $6 per month after a three-month trial period. Her duties were also expanded to include milking three cows, looking after three children, and preparing meals for two hired hands. Every cent of her income was also sent home to her parents because they were so poor that "all they had to eat was rabbit meat, and without bread at that" (p. 90).

Other girls who obtained jobs performed a variety of tasks. For example, L. Cook (1902) of Wishart, Saskatchewan, states that she ran the local post office, assisted with the weekly stagecoach, and also had a job as a housekeeper. The energy and dedication that she put into earning a living kept her and two younger siblings from starving in the West while their father lived in Ontario, thereby proving that she was as tough and determined to succeed as any adult pioneer.

Similarly, Elizabeth Turnbull (n.d.), a girl whose family immigrated to take up farming near Lumsden, Saskatchewan, in 1905 when she was only six years old, held a paid position as a housekeeper with a neighbour when she turned seven. She cared for the baby and stayed at their house during the day. She took on a different job the following year, washing dishes, scrubbing floors, and performing general tasks, and then moved between houses as a cleaning person once her sister was old enough to assist her in handling several houses at the same time. While she and her sister were working as domestics, their father was holding a job with the CPR and her mother was working as a nurse. There is no doubt that all of the Turnbulls took the need to generate income very seriously and devoted as much of their time as was available to paid employment, as the income produced by farming was insufficient to maintain the family.

Most girls worked as domestics for short periods of time, but on occasion, daughters moved in with families who did not have older girls of their own, where they assisted with all of the domestic labour for the household (Barber, 1991). For example, an anonymous sixteen-year-old female contributor to Broadfoot's book *The Pioneer Years* (1976, p. 214) states that she hated handling field work on her family homestead and was thus happy to accept an offer of $20 per month to perform domestic work for a neighbouring farmer. The farmer's wife had died years before and therefore she was responsible for cleaning up years of grime in addition to being up by 5 a.m. to bake and cook meals for the farmer and his sons. Her father would agree to the arrangement only if the entire $20 was paid directly to him. In other words, she would be working "15 hours a day, 6 days a week" for nothing but, anticipating improved working conditions, she was still prepared to accept the job. As noted by Evelyn McLeod (1977, p. 13), "a lot was expected of farm children in those days and they lived up to it."[4]

Raising Animals for Sale

The second form of entrepreneurial labour undertaken by children involved the raising of animals for sale. This type of activity served a twofold purpose: first, the creation of a valuable asset that could add to the chances of family survival and success, and second, reinforcement of the social value placed on work and responsibility. Prairie social norms were such that children were encouraged and expected to assist their families, and, at the same time, society also had an interest in seeing that children grew into adults capable of industrious behaviour in the agricultural West. For these reasons, the socialization or teaching aspect of parental control over children required that children be trained to perform farm work and enjoy farm living. At the same time, the effort expended on such a training task was not wasted since saleable products could be developed and necessary work accomplished while the lesson was learned.

Numerous pieces of advice on these points were directed at parents by experts and other individuals who felt they had a worthwhile opinion to express. However, the situation of male children on the farm was somewhat different from that of females, and thus the counsel provided to parents differed depending on the gender of their children. For example, gender norms of the time determined that work external to the home was appropriate for boys, so assisting their mothers with household work would not provide the skills and opportunities to generate income appropriate to the male sex. Rather, as suggested by Alex McLay (1901) of Horse Hills, Alberta, a father could make life on the farm more worthwhile for boys if they would

> build a good warm workshop, where farm implements, harness, etc., can be repaired on wet and stormy days. There, the boys can be taught lessons of thrift, economy and industry.... And the farmer who has boys and invests in a blacksmith's outfit will soon find them doing nearly all the blacksmithing required. (1901, p. 245)

Similarly, an article in the August 1899 edition of *The Nor'-West Farmer* advised that a father should teach his son to "respect his father's calling" (not his mother's) and "instill in his mind that the great men of all ages were sons of farmers" (Anonymous, 1899b, p. 622). The father was also advised to ensure that there was some play mixed in with the work each day and to encourage all efforts, share plans for the use of the land and the future of the farm, and pay his sons some wage for their work. It was believed that doing so would both give the sons a sense that their labour was worth something and provide them with a stake in the operation through the planning process.

However, one suggestion common to the proper upbringing of both boys and girls was to make children responsible for the performance of duties on the farm, such as caring for one or more animals from birth. It was believed that children in this position would develop a sense of responsibility and devote themselves more fully to the farming lifestyle while developing a valuable commodity for the family. This approach, profiting from the work efforts of children while giving guidance on necessary skills, was mentioned often by those theorizing on the best means to convince children to adopt farming as an occupation and remain on the farms to take over from the parental generation of settlers.

For example, the letters and articles written to prairie newspapers, such as "Interesting the Children in Livestock," published in a 1901 edition of *The Nor'-West Farmer*, and "To Keep the Boys and Girls on the Farm," submitted by "A Father" in 1902, recommend animal husbandry very highly. It was seen as a motivator to encourage children to stay on the farm and contribute to the well-being of the family. Not only would practical lessons in the proper care and feeding of livestock and in the provision of sustenance or income for the family be provided, but, in addition, a child's imagination would be captured at an early age and directed at the farming life as a source of satisfaction. Not all fathers managed to profit from their children's efforts, but coincidentally (or not), raising animals became one of the most common forms of entrepreneurial behaviour among farm children.

Four-year-old Verne Hunt, for example, had his older sister write his story to *The Nor'-West Farmer* in June 1902; among the numerous tasks he performed on the farm was caring for his personal animals. He indicated that he had "a cow called Flora, two pigs and some horses"; while this seems like a large number of animals for a child of his age to own, it was not unusual for parents to present their children with animals to raise (Hunt, 1902, p. 507). In fact, Verne's seven-year-old sister, Winnifred Hunt, also reported that she owned animals, in her case a cow and a calf, and that the family as a whole had "eleven horses and about forty head of cattle" (Hunt, 1902, p. 507).

Calves and cow/calf pairs were the most common types of animal to be raised by farm children, possibly because they were easy to raise (having no special diet or other needs) or possibly because cattle were the most common type of livestock on the prairies.[5] Typical of the dozens of children who noted raising calves were Edwin Hardy (1901), a young man from the Yorkton, Saskatchewan, area who also grew his own cattle feed; an eleven-year-old girl named Elsie Brown (1902) from Winlaw, Saskatchewan, with a cow named Cherry; and a boy named Ralph Clench (1902), with a calf named "King Edward."[6] Ralph's older sister, Elsie Clench (1901), was also a consummate cattle entrepreneur. She planned to turn a $5 present received from a cousin into her own cattle empire by, in her own words, buying "a calf which I have named Barney. I am going to keep it until I can sell it for enough to buy two heifers if they do well I will have quite a number bye and bye" (Elsie Clench, 1901, p. 598).

In a letter entitled "Bob's Calf but Pa's Steer," an anonymous writer tells the story of a family in which the children were encouraged to raise cattle (Anonymous, 1902). The letter tells how the two sons each raised a calf from birth on their father's instructions, ensuring that the calves were fed, watered, had a clean stall, ate properly, and had shelter as necessary. When it came time to sell the animals, the sons were not consulted. It was assumed that the father would receive the $100 purchase price, but on the day of the sale, the steers were not to be found and the father's sale fell through. However, "snug in each boy's pocket was a fifty dollar bill" (Anonymous, 1902, p. 508).

Numerous other youngsters also mention owning animals, including Eddie Northey (1902), an eight-year-old from Holland, Manitoba. According to a letter written by Eddie, he owned a different set of animals. Instead of cattle, he had a horse (named Prince) and several chickens. Chickens existed in abundance on his family farm (the family also had pigs and cows), but Eddie preferred chickens for several reasons. They would largely care for their own needs, reproduce themselves, provide a steady stream of eggs for consumption and marketing, and could be eaten when no longer fit for egg laying—an almost perfect product for any entrepreneur!

Other unusual choices (animals other than typical farm denizens) made by children when setting up their livestock businesses included the forty ducks that Elsie Clench (1901) attempted to raise, thirty-four of which died due to a heavy rainfall (they were virtually battered to death) while others ate pea pods that later swelled up in their stomachs. Walter Brown (1902), a nine-year-old from Portage la Prairie, Manitoba, tried raising purebred Toulouse geese for their eggs, while Florence Griffiths (1902), an eleven-year-old from Yorkton, Saskatchewan, cared for eighteen pigeons (potential roasted squabs). The largest breeder of pigeons among the children referred to in the written memoirs and other documents is Alan Redfern (1902), a fourteen-year-old from Sandhurst, Manitoba. He indicates that he had twenty-five pigeons in stock but had slaughtered and sold another twenty-five in the fall, proving that a market did indeed exist.

However, the most unusual stock choice may have been the animals raised by eleven-year-old John Fardoe (1902) of the Brandon, Manitoba, area: rabbits (plus a calf). What made this out of the ordinary was the fact that wild rabbits were so abundant.[7] Since they were a regular source of food and easily trapped, raising rabbits as a commodity does not seem to have been carefully thought out by John. However, several other children also reported raising rabbits for the market, including Jennie Erickson (1902), a fourteen-year-old girl from Edberg, Alberta; an eleven-year-old boy named Clifford Earl (1902) from Swan Lake, Sas-

Girl feeding calf, n.d. [PAA, B.345]

katchewan; and fifteen-year-old Oliver Wright (1902) of Rose Hill, Manitoba. Only Oliver seemed to have prepared for adverse market conditions by diversifying his stock since in addition to his rabbits (which "live under the granary"), he had two cows, a calf, and a pig of his own (Oliver Wright, 1902, p. 332).

Among the children who wrote of their pride in caring for their livestock were others to whom the raising of animals was simply a practical venture. For example, ten-year-old Martin Henderson (1902, p. 506) of Alameda, Saskatchewan, points out that he liked "working the land…[but at a practical level] must be doing something to help pay for the feed my stock has to eat in the winter." He had a cow given to him by his father on his eighth birthday along with several other animals and enjoyed working them, but Martin saw these animals as would a professional farmer. His cow was not a pet, but stock to be marketed.

These enterprises could generate reasonable amounts of money for those prepared to participate in the process, but as shown by Bert MacPhail (1902), the children might not be the ones to benefit directly from their work. Bert and his sister had raised a steer from birth, but when the sale was completed, the $12 sale price went straight to their mother.

However, two other young entrepreneurs, Elmer Lockhart of Lidstone, Manitoba (1902), and Frederick Arnott of Calf Mountain, Manitoba (April, 1902), were enterprising enough to retain their early income and reinvest it in new ventures. Both chose pigs as their second money-making venture, with Elmer using his wages from acting as the local school's early-morning fire starter to buy his first hog and Frederick using money from a successful small-scale wheat crop to pay his father $1 for a piglet. Because both chose assets that could reproduce and thus increase their numbers, the profit potential was large.

Unfortunately for some, animal husbandry was an entrepreneurial activity not without risk. For example, Norman Moss (1902, p. 741) points out the dangers of the cold weather (it had been so cold in the spring that the calf birthed by his cow Rooney died of exposure in a late-season snowstorm). Eager (1953) notes that a prairie fire could kill animals or destroy stored hay, Watson (1975) indicates that coyotes and wolves could kill sheep, and Christensen (1976, p. 19) refers to a disease called blackleg that could kill cattle.

Gopher Bounties and Trapping

The third form of entrepreneurial activity among farming children involved hunting for animals that had some value in the market. Furs continued to be valuable, but few children had the time or expertise to trap anything other than animals that might come near the homestead. The activity that could provide the greatest cash return for the least amount of effort was hunting gophers to collect the bounty placed on the rodents by the federal government. The bounty was designed to encourage people to kill the animals and rid the prairies of a dangerous pest. They were hazardous for horses and livestock since a misstep into a gopher burrow could result in a broken leg, and they also ate crops and gardens. Given the importance of wheat exports, "the Canadian government offered a bounty of one cent for each gopher tail turned in" as proof of the elimination of that animal (McLeod, 1977, p. 14).[8]

The children most interested in the gopher bounty quickly became quite expert in their executioner's role. Evelyn McLeod (1977) mentions that her younger cousins (she was six years old at the time) were great hunters:

> Usually they snared the gophers with a slipknot at the end of
> a length of binder-twine. After a gopher ran into his burrow,
> the loop was placed around the entrance to the hole and the

Gopher, Saskatoon, 1912. [SAB, R-A16709]

boys flattened themselves about twelve feet back. In only a
few minutes, they had their prize. (McLeod, 1977, p. 14)

Similar action (using the string-trap technique) is also mentioned by Harry Wathen (1975), who indicated in an interview that he would go out for
entire days on gopher hunts and return with enough tails to earn himself a
quarter for his efforts. The string noose was also a favourite of the grandfather of Dorthea Calverley, although this lowly technology eliminated
few of the pests. For more efficient kills, strychnine mixed with wheat was
used as poisoned bait. After warning Dorthea not to use any of the mix for
"prairie chewing gum" (a ball of chewed wheat converted to a rubbery tex-
ture), her grandfather gave her the job of depositing the poison while on
her rounds with her homemade wagon looking for buffalo chips (Calverley, 1985, p. 32). The virtue of efficiency was also a part of George Cox's
(1902) approach to the business of killing gophers. This ten-year-old from
Pincher Creek, Alberta, used a trapline in his quest for the gopher bounty,
staking out likely territory on the family farm and spending the summer
at his work. By the time he was done, 161 of the rodents, enough to fill a
small prairie dog town, had fallen victim to his trapping technique.

The string-trapping and poisoning techniques were not sporting
enough for all gopher hunters. Members of George Still's family, for instance, used both guns and snares. As George wrote in a letter to the
Free Press Prairie Farmer newspaper, he was out hunting with his "uncle
Tom and brother Jimmy" and " shot about 20, and snared some. We were

hunting nearly all day. I like hunting; it is great sport" (Still, 1996). Others, like a Mrs. Cameron, were much more practical about the matter and simply "tumbled over a good many" gophers with a rifle to save their gardens (Turner, 1955, p. 53).

According to his published memoirs, James Minifie was also an enterprising fellow with an eye for money-making opportunities. Since they had earned pocket money in England by hunting down with his pellet rifle house sparrows that ate seedlings and nested in rain gutters, the bounty of one cent per gopher became a natural source of income for James and his younger brother. However, these young entrepreneurs were not satisfied to adopt the habits of their predecessors in gopher hunting. Having decided that the usual technique of putting a noose around a gopher hole and waiting for the occupant to stick its head up was far too slow, the Minifie brothers developed what they thought would be a more efficient technique. They poured water down a hole until a gopher left the burrow through an alternate entry point and relied on their collie, Scottie, to snap up the gopher. At that point, the boys took over; as James notes, "we stripped off their tails with a quick jerk, and packed them into an Old Chum tobacco sack of father's, which we carried on our persons until my mother objected" (Minifie, 1972, p. 103).[9]

The Minifies were able to take ten or twelve trophies per day, but had they been able to add the family cats to their hunting expeditions, or at least been able to rescue the gopher tails from consumption, they may have developed larger deposit accounts at the local bank. As recounted by James Minnifie, the cats were formidable hunters; every morning, each adult cat would capture and kill a gopher, drag it back across one half mile of broken fields, and share its bounty with the kittens playing in the family yard. This would have presented the best opportunity to intervene and rescue the tails, but coming between a farmyard cat, its kittens, and breakfast may not have seemed worth the pennies to be earned. Of course, once the kittens were blooded and hunting on their own, the hunters would not return to the yard with their catch. Instead, they became competitors for the same prey that the brothers pursued. One enterprising young girl named Neen Barr had a different perspective on the best ways of earning money from the gopher bounty: "If she could cut off its tail, set her victim free to grow another, there could be no end to the revenue gophers could produce" (Pratt, 1996).

Beyond the tail bounty set for gophers, furs from beavers, foxes, minks, coyotes, and wolves remained valuable commodities in the market. Demand was not as high as during the fur-trading era that was ended by the influx of settlers into the prairie region and the consequent movement of animals farther into the wild, but for a few families trapping did provide a source of cash that could not be ignored. Boys such as Roy DeVore (1970, p. 28), who brought with him a ".25 Stevens rifle…a single-gauge shotgun and a number of traps" when he entered the prairies with his family, set out traplines during the winter months in the hope of generating large amounts of cash in the spring.

Trapping was somewhat easier at the Reesor (1977) homestead because the traps could be laid close to home. Piles of skinned carcasses of the cattle that had died during the winter were all dragged to a nearby ravine or coulee for disposal. The smell of fresh and rotting cattle attracted hordes of coyotes and wolves into the area to be shot or trapped. William Reesor notes that by laying traps on the most likely paths that could be followed to reach the carcasses, his brothers increased their odds of success. Once the pelts were "stretched on boards shaped for the purpose," they could be sold to a hide buyer for a price set by quality and "a lot of dickering," while the hides of the dead cows could be sold by weight to bring in some cash to compensate for the loss of the cattle (Reesor, 1977, p. 5). Others concerned about the presence of such predators sometimes took more direct action by seeking out the dens of these animals, "crawling into the den wearing a miner's hat with the light in front, a piece of rope around the waist, a revolver and a gunny sack" (Reesor, 1977, p. 9). Whatever the reason for killing these animals, their fur represented potential profits for the family, and hunters could thus serve their families in several ways. As noted by Lewis (1996, p. 9), "[young] hunters, fishers and trappers supplemented family larders with wild birds, fish, and game they shot or caught, and they contributed to family incomes from the profits of their traplines." For example, in a letter written to the *Free Press Prairie Farmer*, fourteen-year-old Ethel Place (1996) says that the family received $50 from the sale of coyote and muskrat pelts that had been trapped on their homestead. Even small animals could generate some income. The pelt of a red squirrel was worth 15¢, a gray squirrel was worth 10¢, and the rarest breed, black squirrels, brought 25¢ each (Broadfoot, 1988, p. 138).

Ellenor Merriken (1999, p. 89) reported much higher prices for the furs of weasels (or white ermine). The furs were mailed to Winnipeg from their home in Alberta, and they received between 25¢ and 65¢ for each skin, depending on size. However, badger furs were kept for family use: once the hides were tanned, stretched, and made pliable by rubbing them with stones or pulling them back and forth across the beam of a sawhorse, the furs were used to line outdoor clothing for winter use.

Sales of Fruit and Other Produce

The fourth form of entrepreneurial labour performed by children provided some cash for the farm but also actively trained the children in gardening and harvesting techniques that would allow them to make maximum use of their physical environments. At the same time, this type of training and honing of their entrepreneurial skills could be enjoyable and provide adventures for the participants. For example, fruit-picking expeditions to appropriate berry sites could include very young children since the work was not heavy or dangerous, and in addition to exploring new territory and eating their fill of fruit, the children also served a need for the family. As reported by Maryanne Caswell (1968) to her grandmother in a letter written in 1887, a bushel of raspberries and a grain sack full of saskatoon berries were easily obtainable by the six youngest children of the family. This activity was squeezed into the spare time during the course of a hectic day in which the family was travelling to deliver eggs to a farmer with no chickens and to pick up their mail at the local post office. This efficient use of time to take care of personal matters while also promoting their business of selling foods was a hallmark of prairie settlers. There was little time to waste in a day if the farm were to remain in operation.

As reported by Rowles (1952), berry sales were an important part of the family income stream for the Neville family, who farmed near Lumsden, Saskatchewan, in 1884. The family, already involved in direct sales of vegetables to the families of the North West Mounted Police officers stationed at Regina, also took advantage of the "great quantity and variety" of natural berries and fruit in the valleys near their homestead. The children and Mrs. Neville would locate and harvest the fruit and pack it into pails for their father to sell in Regina for up to $2 (or its equivalent in bartered sugar or tea) per pail (Rowles, 1952, p. 2). Additional processing of the fruit on the homestead allowed the family to charge more for their produce; Mrs. Neville sometimes took a portion of their raspberry harvest, some dried apples, and a lot of sugar to create her own jam, a product that could be sold "to the C.P.R. for twenty-five cents a pound" (Rowles, 1952, pp. 2–3). The railway valued this access to fresh products so highly that they even supplied the pails for the family to use while picking berries and for storing the homemade jams.

Another farm child, fifteen-year-old Annie Penhall of Bear Creek, Manitoba, was also successful as a vendor of natural fruits. In a letter, she wrote of her excursions into the brush in search of fruits and berries, both for the family table and for selling to townspeople. While she did not note

Henry Peltier, Uncle Bill, and Alcie and Jordan McDougall,
saskatoon berry picking, 1905. [SAB, R-A7570]

her profit level, she does indicate that she had "sold quite a lot of currents [*sic*] in town," suggesting that she was earning needed money for her family (Penhall, 1902, p. 829).

While most children preferred collecting and selling berries, one boy chose to grow vegetables for the market. Ten-year-old Alfred Jones (1902) was in the right place at the right time to obtain a job paying 5¢ chasing a neighbour's cattle away from his father's haystack, but rather than squander his new-found wealth, he turned it into investment capital and purchased part of a bag of onion seeds with his money. Establishing his own small garden, he planted the onions alongside seeds for other produce donated by his parents so that when the growing season ended, he would have a broad assortment of vegetables to market, in addition to a few acres of oats, wheat, and barley that his father had planted in a separate area on his behalf. His ultimate goal was to obtain an air rifle and a pony, all with funds derived from his original 5¢ job (and a bit of help from his father), revealing him to be a truly dedicated and ambitious child. By investing his money in diverse farm assets, he hoped to multiply his original capital as a means of achieving his goals.

Summary

As was the case with productive labour tasks, children entered into entrepreneurial activities with the family's well-being in mind. While this type of activity raised funds for use on the farm, participating children also learned a lesson that would be important to them as future farmers and farmers' wives: animals on the farm were not pets, but assets to be used as necessary to raise money that would improve the family's financial position.

FIVE

Subsistence Labour

A S ILLUSTRATED IN PREVIOUS CHAPTERS, child labour power could make a meaningful contribution to the production of cash crops, marketable livestock, and other goods and services that might generate income for the family farm. However, long-term success on the prairies also required an investment of family labour in the tasks necessary for physical survival. This work was vital because if the farm was to continue its day-to-day operations, the people and animals involved in the process had to receive the materials essential to life.

The importance of subsistence labour to the entire family is made clear by the fact that large numbers of both boys and girls contributed their efforts to the tasks needed for survival. As shown in Tables 10 and 11, both genders took on equal responsibility for obtaining water and fuel, and for protecting family members from insects and wildlife. However, more boys than girls took up hunting and fishing and helped to fight fires. Girls dominated the remaining activities of producing animal products for family consumption, gardening, and harvesting wild plants. Regardless of the task performed, and whatever the gender of the worker, these children helped to ensure family survival and thus the successful expansion of the farming economy across the region.

Subsistence Labour:
Boys' Contributions by Age and Type of Work

AGE	Animal Products	Obtaining Fuel	Obtaining Water	Hunting & Fishing	Gardening & Harvesting Wild Fruits & Vegetables	Protection from Insects & Animals	Protection from Fires
4–5	0	1	0	0	0	0	0
6–8	3	2	1	2	2	1	1
9–11	18	7	6	6	5	1	2
12–14	14	5	7	9	9	0	6
>14	2	1	4	3	0	0	3

TABLE II

Subsistence Labour:
Girls' Contributions by Age and Type of Work

AGE	Animal Products	Obtaining Fuel	Obtaining Water	Hunting & Fishing	Gardening & Harvesting Wild Fruits & Vegetables	Protection from Insects & Animals	Protection from Fires
4–5	0	2	0	0	0	0	0
6–8	4	1	1	0	1	1	1
9–11	21	6	6	1	10	1	0
12–14	23	2	6	3	18	1	2
>14	4	2	4	2	3	0	2

Obtaining Water

One of the main goals when farming in the dry areas of the prairie region was to ensure that a steady supply of water was available to the farm and family. Children's labour was used freely to fulfill this need. Small supplies to be used while undertaking the work necessary to establish the farm could be obtained relatively easily, but for use in an ongoing farm with the needs of the family, livestock, and gardens to consider, the supply had to be extensive enough to meet all of the requirements without fail. It was also preferable that the water be clean enough that it did not have to be strained and boiled before being consumed since having to treat the water would add a further burden to settlers' lives. However, in the absence of a stream or river with water that moved too quickly for contaminants to accumulate, or a large lake relatively free of concentrated problems, potable water was rare.

The water that was available in the areas of the prairies that received reasonable rainfall was generally found in the numerous sloughs and ponds that dotted the landscape (Dawson and Younge, 1940). These reservoirs held stagnant water-hosting plants, animals, birds, and insects and their larvae, so water from these sources had to be filtered and boiled for aesthetic as well as health reasons. For example, Mary Cummins (1975) relates a story about her trip to the new family homestead near Grenfell, Saskatchewan, in 1883. The hotel where they stayed on the night before driving across country in a wagon to their homestead used a nearby pond for its drinking and bathing water. Mary refused to put her clean washing sponge into the water as it was "full of 'wigglies' since it had not been filtered or boiled before being delivered to their room" (Cummins, 1975, p. 30).

A number of individuals report similar stories about their experiences with water. Lars Larson (n.d.), for example, indicates that in some areas, only slough water was available for drinking, and when that was the case, precautions had to be taken to avoid illness and parasites. The precautions they did take were insufficient (they did not boil the water before drinking) but would have eliminated at least the larger-sized pests from the drinking water. Their water purification system was based on dipping a handkerchief under the surface of the slough, folding the corners up to trap a pouch of water, pulling the pouch out of the slough, holding it overhead, and then drinking the water as it leaked through the cloth. The bugs that would otherwise have been ingested remained in the pouch to be shaken out later.

Such filtering methods were also used by the family of Russell Braithwaite, who homesteaded in the Yellowgrass, Saskatchewan, area in the 1890s. They did not have a reliable well at the time, and thus, whenever a storm passed through the area, the family put barrels out to catch as much water as possible. When the storms ended, the children were sent out with an empty barrel on a stoneboat to gather as much additional water as they could before it soaked into the soil and was lost. They would drag the barrel out to the fields looking for ditches and depressions that might hold a couple of gallons of water that could be salvaged. However, the water scooped up off the ground had "all kinds of red bugs in it"; these were eliminated by filtering the water through a flour sack stretched over the opening (Braithwaite, n.d., p. 1). Because flour sacks had to hold finely ground powder, the mesh would likely have been tight enough to filter out the bugs and even particles of dirt. Thus, some sort of drinkable water could generally be found or created on the prairies, but as with most other obstacles that had to be overcome, additional labour had to be expended on the solution.

Rodwell's (1965) analysis of government homestead records respecting the reasons settlers gave for abandoning their homesteads produced numerous examples of failures tied directly to water issues. At one extreme, floods and extensive sloughs drove some settlers away from land that was "only fit for ducks," while at the other were homesteads with "no water to be found" (Rodwell, 1965, p. 13). Other typical comments found on homestead abandonment forms include driving cattle "4 or 5 miles to a watering place…[and travelling] 5 or 6 miles for drinking water," and the need to dig or drill wells to a depth of hundreds of feet before a reliable water source was tapped (Rodwell, 1965, pp. 13–14). One settler (who did not abandon his homestead) had a spring that ran through his homestead during the spring, summer, and fall, but in the winter, when the spring froze, he was so desperate for water that he was forced to spend a great deal of valuable time melting snow (Stringer, 1888).[1]

Stories of families reusing the same water for cooking, bathing, washing clothes, and scrubbing floors (in that order) were not an exaggeration in a region where every drop of water might have to be hauled over long distances (Jones, 1987). Use was rationed, and the McNaught sisters (1976) say that since dishwater picked up scraps of food and grease from the family's plates and utensils, dishwater could also provide extra nourishment for the pigs she was raising. One of the McNaught sisters also mentions that an older sister conserved water by using the water from a vase of flowers to wash her face and clean her teeth.

The scarcity of water was confirmed by survey results (Rowles, 1952, pp. 4–5) revealing that almost one-third of the 217 respondents hauled water in barrels for use on the homestead. Twenty-one had to haul the water more than one mile and one respondent was eleven miles from a source of reliable drinking water. Lucy Johnson's (n.d.) autobiography indicates that she and her father found themselves in a similar situation. They normally obtained barrels of water for their livestock from a nearby river, but with the river running low during the summer, the two were forced to expend a lot more effort than usual. They scooped the water up in buckets from low spots in the riverbed and poured it into barrels for transport back to the farm.

For others, drinkable, if unpalatable, water was readily available, but in such cases, the taste sometimes had to be hidden in some fashion. Blending in powdered ginger or drinking the water only when it was brewed with tea, coffee, or a homemade substitute such as burnt toast or roasted barley and wheat, made it more palatable (Rowles, 1952). It reached the stage for the Pinder family that "tea made from tasteless water seemed flat" (Hiemstra, 1997).

In the absence of a convenient natural source of drinkable water, many settlers undertook one of the most dangerous endeavours for inexperienced workers, the digging of a freshwater well. Wells were deadly in a variety of ways since aside from the potential for the accumulation of lethal levels of noxious gases,[2] collapsing walls could bury the digger, and accidents with explosives could endanger his life. Digging without a partner could mean digging one's own grave if an exit route was not planned (Minifie, 1972).

The latter problem stopped work at a neighbour's well on which Roy DeVore's father and fourteen-year-old brother, Hugh, were working. They were using dynamite to loosen the dirt in the well, and on the day that they hit the 102-foot mark, three charges were set and triggered before the work crew quit for the evening. The following morning, the two DeVores were the first down the shaft; while digging, they set off a charge that had not actually fired the night before and were severely injured. The father's face was "swathed in bandages" and "the end of one thumb was blown off, two ribs were cracked and his face was filled with fine pieces of sandstone" (DeVore, 1970, p. 49). Hugh had a superficial leg wound, "an injured eye, both forearms penetrated by sandstone particles, while the right hand appeared to be shattered from the inside" (DeVore, 1970, p. 49). Luckily, neither was killed, but the fact that a fourteen-year-old would be allowed to participate in such a dangerous operation suggests that children's labour was of importance on the frontier, that it was needed badly enough that parents would allow them to take on dangerous tasks.

The brother of Lucy Johnson (n.d.) was also drafted into working on a well with their father, but this well was on their own property, so they were risking their lives for their own benefit. The two took turns going down into the well to dig since there was not enough room for two to work at once. Eventually, they were deep enough after several days' work to necessitate the use of a bucket to haul displaced dirt to the surface for disposal.[3] The person out of the well had to pull the dirt out of the excavation and, in addition, to help the digger out of the well using the rope since they did not have a ladder long enough for the depth they had reached. One morning, after completing the regular chores, Lucy's father volunteered to dig first and her brother was to join him at the well as soon as he finished eating lunch. However, rather than going to the well, the brother was distracted by the thought of a food shortage and decided to walk to Saskatoon (a five-day trip) for supplies. Luckily, he came to his senses within a few miles and got his father out of the well, but with dust storms, unceasing farm work, and an ambitious building program, including a sod barn and a two-storey wood frame house, there was little time for recriminations, even over a potentially deadly mistake.

After a well was completed, children often assumed the job of hauling water from the well to the house or barn, depending on need. One enterprising young boy, twelve-year-old J. MacDonald (1901, p. 597) of Poplar Grove, Saskatchewan, developed a labour-saving method of hauling water the three hundred feet from the well to their house. His dog, a pointer, was used to pulling him on a sleigh in the winter; he adapted this so that the dog pulled a cart with a pail of water on board during the summer.

Of course, hauling water was not the only task assigned to children, and when other jobs fit for a child came up, the child had to perform them no matter how distasteful. Thus Helen Koett, the older sister mentioned in the memoirs of Augustine Koett (n.d.), was called on to ride a bucket down into a well to remove another bucket stuck in the hole. The opening to the water at the bottom of the well had been shrinking all winter due to ice buildup on the walls, and when the first bucket was accidentally dropped, it hit at an angle and blocked access to their only source of water. Helen was small enough that when dressed warmly in a coat, hat, and mittens, she fit in a second bucket and still had enough room to move around and wiggle the stuck bucket loose so that the access could be reopened. (The memoirs do not mention whether anyone had considered how they would get the child out if the second bucket also became stuck in the narrow opening.) Helen was promised a quarter for doing the job and then placed in the bucket to be lowered into the hole, but at that point, Augustine (Koett, n.d., p. 5) indicates,

> Helen, who had that terrible experience at the camp [she had run across a board over a ground-level well at a CNR construction camp and slid into the opening, barely hanging on to the edge of the board until rescued], was afraid of wells and screamed "Mama, I'm choking, I can't get any air!" although she was still on top of the well. [When Augustine heard Helen screaming, she] ran to the well crying, "Mama, Helen is dying, let me go down." Then mother took Helen out of the pail and put me in—without a coat, cap or mitts, and let me down. When I got down, I grabbed the pail from the hole with one hand and held onto the rope with the other, then mother pulled me up, pail and all. But I didn't get the

quarter that had been promised Helen, nor did I ask for it. It was enough for me that I saved Helen's life, as I thought.

Finding water when digging a well did not necessarily mean the end of difficulties since wells had to be maintained for use and, if not protected from wildlife, could become spoiled. For instance, Olive Lockhart, a seven-year-old British immigrant living on a homestead near Saskatoon, Saskatchewan, in 1908, mentions in her memoirs that her father had struck drinking water when the well he was digging hit the eight-foot level. However, mice, frogs, and other animals often found a way into the well, and "one spring, the water tasted 'queer' so Father emptied the well, and found twenty-seven rabbits at the bottom of it" (Lockhart, 1978, p. 8). The dead animals were removed, saving the family from illness, but without a box built around the well to shift the opening above ground level, animals continued to find their way into the water.

Obtaining Fuel

Another major concern for prairie residents was to secure a dependable source of fuel for both heating and cooking purposes, but in some areas, this was difficult to do,[4] as is confirmed by Rodwell (1965), whose report on homestead abandonment indicates that one of the more frequent causes for leaving a homestead was the lack of available wood, let alone the coal that the advertisements said could be easily found in the region.[5] Lack of fuel was not a concern for those in the more northern zone of black park soil, where abundant tree cover existed, or for those in the southern light-brown soil zone, who farmed in proximity to surface deposits of coal near Estevan, Saskatchewan, or Lethbridge, Alberta. For example, the family of Kathleen Smith (n.d.) homesteaded near Weyburn, Saskatchewan, and thus had access to as much coal as they could afford. A deposit of coal was close enough to the surface that a farmer only five miles from their location had started his own mine, which supplied people in the area. Kathleen's father built a coal shed at the side of their house and for winter filled this to the ceiling and then created a large pile of additional coal near the house that was buried in hay to keep it dry throughout the winter. For the rest of the region, however, fuel was relatively scarce, yet settlers had to have it for cooking and to maintain a livable temperature in the home during the winter. It was a priority item to be obtained whatever the cost in time, effort, or money.

For some settlers, for instance Mr. K.J. Smith of Watertown, Saskatchewan, the lack of readily available fuel meant a trip of thirty-five miles to gather wood from the valley of Last Mountain Lake, where the availability of water meant denser vegetation (Turner, 1955). For others, however, a degree of ingenuity and the help of a child were needed. Cora Montjoy tells of how her job as a three-year-old was to help her brothers search the rail line that ran near their home in the Weyburn, Saskatchewan, area for pieces of coal that might have fallen from the trains as the crew stoked the boiler fires for their engines. She was convinced "the trainmen spilled a bit" when they saw the children gathering the pieces of coal to take home (Montjoy, 1901, p. 2).

Dorthea Calverley (1985), who homesteaded near Swift Current, Saskatchewan, at the turn of the century was also assigned the task of gathering fuel as a child. However, she found it a difficult task, given the lack of trees and brush in the area. Their fuel problem was eventually solved when a new family homesteaded in the area in 1906. Although new to the prairies, the newcomers had learned about the use of buffalo chips for cooking and heating[6] and shared the knowledge with Dorthea's grandmother. Soon after, collecting chips became Dorthea's chore.[7] In her memoirs, she indicates that her grandfather

> made a light cart out of a wooden apple box which I pulled
> by a string. On it he fixed four wheels, made out of syrup pail
> lids. He also fashioned a long handled wooden paddle. Under
> my mosquito-netting anti-insect ankle-length tent, with slits
> cut out for hand-holes, I sallied forth to keep the homefires
> burning. Old dry flops were paddled into the wagon. There
> were very many of them for we were on the old trail from
> ranch to railway siding. When there had been a rain, the
> carboniferous, plate-sized objects were raised with the paddle,
> turned over to dry, and be "harvested" later for the coal
> bucket beside the kitchen stove. Grandma was sympathetic
> enough to my squeamishness not to make me lift them by
> hand, for she herself also used two sticks as tongs. Sometimes
> they didn't quite make the transfer intact. Grandma's lips
> would tighten ominously...[and] grandfather made several
> trips to the railway for more discarded "ties." (Calverley, 1985,
> pp. 22–23)

A similar story is related by Vivian Russo, who was also assigned to chip-collection duty. She was ten years old in 1915 and living in southern Alberta on the family homestead. As she describes the situation,

Down near that Montana border it was very flat. It was a long way to get any coal, sort of barren; no wood around so we used to hire a stoneboat...and go out and pick buffalo chips....You went out and when they were dry you picked them up, and if they weren't dry you turned them over and went back. It makes wonderful fires, and it's clean. When it was dry, there was no smell. My uncle had a lean-to with a sliding door into the kitchen, and stored them all there. (Silverman, 1984, p. 16)

While the use of chips as a primary fuel seems unlikely given their size, Russo notes that three chips set on fire in a stove were sufficient to make a hot fire suitable for baking bread.

Girls were not the only children assigned to fuel duties. John Watson (1975), born in 1900 in Scotland, immigrated to a farm near Calgary with his parents in 1904 and proved to be an adaptable worker. He handled cattle and assisted in gathering firewood and buffalo chips at age four when coal was not available (wagonloads of coal had to be purchased at a mine and such cross-country trips were a lower priority than necessary farm work). A similar story is told by Harry Wathen (1975), who began his childhood duties on the family homestead near Okotoks, Alberta, by gathering firewood and shovelling coal for the stoves when he was seven. However, Harry indicates that by the age of fourteen, boys were expected to have moved on to performing serious farm jobs such as driving wagons, ploughing the fields, and taking part in cropping activities such as harvesting oats and barley.

Unfortunately, neither the chips so dutifully collected, nor the railway ties appropriated for fuel, nor the scraps of coal gathered from the railway right-of-way could satisfy the needs of all families throughout a winter. Further, since trees were almost non-existent in much of the southern plains area, coal was the only other potential source of warmth during the bitterly cold winters. Dorthea Calverley (1985), speaking of the 1906–1907 winter, makes this point clear when she tells the story of a strike at the Alberta and British Columbia coal mines. This work stoppage had ended deliveries of vital fuel to the Swift Current area, so the area residents felt justified in entering into a mass criminal conspiracy to save lives. Thus, railway workers and "every able-bodied man in town including the policeman and the preachers" worked together to steal a load of special high-grade coal that was being shipped east for study, and by the end of the night, every family in the area that needed fuel had a supply hidden on their property. Coal shipments from the mines resumed shortly afterwards, but every town resident and farm family in the area became a criminal that night although "nothing ever came of it" (Calverley, 1985, p. 38).

Although few children reported being involved in felling trees for use as firewood, likely because of the danger that the job posed or their lack of the required physical strength, they were involved in processing the logs into usable form. While this task would seem to have been one requiring the strength of an older child, boys as young as ten-year-old George Cox (1902) report being involved with cutting logs into a size that fit into the family stove. George spent each Saturday cutting wood, but others were not so specific as to the amount of labour they devoted to this job. For instance, a twelve-year-old boy from Kinsmore, Manitoba, named Wesley Barr (1902, p. 740) notes that he "cut most of the wood" used by the family. Similarly, eleven-year-old Clifford Earl (1902) mentions cutting up wood for two family stoves, and Ralph Clench (1902) indicates that he helped his father cut green wood in the summertime, presumably so that it would have some time to dry before being used in the cold season.[8] However, if the wood had to be used before it had a chance to dry out, this was done, since the heat that it could provide was more important than worrying about the wood burning unevenly, excessive smoke, or having to deal with more popping and gas explosions than usual. Such was the situation for the family of Viola Cameron (1975), whose wood was delivered by an uncle from time to time over the course of the year. They were not able to develop their own woodpile due to a lack of trees on their property, and they were grateful for any wood they received, even if it was green. Viola cut the wood into stove-sized pieces when her uncle arrived with a sleigh-load of eight-inch-round poplar logs. She "put the green wood up on the sawhorse and saw[ed] it" with "an old Swedish saw" and then hauled wood into the house to replenish their supply (Cameron, 1975, p. 10).[9]

Once logs were cut to the proper size, any child could be assigned to haul the wood into the house so that the woodbox was always kept full. For example, Gordon Frook (1901), a ten-year-old boy from Burnside, Manitoba, indicates that this was one of his regular duties. The same instructions applied to an eleven-year-old girl named Florence Griffiths (1902) from Yorkton, Saskatchewan. Eight-year-old Eddie Northey (1902) of Holland, Manitoba, seven-year-old Winnifred Hunt (1902), and four-year-old Verne Hunt (1902) were also involved in hauling wood into the house, suggesting that this task at least was not assigned on the basis of the sex or age of the child providing the labour.

Animal Products

Based upon the materials reviewed in Chapter 3 respecting children's productive labour, it is evident that many family farms in the prairie region possessed a range of animals and poultry that were sold on the market. However, animals and poultry were also kept by farm families for personal consumption and for their products such as milk and eggs. Almost every child whose writings were reviewed indicates that the family, or the child personally, kept animals for food. As with the sale animals, children were made responsible for watering, feeding, milking, collecting eggs, and cleaning up after the family herd and flock.

Comments on each aspect of animal care are recorded by numerous children assigned to these tasks, including eleven-year-old Hugh McIver (1902) of Virden, Manitoba, who reports waking at 5 a.m. to care for the family's horses and cattle. He describes providing water, straw, and grain for the animals and cleaning the stable area. Such stable chores are also mentioned by W.E. McIntyre (1902), Elmer Lockhart (1902), and Ambrose Dowkes (1902), who, at seven years of age, was the youngest boy to mention assisting his father with handling stable chores on their farm near Meridian, Saskatchewan.

Tasks were more difficult for some children than others, since, in many cases, neither the settlers nor their children had experience in this type of labour and had to learn from problems as they presented themselves. For instance, as discussed in the memoir written by Mary Waddell (n.d.), no member of her family had participated in farming endeavours of any kind prior to immigrating to Canada in 1909. Thus, when they acquired a milking cow for the family, no one knew anything about milking or caring for the animal. Mary proved to be the only one not frightened by the cow, so she was assigned the milking chores. Unsurprisingly, given the family's lack of experience, they had not purchased a cream separator. However, Mary improvised and left the milk in a flat basin each night, skimmed off the cream each morning, and put it in a sealer jar. When enough cream was accumulated, Mary shook the jar to make butter for the family.

A similar situation is reported by Lucy Johnson (n.d.). She wrote that when her family was in England, no member of her family had spent time on a farm. Thus, when her father bought a cow after arriving at their homestead near Saskatoon, Saskatchewan, every member of the family was tested to see who had the ability to deal with milking. Since "can't milk means no milk," they all soon learned how the system worked. However, because her father believed that milking was a girl's job,[10] Lucy soon became the family milkmaid; she notes in her memoir that:

Milking the family cow, n.d. [PAA, OB.671]

> I was secretly pleased at this arrangement because I disliked
> washing dishes, and just as soon as mother started to wash
> dishes in the evening, I grabbed the milk pail, saying as I
> went out…"father likes the cow milked at the same time every
> night." This always worked because we had supper at the
> same time every night. (Johnson, n.d., p. 36)

Many other children in the prairie region were given the task of dealing
with the family cows and poultry. Dozens of girls and boys mention milking
cows, separating cream, and churning butter as part of their daily duties, including eleven-year-old Marion Turner (1902) from Carroll, Manitoba, and
twelve-year-old Eva Cox (1902) of Pincher Creek, Alberta, who milked four
cows on a daily basis. Typical of the boys involved in performing this work
for the family are eleven-year-old George Smith (1902) of Alexander, Manitoba, and Norman Moss (1902) of Shepard, Alberta—an eleven-year-old
who milked three cows after locating them and herding them to the barn
each day. While each of these young milkers also worked to process the
product, others such as Selena Tucker (1902), who owned her own milk cow,
were also called upon to assist. Thus, while eleven-year-old Selena churned
the cream from her cow to make butter, she also worked with the cream
from the rest of the cows on the homestead near Margaret, Manitoba.

Caring for the family's chickens and collecting the eggs they laid was
also a job commonly assigned to children, as evidenced by the large number of boys and girls who report involvement. For example, Stanley Taylor

(1902) of Neepawa, Manitoba, reports taking care of nine chickens, while eleven-year-old Florence Griffiths (1902) of Yorkton, Saskatchewan, was responsible for ten chickens and their eggs. Edna MacPhail (1902), a ten-year-old girl from Belmont, Manitoba, indicates that she had twenty-five hens; B.A. Moss (1902, p. 332), a nine-year-old girl from Shepard, Alberta, fed the hens and collected "a lot of eggs,"[11] and twelve-year-old Alice Campbell (1902) from Pomeroy, Manitoba, collected eggs from twenty-five hens and also cared for five turkeys and three roosters. Other children also indicate having chicken responsibilities, such as fourteen-year-old Florence Rayner (1902) from Elm Valley, Manitoba, ten-year-old Lillian Williamson (1902) from Regina, Saskatchewan, and eleven-year-old Albert Wright (1902) from Rose Hill, Manitoba.

As well as milk cows and laying hens, other animals on farms were kept for slaughter. While chickens and turkeys could be eaten in a single meal and thus could be killed and cooked as required, the slaughter of pigs, cattle, sheep, and goats had to wait until the fall or winter, when the natural cold would preserve them for a longer period of time, since the meat of these larger animals lasted far longer.[12] For example, Sue Harrigan (1980) reports in her memoir that her family ate fresh meat in the late fall and much of the winter, but as warm weather approached, the remaining pork and beef had to be cured or canned if it was not to be wasted. In her household, Sue was responsible for curing the pork by covering it in a mixture of saltpetre, brown sugar, salt, and pepper until it permeated the meat. As for the beef, it had to be marinated in brine before being sealed in jars. Unfortunately, learning the process was expensive for the family because Sue, not knowing that salt could kill pigs, put the used beef brine into the pail used to water their hogs and one sow died when she drank the mixture.

While information concerning children working with pigs is less prevalent than for cows and poultry, some children were charged with their care. For example, fourteen-year-old Clarence Vance (1902) of Brandon, Manitoba, had the job of looking after the farm animals, including the pigs. This chore was relatively light since he fed them only once a day (before his own breakfast), but he was also responsible for several cows, horses, and even the chickens. Caring for the pigs was also a secondary job for Gertie Anderson (1902) of Lenore, Alberta, since the ten-year-old primarily performed housework.

Hunting and Fishing

Another chore often assigned to the children of a family was the hunt for small game suitable for the family stewpot or roaster.[13] One child who took his charge very seriously was John Henry Wood (1976), the eight-year-old son of American immigrants who came to Canada at the turn of the century. Despite his young age, John was prepared to handle his part of the workload; when he spotted a flock of geese in a nearby field, he went in search of a gun:

> Running to the house he got...[a] ten gauge double barrel
> shot gun and one shell was all he could find. He shot at the
> geese and they flew into another field a short distance away.
> Running to the Logan store he got more shells and crawling
> through the field he braced his gun on a fence post and let fire.
> He killed three. They were so heavy he had to fetch...[his]
> mother from the house to help him carry them....mother was
> overjoyed with her little hunter, but...much to her dismay
> found they were banded. John had shot Mrs. Cookson's geese!
> Confession was made and...dad paid the bill. (Wood, 1976, p. 2)

The brothers of fourteen-year-old Maryanne Caswell (1968, p. 14) were more efficient in their goose hunt, according to her published letters, avoiding the privately banded birds and bringing home three geese that "looked like an order of priests with their black collars and cowls." Similarly, the brother of Nellie Hislop bagged prairie chickens[14] with no difficulty and could kill two or three ducks with a single shot if they were swimming in formation (Nuffield, 1987). Although ducks were smaller than geese and thus provided less food value, they also offered a different taste for those tired of standard fair. Christensen (1976) reports hunting ducks, which were easy to locate and hunt given the number that frequented his family farm in the summer.

When not hunting ducks or prairie chickens, young Mr. Hislop was searching for duck eggs in the trees near water sources to incubate on the farm for the purpose of raising domesticated water fowl for future consumption (Nuffield, 1987). The eggs of wild birds such as crows could also be collected, although they were eaten immediately rather than hatched (Merriken, 1999).

An interesting tale respecting the use of birds as a source of food is told by Augustine Koett (n.d.), who says that she and her sister Helen used a box full of oats as a lure for blackbirds. Once a bird had entered the box, Helen climbed in to capture their prey while Augustine held an old cape over the opening to prevent escapes. When enough birds were trapped, they were taken to the girls' mother for preparation as fried blackbird, a peculiar but life-sustaining dish that the family could acquire despite their lack of money. When blackbirds were not captured and fried for lunch, their brothers scolded the two girls for being too lazy to set up a good meal for them to eat.

While the Hislop family was not in such desperate financial straits as the Koetts, Nellie's brother was prepared to kill anything that flew, and since he knew the rhyme about the four-and-twenty blackbirds, he decided to hunt down enough birds for a pie. Unfortunately, he conducted his hunt with his two smaller sisters looking on, and when he used a shotgun on twelve birds, the girls were shocked by the many small bloody pieces of blackbird that landed throughout the farmyard. Despite the "four-and-twenty blackbirds baked in a pie" defence that he tried to use with his furious mother, she told him it had been a poor idea and he should stick to fruit for his pies in future (Nuffield, 1987).

Boys, while forming the majority of hunters, did not have an exclusive franchise on the ability to shoot. A fourteen-year-old girl from Glenboro, Manitoba, named Annie Marsh (1902) was also quite proficient, even though she spent most of her time working in the house. She managed to obtain a goose for supper one day using only a single shot from her rifle. Another girl not reluctant to shoot was Leddie Wilson (1902) of Circus Coulee, Alberta. She wrote to her sister in November 1902, to tell her that she and the family had shot seventeen prairie chickens in less than two hours. Her letter went on to describe the culinary qualities of prairie chickens, describing the birds as "plump and tender" and without a pronounced "wild" taste to them (Wilson, 1902, p. 2). However, not all girls were great, or even mediocre, hunters. Mary Hiemstra (1997), for example, went hunting with her father, but given her lack of skill, she was put in charge of the evening's transportation chores. The gully where the local farmers hunted was some distance from their homestead and Mary's job was thus of some importance, but she failed in her task due to impatience and a lack of perseverance and left her father stranded. As Mary describes her shameful conduct,

> Going to the gully was fun, but when Dad left me with the team my troubles began. The mosquitoes came in clouds, and the horses got so restless I finally decided to go home. Dad got two mallards, but he had to walk all the way home, about two miles, through a mist of mosquitoes. (Hiemstra, 1997, p. 164)

The proficiency of the Minifie boys in hunting gophers (discussed in an earlier chapter) also enhanced the family diet. Fresh meat was a rarity without refrigeration, but gophers caught, skinned, disembowelled, and cooked the same day filled that gap in their diet. Feasting on gopher continued even after the family discovered that other settlers considered gophers as repulsive as rats on the menu; they had found that the rodents tasted like rabbit and could see no reason to forsake this manna from nature (Minifie, 1972). Indeed, during years of drought or crop failure, attitudes toward eating gophers changed quite dramatically. As noted by Clarence Zeller in response to a questionnaire distributed by the Saskatchewan Archives Board, life on the frontier was either "feast or famine." In one particularly tough year, the community picnic that usually featured lemonade, sandwiches, cake, salads, and fried chicken was somewhat limited. With the food shortage, they "all brought gopher's fried hind legs" (Morgan, 1965, p. 49).

While hunting was a common pastime for young people in the West, guile rather than guns was also used to fill the supper pot. For example, G.F. Chipman wrote of visits to houses of his pupils where he spotted the subterfuges used in rabbit hunts. Rabbit pits were dug relatively close to the home and were cunningly covered with hay. Some turnips or cabbage leaves were thrown in the middle for bait, and when the unsuspecting rabbit went foraging, it fell through the hay and twigs into the pit, where it was hailed with joy on the following morning. Soon its flesh was stewing in the pot for dinner (Chipman, 1969). While Chipman does not note the degree of success that his pupils enjoyed with their rabbit traps, other families using the same methods reported anywhere from seven to fifteen rabbits being taken on some nights (Lippert, 1981). This would have represented a bountiful harvest of free food and might make the difference between survival and starvation.

Similarly, fish from the lakes, rivers, and streams of the prairies could also help to fill the food needs of settler families. As reported by a twelve-year-old girl named Ida McConnell (1902) from Hamiota, Manitoba, news that a lake was filled with fish could inspire immediate trips to the local fishing hole. Ida, for example, quickly gathered her fishing equipment and set out to harvest as many fish as possible. Her gear consisted of nets rather than fishing line, to ensure that she did not allow any fish to escape.

Such an approach was also advocated by Aaron Biehn (n.d.), who lived in the Humboldt, Saskatchewan, area in the early 1900s. A creek near his family's homestead that emptied into a nearby lake was reported to be teeming with fish. Rather than treating the hunt as a means of relaxation with a fishing pole, Aaron and his father took nets to the creek and trapped every fish they could find. On a different day, they drove their wagon into a deep section of the creek, opened the back, and allowed the fish to swim

Rabbit hunt, n.d. [PAA, A.6694]

straight into a net at the back of the wagon that prevented them from swimming back out of the box. When the wagon was full, they drove out and hauled the fish home to be processed into canning jars for future use. The fish were thus harvested as effectively as grain rather than being treated as a sporting opportunity and, thanks to the labour of Aaron and his father, helped the Biehn family to achieve its goal of increasing the variety of their stockpile of preserved foods.

Gardening and Harvesting Wild Fruits and Vegetables

As in all other areas of subsistence labour, children contributed their efforts to a mainstay of the family food supply, its garden, and the collection of wild fruits and edible plants. Fresh and preserved vegetables provided variety in settler meals, and the occasional canned fruit or jam added an element of luxury.

Delia Woolf (1974) deals with the specific duties performed by settlers' children in providing vegetables for the family table in some detail and covers the types of work that she, her siblings, and her mother performed on a regular basis on their family farm near Cardston, Alberta. Delia and her siblings helped their mother tend the family garden. A variety of basic vegetables such as carrots, beets, peas, and potatoes were grown, with the children working to ensure that plants were watered, weeds pulled, and insects killed, if found. When the garden was harvested, the crop was carefully stored in the produce cellar over the winter (Woolf, 1974).

For those who did not dig their root cellar deep enough or could not keep it warm enough to avoid freezing, the stored potatoes, carrots, beets, and most other items would be ruined by the cold. Olive Lockhart (1978) suggests that only turnips could survive a night of freezing and remain edible. If defrosted, they turned to mush but if cooked while frozen, they could be used for animal feed. However, Kenneth Doolittle (1978) indicates in his memoirs that his family found a common-sense solution to the problem of vegetables freezing in the root cellar. On the colder nights, when they could not count on the stove to keep the house warm, a coal-oil lamp could be placed in the cellar on a low flame to maintain a warm environment for the food.

The weeding of the garden appears to have been one task consistently assigned to children, possibly because of its simplicity. In any case, numerous children mention weeding duty, including fourteen-year-old Alice Lyons (1902) of Montgomery, Saskatchewan, who notes that she was out of bed at 6 a.m. each day to milk the family cows and then filled the rest of her schedule with weeding, baking, cooking meals, washing and ironing clothes, and performing other housework until it was time for the cows' evening milking. A similar schedule, complete with weeding of the family garden, is also reported by a ten-year-old boy named Raymond Roff (1902) from Plum Coulee, Manitoba, and by A. Kirk (1902) of Portage la Prairie, Manitoba. Of course, not all children were good at their tasks, as shown by the admission of Ruby Stewart (1902, p. 1020), an eleven-year-old girl from Brandon, Manitoba. She indicates that her own garden was not "weeded out good and things in it do not get on very well."

The decision as to which plants would be grown in the family garden was a personal one, and a great deal of variety could be expected. For example, Charlie McLeod (1902) observes that the garden on their family homestead near Virden, Manitoba, contained carrots, peas, and potatoes (an entire acre of ground was devoted to this dietary staple), plus beans, radishes, onions, cabbage, cucumbers, tomatoes, pumpkins, and citrons. In addition, they had planted a cherry tree and transplanted wild fruit to their patch, including red, white, and black currants, gooseberries, and cranberries. The garden was thus similar to but more extensive than that of the Woolf family. Similarly, Vernon Bassett (1902) of Glenlyon, Manitoba, remarks that carrots, peas, potatoes, beans, onions, tomatoes, cauliflower, and parsnips were planted in the main garden, as well as berry plants and rhubarb. Elmer Lockhart (1902) of Lidstone, Manitoba, was also quite ambitious with his garden planting: he grew carrots, peas, beets, potatoes,

Denys Bergot's first home and garden in St. Brieux, Saskatchewan, 1904. [SAB, R-B8896]

beans, radishes, onions, cabbage, cucumbers, tomatoes, cauliflower, parsnips, pumpkins, and citrons in the vegetable garden, and also spinach, lettuce, celery, squash, corn, and turnips. Rhubarb and various berries were planted in a fruit section.

While many children report being assigned to gardening work and most seem to have enjoyed the labour, only one reveals a true expertise in growing plants. This young girl, Elizabeth Ebbern (1901) of Balmerino, Manitoba, provides a detailed description of one aspect of her garden set-up, her special cucumber patch. She stated that she prepared the seedbed with crushed soil mixed with rotted manure for vitality and ashes for protection from insects.[15] The technique that marks her efforts as special, however, is her automatic fertilizing system created out of an old barrel. The barrel was filled with rotted manure and placed on a raised area in the centre of the seedbed. Elizabeth poured water through the manure, and nutrient-rich water then leaked from the barrel and flowed down to the plants. Presumably, this also worked automatically when it rained. As Elizabeth describes it, her system helped "to invigorate the plants which are very strong and the way they grow is astonishing" (Ebbern, 1901, p. 597).

The early fall was the time for harvesting the family garden, but before work with the vegetables began, the harvest of ripened wild fruits had to be completed. Delia Woolf describes an early memory of going with her siblings on berry-picking expeditions. They had to cross a river on their ranch and then pick "strawberries, serviceberries, gooseberries and wild raspberries" from an area with "acres of bushes" (Woolf, 1974, p. 9). Huckleberries were a rarer commodity, but overnight trips to the nearby mountains provided enough of this fruit to make the travel worthwhile, and the preserved fruits made it possible to cook wild berry pies year-round (Woolf, 1974).

Gathering and growing food, particularly berries, were also the most common forms of subsistence labour performed by Elmer Spackman as a young boy after his family settled in the prairie region in 1902. For the Spackmans, natural foods cost nothing but effort and could provide both variety and freshness in an otherwise mundane diet. When they first arrived in the area, the Spackmans planted the fruit plants they had brought with them from Utah, but until the plants matured, they had to purchase dried apples and prunes for eating, referring derisively to prunes as "Canadian strawberries" (1975, p. 17). These dried rations were supplemented by crabapples, chokecherries, and saskatoons that Elmer gathered from bushes near a river.

The chore of gathering a supply of berries large enough for the entire family is also recounted by Evelyn McLeod (1977) in her memoirs:

> Wild berries were plentiful. Strawberries were to be had in season by the dishpan-full, provided one didn't mind crawling around the low hillsides in the hot sun and we children came in handy for this little job. (McLeod, 1977, p. 16)

Other young girls, such as Alice Campbell (1902) from Pomeroy, Manitoba, and Mabel White (1902, p. 740), an eleven-year-old from St. Charles, Manitoba, were also responsible for locating and collecting wild "plums, cherries, black cherries, gooseberries, saskatoons, raspberries and haws" that grew close enough to their homesteads. What could be found in the wild was also often imported into family gardens, since gooseberries, red and black currants, and raspberries all grew well in the prairie climate (Myer, 1978). The transplanted berry plants, receiving regular watering and fertilizer, could also outperform their wild cousins and supply fruit without the long trek into the country (Dinsmore, 1901). Fourteen-year-old Maryanne Caswell (1968) was also involved with transplanting several plants, but unlike the berries mentioned above, the roots for these rhubarb, currant, strawberry, and iris plants had been transported across the country when the family moved west.

Wild fruits were a source of nutrients but were also important because of the change that they allowed in the daily diet of the typical settler. The individuals and families who embarked on journeys into the wild to establish their own farms did not have a great deal of cash to spare on unnecessary items; a standard "grubstake"—a term used by Isabel and Betty McNaught (1976) to describe the basic food supply people purchased each winter from the general store in Edson, Alberta—was made up of fairly basic, durable, and transportable food. A grubstake would last a family for one year and cost approximately $300 in 1912. The McNaught sisters describe the goods their family had purchased as

> everything that would swell as much food as possible for the poundage...all by the case, wholesale by the case. Dried fruits, they got prunes and plums and apples and rice and tapioca and sego, horrible stuff, and beans and oatmeal and sugar. (McNaught, 1976, p. 8)

Such supplies were generally bland, and wild berries and other plants could help to cure this deficiency. For example, Bertha Myer (1978, p. 3) reports that one of the tasks assigned to her was the collection of edible mushrooms that she found growing "on sod buildings, in the prairie grass and in edges of wheat fields." A similar job fell to Olive Lockhart (1978), who was responsible for collecting mushrooms and also pigweed (wild spinach) and dandelion greens for the family table. Another child raised on the prairies notes that children collected other plants as well:

> In the fall, we'd pick rose-hips on the way home and my mother would make some kind of tea....I think they got it from the Indians. The rose-hip tea was good for all sorts of illnesses. (Broadfoot, 1988, p. 137)

Although stories about berry picking do not reveal the dangers of children entering the bush, family members had to remain aware of the danger that the prairie itself presented for younger children. For example, McLeod (1977) discusses the case of a young girl from a neighbouring farm who went out in a light rain to collect mushrooms and other edible plants for a meal. She did not return home and, despite a search, was not found for two days. When she was finally discovered, her basket contained a few wild mushrooms, but she had died from exposure and starvation because the family had been rationing its dwindling food supply before she went out on her search.

Protection of the Family from Insects and Other Animal Life

While creating an infrastructure of buildings, fences, and fields, and locating sources of necessary supplies such as water, fuel, and food, was vital to establishing a viable family farm, protecting what had been built was equally important because no operation could otherwise remain viable. Among the more important duties of all family members was the devotion of as much time as possible to ensuring the safety of the food supply and members of the family. Protecting the crops and gardens from pests meant that traps, guns, poison, and other protective measures were as common as rabbits, gophers, cutworms, and grasshoppers.

However, settlers faced a problem in that the state of knowledge at the time provided no solution for many of the problems. They had to be accepted and the operation rebuilt afterward. For example, grasshoppers could eat a crop to the ground (Owram, 1980), cutworms could completely destroy acres of wheat (Report on the Census of the Northwest Provinces, 1906), and hailstorms could ravage crops and kill animals (Kennedy, 1970).[16] No investment of time or labour could prevent such harm, but sometimes the careful application of labour could at least reduce the damage.

For example, the most common defence against mosquitoes was to use their dislike of clouds of smoke as a defensive barrier. Smouldering bonfires ("smudges") lit upwind of the pasture, barn, or house to be protected provided billows of thick smoke that held mosquitoes away from anything within the protection of the smoke cloud (Harrigan, 1980). Of course, it was not necessarily pleasant within the cloud since coughing, stinging eyes, and the smell of smoke could themselves become irritants, but it at least provided an option other than suffering continuous mosquito attacks. The effectiveness and convenience of smudges could also be improved by making a smudge portable or of a smaller size with a smudge pot[17] to provide individual protection (Lehr, 1996; Harrigan, 1980).

With portable smudges, even individuals driving out into the countryside away from concentrations of people and animals who might attract clouds of the insects could protect themselves by lighting a smudge pot if the insects did appear. The effectiveness of such a strategy is shown in Evelyn McLeod's (1977) description of the activities of her neighbour. This woman, a housewife named Molsberry, hitched up her horse each morning during berry season at five o'clock and drove the eight miles to the coulees where the bushes grew. She then spent the entire day picking pailfuls of the "raspberries, saskatoons, gooseberries and chokecherries [that] were to be had for the taking in those early days," but at all times, she used her prepared smudge (in a metal pail for ease of carrying) as a personal form of insect repellant. The smoke that followed her all day held off the mosquitoes that might otherwise have driven her from her quest (McLeod, 1977, p. 17).

In addition to the use of smudges to keep the mosquitoes away from people, reports also discuss the effectiveness of netting as protection. As was noted earlier, the case of Dorthea Calverley (1985) suggests that netting could provide protection from bites, but as she describes her outfit as a tent of netting, it was probably unrealistic for those whose work required them to be active. However, a veil over the face could protect a person from inconvenient bites from the clouds of mosquitoes that "waited for you at the door in the morning" (Graham, 1974), and, as noted by Mitchell (1976), wearing a pair of gloves as well as a head veil could protect the skin usually exposed during the day. Putting a layer of paper under the clothes at sensitive spots could also improve the situation, since mosquitoes could not bite through the paper (Merriken, 1999).

Unfortunately, while clothing and netting could provide some protection for individuals, farm animals also suffered from the attacks of these insects, and protected farmers could do little work if their animals were unsettled by constant biting. One recorded solution was to make covers for the animals as well. Potato sacks strategically cut and stitched back together could provide effective cover for the animals that had to be taken out of their sheds to perform their work during mosquito season (Turner, 1955).[18]

Lathrop Roberts indicates that as difficult as it was to protect oneself against mosquitoes, it was impossible to establish any control over the flies that invaded homes, barns, and any other location, indoors or out, without killing them, and there were simply too many to kill them all:

> As for the flies, we were absolutely at their mercy. We could not smoke them out, or drive them out or keep them out, though we waged perpetual war upon them and, at mealtime, did more fighting than eating. (Sarah Ellen Roberts, 1971, p. 33)

In essence, during the warm months, the prairies could become a rather irritating environment as the various pests came out of hibernation or were hatched. Holding on to his sense of humour despite the conditions, Lathrop's father suggested that they should delay dinner until dark all of the time, because, that way, at least they would be unable to see what they were eating, including any flies that might have settled on the food (Roberts, 1971).

One additional problem faced by most settlers due to their living conditions, but one that could be controlled through the use of common products, was fleas. These parasites were carried into the home on pets and on the clothing and bodies of those in contact with farm animals, but diverting flypaper to duty as a flea killer could solve the problem. By covering a mop or broom with the paper and using this sticky implement to sweep the floor, fleas could be trapped in the glue along with the dust and other debris that was found. To cover the possibility that some of the insects might jump onto the legs of the sweeper to escape death, flypaper would be pinned onto the pant legs to trap fleas as well. The whole process was completed by placing flypaper under the beds to trap new insects as they tried to reach the bedding where they could feast on people during the night ("What Other Women Have Found Out," 1908).

Luckily, the more dangerous pests such as poisonous snakes in southern Alberta (Marquis of Lorne, 1886) and larger predators such as wolves and bears, which could make life dangerous rather than just unpleasant, did not tend to seek out human victims (Lehr, 1996; Jones, 1987; Potyondi, 1995; Roberts, 1971). However, even coyotes might attack stock, and while they might be relatively easy to kill (the fourteen-year-old sister of Sue Harrigan killed a coyote with rocks while her dog distracted it), wolves and bears that attacked the animals were in a completely different class of predator (Harrigan, 1980; Chipman, 1969; Hiemstra, 1997). There is no doubt that these larger predators frequented the same areas as the settlers (for example, eleven-year-old Ina Mumby [1902] reported that wolves attacked the family's chickens and turkeys at night) and could not be defeated without guns. Archie Althouse (n.d.), whose family homesteaded near Handel, Saskatchewan, describes a problem with a weasel that could not be kept away from the henhouse. Archie and his mother, tired of their continuing losses, decided to put an end to the chicken thief, but after holding it away from the chickens with long sticks, they found they could not kill it. The weasel was therefore held until the father returned that evening and shot it with a rifle.

Protection of the Family from Prairie Fires

Of all of the preventable hazards present in the prairie region, the most dangerous and mortally terrifying were the prairie fires that shattered lives and property with an immediacy that none of the other impediments to farming could match (Eager, 1953; Ruthig, 1954). However, settlers' property could sometimes be defended from the effects of such natural disasters. While such fires might begin with a lightning strike, a careless campfire, or a spark from a train engine or the steel wheels of the railcars (Cotton, n.d.), the general lack of accessible water on the prairies meant that the most common defence from fire was a firebreak or fireguard. A firebreak could be as large or small as a person desired, but in general the term denoted a deliberately created gap in the source of fuel available to the fire.

In the case of prairie fires, the fuel was made up of "prairie wool," as the pioneers named it—the continuous stretch of wild grasses running across the prairies (Mitchell, 1976, p. 1). A single fire could theoretically burn hundreds of thousands of square kilometres of land, spreading through the "wool" with the speed imparted by the wind to the wavefront of the fire,[19] stopping only when reaching a natural barrier such as a stream or a patch of land with no unburned fuel close enough to the fire to ignite. Even then, the fire would die only if the dead patch were wide enough that embers could not reignite the blaze beyond the barrier.

Given the simplicity of the concept, a number of different approaches could be taken to creating firebreaks. For example, building a sod house on the land from which the sod bricks for the walls had been cut would leave the home at the centre of an area from which all fuel had been stripped. Similarly, firebreaks of bare land ploughed around important areas could perform the same function, starving a fire of the fuel it needed to sustain itself. How wide the ploughed area should be was a matter of judgement and terrain, but with any wind at all, sparks from a fire would fly at least several feet before landing and possibly starting a new fire within a pro-tected zone. The only valid defence strategy once sparks crossed the bar-rier was to have every available individual standing by with wet cloths or gunny sacks to smother any sparks and beat out any flames. The lack of water on the prairies could lead to the failure of such tactics, but no other realistic option was available. In her memoir, Hazel Dennison (n.d., p. 4) tells a story of her family's fight against a prairie fire started by a spark from a train engine. Her family was homesteading near Assiniboia, Saskatchewan, one of the drier sections of the area, and to fight the fire, barrels of water had to be obtained from a small stream "to keep the gunny sacks wet to fight a blaze two feet high. We had to fight to save the pasture and cultivated land." They had no choice but to court injury or death if they were to have a farm left to operate.

When faced with the problem of wind-carried sparks, the solution of the settlers in the Lloydminster area was to construct a firebreak two miles wide to the south of the town by ploughing strips of land two miles apart and then deliberately burning the area inside the two barriers. This created a wide dead zone that they believed would halt or at least divert a massive and fast-moving prairie fire that was bearing down on the town in the spring of 1905 (Strong, 1968). Even with this massive effort, burning bits of grass and turf blew into town, but as these landed, the second phase of the defence came into play. Men, women, and children from the town and surrounding evacuated areas fought the embers with water-soaked gunny sacks. The town was saved, but as Strong indicated in her memoirs, the terror was visceral:

> Unless one has seen a prairie fire it is difficult to describe
> the horror of one, we were on the edge of it but as far as
> one could see, for thirty miles was told us after, it appeared
> as a sea of waves of fire. The heat and smoke were terrific.
> (Strong, 1968, p. 9)

For those who failed to take such precautions and those without ploughs to set up a defensive ring around their buildings, a fire could mean ruin or death (Eager, 1953). For example, the papers of G.F. Chipman (1969) relating to his teaching experience near Edmonton, Alberta, during 1903–1904 discuss the situation at the school when a prairie fire drew within thirty feet of their location. The building was of log construction, but as with most buildings in the West, the roof was not built so well. Simple cut boards had been used, but no other protection from fire existed and the wind was blowing the fire closer all the time. Chipman indicates in his notes that "but for the good work of the pupils, their 'academy' would have passed into history" (Chipman, 1969, p. 6). Rather than panicking, the boys went to the nearest neighbour's house, filled two barrels with water, and hauled them back to the school site like a junior volunteer fire brigade:

> By means of a primitive bucket brigade, we accomplished
> what seemed to be impossible. Three of the boys on the roof,
> some on tables under the eaves, and the rest handing the
> water made the system complete....And when the fire had
> passed the danger zone it was a tired but happy group of
> school children who wended their way home, all proud of the
> work they had done. (Chipman, 1969, p. 6)

Even with the rapid increase in the settler population during the first decade of the twentieth century, prairie fires continued to prove a menace. This seems illogical given that settlement meant the breaking up of long open stretches of prairie grasses in favour of protected quarter-mile squares, but, even so, reports continued to refer to these fires with terror. The family of Mildred Hyndman (1979), for example, moved to the prairies in 1910 when she was ten years old. In her memoir of her early years on the homestead near Morse, Saskatchewan, Mildred writes that the prairie grass was not as tall or thick as she had expected based on the information provided by her teachers about the West. In addition, they had many neighbours within walking distance, and creating ploughed firebreaks was common practice. This would logically suggest that fire should not have posed as much of a threat, yet she goes on to say,

> prairie fires in summer were something to fear. At the first smell of smoke, our eyes would search over the horizons to locate the source. If a fire was found to be advancing in our direction, every one would rush to be prepared to fight it. Fresh sod be plowed while gunny sacks were wct [sic]. Then a fire set between the two rows of freshly turned sod in order to protect the buildings from the advancing fire [sic]. If there was a high wind, and it seemed that the fire would create its own wind [sic]. It would sometimes jump the fire guard to be quickly snuffed out with the wet sacks. (Hyndman, 1979, p. 5)

However, even when firebreaks were created, conditions sometimes meant that they did not always work to hold back the fires and each individual then became responsible for protecting whatever he or she could. For example, in her autobiography, Kennedy (1970) reports that the first fall spent on the family homestead saw a prairie fire jump their ploughed fireguard. Even though they attacked the fire with wet gunny sacks and brooms, their tent home was burned out along with all of their possessions, but luckily there were only a few minor injuries to family members. The situation described in the memoirs of Evelyn McLeod (1977) is similar, but in a very short period, she and her family faced two fires. The first, encountered on the trail to their new homestead, was a total surprise. It was early spring, and the family had been travelling for three weeks, spending two days in a snowstorm and the balance of the week waiting for the snow to melt and the waterlogged trail to dry, and then two weeks moving toward their property. At that point, they discovered that the prairies could dry very quickly after a snowstorm and sudden melt, since a prairie fire was being swept in their direction by the wind:

> We halted, the horses were hitched to hand plows unloaded from the wagons and furrows cut for a firebreak. But time

had run out. The strip…was not sufficiently wide and in
some places the fire jumped across and had to be beaten out
with wet gunny-sacks.…Afterwards there was concern that
there would be no grass for the livestock when we reached
the homesteads. (McLeod, 1977, p. 4)

On reaching their land they discovered that it had not yet been burned
and the family rushed once again to break out the plough and set up a
proper firebreak around their entire quarter section to protect the grass
for their cattle to eat. Additional breaks were ploughed nearer the wagons where they would live until a house was built, in case the first barrier
failed. Only three days after the work was done, a second fire "burned off
the rest of the prairie," and their quarter became the sole source of food for
local wildlife until new growth began (McLeod, 1977, p. 5).

Of course, not every effort to protect lives and property was successful.
For instance, McElhone (1975) comments on the relentless pressure of the
fires that swept the prairies, particularly one that started near Medicine
Hat, Alberta, and then swept through the area of their family farm. A
neighbour woman and her two children were trapped by the wall of fire
and perished, and, while no members of his family died, McElhone recalled
the fire vividly:

This fire was about a mile or more wide and it rolled with a
tremendous wind behind it. The warning about the fire was
the smoke that preceded the fire itself. It was rolling so fast
that it would roll right over a building without burning it. If
it rolled over a haystack it would leave the haystack on fire.
This way, my father lost all his hay. He was left with a bunch
of horses and very few cattle and had nothing to feed them
with. (McElhone, 1975, p. 5)

After such a devastating blow, the only decision to make was whether to
quit the farming life or to carry on as best one could. No amount of planning, no amount of labour by family members, and no amount of foresight
could protect a farm from such an elemental force.

Summary

Despite the occasional failure, the labour power of a family was a factor
that enabled many farms to survive the harsh prairie conditions, and children made major contributions to the welfare and survival of farm families

with their work. Pansey Pue (1975), a twelve-year-old girl whose family migrated to the Cheadle district of Alberta in 1911 after her father's death, is an ideal example of the importance of child labour. Pansey found herself in a position where her labour, along with that of her younger brothers, her older brother, and her mother, was necessary to family survival. For Pansey, this meant caring for chickens and helping with the milking of the family cows but also performing tasks within the house. "There was a good deal to do in the house [and she] was the only girl to help [her] mother…[and her] brothers were so very young" (Pue, 1975, p. 3). When asked whether the homestead could supply them with sufficient food and other resources to take care of the family needs, Pansey responded, "It had to….Nothing else could be done….It was our only means of support" (Pue, 1975, p. 4). Certainly, adults supervised this labour and trained the children in the necessary skills and knowledge, but by working on everything from the home to food to fire and water, children made a difference.

SIX

Domestic Labour

As WAS THE CASE WITH PRODUCTIVE LABOUR, domestic labour (work tasks that supported the comfort, well-being, and morale of the family) was quite sharply divided between genders. As revealed in Tables 12 and 13, these jobs fell overwhelmingly to the female children on prairie farms. Only token numbers of boys helped with food preparation, washing clothing and other items, sewing, and child care. Only in the area of housecleaning did a meaningful number of boys help the girls who were also involved in this task.

TABLE 12

Domestic Labour:
Boys' Contributions by Age and Type of Work

AGE	Cleaning House	Washing Clothes & Making Beds	Child Care	Food Preparation	Sewing
4–5	0	0	0	0	0
6–8	2	0	0	0	0
9–11	9	2	2	2	0
12–14	2	0	2	0	0
>14	0	0	1	0	1

TABLE 13

Domestic Labour:
Girls' Contributions by Age and Type of Work

AGE	Cleaning House	Washing Clothes & Making Beds	Child Care	Food Preparation	Sewing
4–5	0	0	0	0	0
6–8	4	3	1	5	1
9–11	29	20	7	19	6
12–14	43	40	10	30	13
>14	7	3	3	7	3

Gendered Roles

Given the fixed gendered labour roles in the domestic sphere among adults, discussed earlier, it would have been surprising if such a division of labour did not also exist among children. The nature of the labour involved and the skills required were those that society expected of females, a biased social attitude that can be seen in newspaper articles published at the time. For example, a letter submitted to *The Nor'-West Farmer* by a correspondent named Ruskin (1900) advocates that females be trained to know the qualities of the foods available (and how best to cook or serve them). However, the article does not suggest any need for such skills on the part of boys. This was not an unusual submission, as shown by the fact that approximately one year later, A.X. Hyatt (1901) makes similar pronouncements respecting the proper types of labour to be performed by females in the West. In Hyatt's case, the argument revolves around washing and ironing clothes, preserving fruits or other produce, sewing, creating a bountiful garden, and cleaning and cooking chickens for the table, but the intent is the same. All labour that could be designated housework or interpreted as caring for others was to be identified as the exclusive duty of women and their girl helpers. In fact, it was assumed that a thorough grounding in domestic labour would be of greatest benefit to girls because "about 85 per cent of the girls on the farm [were] predestined to become homemakers and homekeepers before they [reached] the age of 28. This is the way of the world" (Florence, 1901, p. 182).

Given this predestination, it was anticipated that farmers' daughters would acquire the skills necessary for the proper running of a home and become hard-working, caring people happy with their place in life. This idealized version of the perfect daughter was expressed in a poem by an anonymous author at the turn of the century published in *The Nor'-West Farmer* (1899a, p. 341):

You should see her in the kitchen,
Cap and apron white as snow,
In her eyes the love-light shining
On her cheeks a rosy glow.

Sleeves rolled up above the elbows,
Sweeping here and dusting there,
This fair daughter of the farmer,
For the household hath a care.

And her song is just as tuneful,
And her step is just as light,
As when she, sweet merry-maker
Joined her mates in play last night.

Oh the little farmer's daughter,
(Heaven bless her as she goes)
She is fairer than the lily,
She is sweeter than the rose.

Given such attitudes, it is not surprising that the proper training and work for females was seen to be in basic domestic concerns. Her birth family could benefit from her valuable efforts while she was single, and her marital family would benefit from them in due course. Even if the daughter never married, the skills she learned in food preparation, baking, and sewing, all of which training could be obtained by working on the family farm, could be put to use commercially through employment as a domestic servant (Florence, 1901). As one mother proudly noted about her own daughter,

Go to her house to-day, eat at her table and you won't dispute me. She learned to cook, to make, to mend, to wash, to iron, to put up fruit, to make gilt-edged butter, etc. She could harness and drive a spirited horse, milk a cow, teach a calf to drink; she could sing and play on an organ, and when strangers ask her where she graduated she says she did most of her graduating at home with her father and mother. (Hyatt, 1901, p. 100)

The acquisition of the skills that would prepare young girls to fit the roles designed for them by the society of the late nineteenth century began at the knee of their same-sex parent. Children were influenced constantly, not only by deliberate lessons, but also by the example set by the parent in his or her daily life. Of course, the advice given to mothers on what to teach their daughters differed substantially from that for fathers on what to teach their sons. Rather than encouraging a sense of involvement in the planning of the future of the farm or an expectation of financial rewards, the "wise" mothers ensured that their daughters were trained in useful skills from the earliest possible age (Anonymous, 1899b, p. 622). This was done by prompting girls to play house and copy their mothers' actions. Thus, a small pie could be prepared and a single item washed with her own tub and washboard; she could also observe how beds were made, learn to set a table using her own miniature tea set, and help with the dusting and sweeping at a very early age. Skill and pride of accomplishment would flow from the play, and even if the girl did prefer "her book, her piano, her pencil…she is [also] ready and equal to her broom, her saucepan, and her flat-iron" (Anonymous, 1899b, p. 623).

Aside from such general knowledge and skills, domestic apprentices (daughters) would also have learned the numerous special processes and helpful techniques that made work simpler in the West or solved some of the problems special to the region. For example, girls would learn that adding carbolic acid to whitewash prevented the smell of the paint from permeating stored foods, an important point given that many soddies were whitewashed. Using borax as a coating for fresh meat and chicken to delay rotting would come in handy since no refrigeration was readily available except for the local stream.[1] Flannel was recommended as both the proper type of cloth for washing walls and for winding tightly around a baby's stomach to cure diarrhea. Dirty papered walls could be effectively cleaned with stale bread (a possible use of the penicillin produced by some bread moulds was to kill bacteria within pioneer homes), while vinegar could neutralize the smell of onions when cooking ("Useful Hints," 1900).

Other tricks of the domestic trade for girls to learn included the fact that a flatiron washed occasionally with water and melted lard (two quarts of water to one tablespoonful of lard) would not stick to clothes, and that salt dried in an oven and ground fine in a mortar would not clump in damp weather. The column "Household Hints" also recommends the use of paper pasted to the tops of jars of preserves rather than metal or glass covers to eliminate the chance of mould developing, and instructs readers on the process to be followed to make waterproof glue that would be useful for the home and farm. This involved soaking ordinary glue in water and then dissolving the mixture into warmed linseed oil and letting it set ("Household Hints," 1897, p. 30). Clearly, the well-trained girl had much to learn from her mother if she was to fulfill her socially mandated role in an agricultural society. As noted by an anonymous contributor to the June 1908 edition of *The Grain Growers' Guide* (p. 45), "[there] is no school better than the home for training girls for the womanly duties of life, and no teacher like a capable and patient mother."

This social attitude favouring the well-trained hard-working girl dedicated to the welfare of her family was reinforced by the negative stereotype assigned to girls who did not fit the role. In fact, comments made in newspaper articles suggest that the worst thing that a man intending to farm could do was marry a "doll" (Anonymous, 1897, p. 196; Anonymous, 1900, p. 635). It was believed that such women were more worried about their appearance than the need for hard work in a farm setting. Instead of acquiring skills directed at maintaining order and keeping the farmhouse presentable and well stocked with homemade foods, they were concerned with being "showy creatures" and in making "trips to the village store to admire the latest styles" (Anonymous, 1900, p. 635).

Thus, advice columns suggested that men use other standards than looks in assessing a possible farming mate. For example, Mrs. M.E. Graham, a contributor to *The Grain Growers' Guide*, writes that in choosing a bride, young farm men should be practical and search for a woman who has the ability to assist them in their endeavours. From her perspective, a man should "use just as much common sense as...in buying a cow or a horse" rather than falling in love with the first pretty girl he notices (Graham, 1909, p. 24). Using an analogy borrowed from the horse-breeding field, she argues that it is important to find a woman with the right personality, abilities, and skills to be helpful on the farm, indicating that a practical man has to realize that he needs a Clydesdale rather than a Percheron for some tasks:

> While some men see nothing but the grooming and the harness, a more sensible man would select his ideal type, then look for good lungs, with good staying powers, good limbs, good feet, good heart action; in fact a well developed and proportioned body, with enough fat to show an appearance of being well nourished....She should have good teeth and breath, a healthy color, clear intelligent eyes and a pleasing expression. (Graham, 1909, pp. 24–25)

The same sentiment is expressed by a contributor named Bill Johnson in a poem published in *The Nor'-West Farmer* in August 1897 (p. 289):

> I've allus notissed fellers
> Hit's a risky thing to do
> To kalkalate accordin'
> To how things looks to you.
> The man 'at talks the nicest
> Don't help you up the hill;
> The one 'at prays the loudest
> Don't allus pay his bill.
> Sometimes the biggest fishes
> Bites the smallest kinds o' baits;
> An' mighty ugly wimmin
> Can make the best o' mates.

This was not to say that beautiful women would automatically fail the test as potential farm wives, but rather that qualities other than beauty should determine the choice of a partner.

Given this social imperative, a girl like Alice Campbell (1902) would have been considered an optimal catch as a future bride. Alice was a twelve-year-old from the area of Pomeroy, Manitoba, a multi-talented youngster performing work both within and outside of the home. As she describes her skills and work activity, she provides virtually every conceivable type of labour that could be expected:

> I can scrub and bake cakes and make beds and get meals
> ready and peel potatoes wash dishes clean the stove and help
> to wash clothes and sweep floors and iron. We have a cream
> separator. I can turn it when putting milk through it and feed
> calves carry in wood and feed hens. We have about 80 hens
> and five turkeys and three roosters. I gather eggs...and feed
> my horse. I drive a black pony In the fall and summer I bring
> home the cows to be milked and sometimes I help to milk and
> I get supper and carry in water and all the wood that's used.
> (Campbell, 1902, p. 333)

There is no indication of what Alice looked like, but her skills and lack of fear of hard work on the farm ensured that she would be a prime candidate, whatever her appearance.

A letter written by Dora Darwood (1902) of Meadow Lea, Manitoba, expresses the same type of industry as she describes the numerous chores and tasks for which she and her mother were responsible in the house and yard. At fifteen, Dora took on the duty of performing all of the basic housework, including cleaning, scrubbing floors, sweeping, washing and ironing clothes, and some of the baking and cooking. In addition, she helped milk the family cows while her mother concentrated on food preparation and converting the raw milk into cream and butter for the family's use. Thus, Dora states (1902, p. 507), "[any] girl who lives on a farm knows what a lot of work there is to do." In other words, she was cognizant of the fact that as a potential farmer's bride, her role would likely prove to be a difficult one since she was likely to receive little assistance in her domestic work from the men or boys in her life. This fact was illustrated by Dora's younger brother, Willie Darwood. Willie primarily worked in the fields with his father and cared for animals. To Dora's consternation, his only connection to the performance of domestic or subsistence work was operating the cream separator.

The reward of marriage for a girl's industry and acceptance of her role is substantiated by the experience of Gladys Holmes when she was a teenager. As she describes the scenario, she was "scrubbing wood floors with soft soap and a scrubbing brush," and "while [she] was down on [her] knees scrubbing the kitchen floor [she] received [her] first proposal of marriage" (Holmes, n.d., p. 7), perhaps proving the argument of Mrs. M.E. Graham that men should admire girls with practical skills rather than covet beauty (Graham, 1909).

Food Preparation

While cleaning the floor was a practical skill, one of the most necessary domestic talents to be acquired was the ability to provide wholesome meals for the family. Such cooking abilities were seldom attained by boys, although they should have been taught as a matter of survival given that eighteen-year-old boys were entitled to claim a homestead and move out on their own. These boys needed food as well as the ability to build a house and plough a field, but only one boy, nine-year-old James Brander (1902) from Nesbitt, Manitoba, makes any mention of being somewhat prepared for the future. He states that he was able to peel potatoes but did not know how to cook them. If this example is any indication of the cooking skills of the young men of the era, it is not surprising that many single male settlers found themselves in dire straits. For example, Mildred Hyndman (1979, p. 3) tells of the bachelors in her area coming to her mother for advice on cooking:

[They] had never cooked a meal before, and the disasters
they had from their efforts was hilarious. They took it all
in good fun and came to my mother for help with it. One
of them tried to bake bread using baking powder instead of
yeast, and couldn't understand why it wouldn't rise like his
mother's did.

Her mother helped them, but Mildred doubted that any bachelors ate as
well as her family, even with their updated knowledge. In fact, she specu-
lated further that because of their lack of training and time to prepare
stockpiles of preserved foods, single men would be unable to respond ad-
equately to unexpected events such as a crop or garden failure. She came
to this conclusion because of her family's own experiences with the loss of
their food crop the year before. Her family was able to survive this disaster
by relying on the homemade products they had stored, including smoked
ham and jars of preserved fruit and jams. Given that bachelors did not
know how to cook, she believed that it was unlikely that they would have
been capable of making similar preparations. Had they spent more time in
the kitchen as children, the situation might have been different since they
would have been more self-sufficient (Hyndman, 1979).

The advantage held by Mildred's family and others resulted from the
training that their female members had received as children. For girls,
learning how to bake cakes, pies, and bread and to prepare meals for the
family began at an early age, but the order in which they learned specific
cooking tasks differed from family to family. For example, being able to
bake seemed to be of the greatest importance in some households. Thus,
while fourteen-year-old Lottie Kent (1902) of Wawanesa, Manitoba, was
old enough to have received training in cooking meals, her only comment
is that she took part in baking. Similarly, Annie Lambert (1902) of Bois-
sevain, Manitoba, began baking when she was twelve years old, and fourteen-year-old Agnes White (1902) mentions that she baked for her family
in a letter discussing her work on the homestead. One somewhat anoma-
lous report is provided by May Leece (1902) of Holmfield, Manitoba. She
indicates that she was capable of performing every household task (and
could milk cows and care for livestock) *except* baking. She does not indicate
whether this was a matter of personal preference or a lack of skill.

It may well be that such limited participation in food preparation for
these particular girls was a result of caution in having them take on the
full load of cooking for the family or the need for a longer period of training before they were ready to cook palatable meals. However, given that
girls both younger and older than those discussed above did take part in

all aspects of the cooking process in other families, the more logical answer to the question of why there were widely differing skill levels among girls is that training began at different ages at the whim of the mother. For example, Gertie Slater (1902, p. 420), a thirteen-year-old girl from Portage la Prairie, Manitoba, worked hard in the home and took part in "baking bread and cake and cooking meals" as well as washing dishes. Similarly, Annie Gilliland (1902) of Bowden, Alberta, was trusted to get up each morning at six o'clock to make breakfast for the family when she was thirteen, and then spent much of the rest of her day baking bread and cakes and cleaning the home. The youngest girl to mention cooking meals is Meta Williamson (1902), who, at eleven years of age, was responsible for helping her mother get dinner ready for the family on their farm near Regina, Saskatchewan. As she was more of a helper than an independent cook, it is likely that she was beginning her training before graduating to feeding the family herself.

However, this emphasis on training did not mean that all women were proficient cooks when they first arrived in western Canada. The mother of Mary Waddell (n.d.), for example, had never made bread in the past, always having had servants to perform such tasks. She had many failures (the family kept one notable loaf that turned out hard as a doorstop), and the family cow, Beauty, was generally happy to consume the other less-than-perfect batches. Many of the failures resulted from letting the dough sit overnight to rise during the winter since the cold temperatures in the house made the dough tough. One experiment in maintaining the proper level of warmth by keeping the tub of batter under the covers on her parents' bed worked all too well. The dough overflowed the tub at the bottom of the bed, but as Beauty enjoyed uncooked dough as well as she did the overcooked variety, at least part of that batch was not wasted.

Unfortunately, by the time her mother had become skilful in baking, her strength had failed her and Mary had to take over the kneading and, later, all of the baking. After six years of practice Mary became good enough that she began to win prizes at local fairs, including 100 pounds of flour from the Women's Grain Growers Club when she was sixteen, beating out jealous older women who thought her too young to be in the competition.

Despite the drudgery of working indoors much of the day and standing over a wood-fired stove baking bread and preparing meals, many of the girls who noted such labour in their memoirs, diaries, and letters seem excited, or at least pleased, by the chance to help their mothers and learn these skills. For example, fourteen-year-old Bertha Cheavins (1902, p. 740) from Chatter, Saskatchewan, writes that she enjoyed domestic labour "very much," while others such as fourteen-year-old Rose Shaver (1902, p. 917) of Minnedosa, Manitoba, say that they "liked" the work they were assigned. Bertha Myer was more eloquent in her expression of happiness over her assignment to help her mother with preparing meals, particularly during harvest season when huge meals had to be prepared for the threshing crews. Bertha and her mother baked and cooked for days to prepare for the arrival of the crew. "[B]utter was churned and stored in crocks which were lowered into the well to keep cool and fresh," hams were cooked, pies were prepared and water supplies were checked to be sure that adequate provisions would be available. Her pleasure in domestic duties may have been partially the result of having new faces around the farm and a sense of excitement as another farming year came to a close. Regardless of the reason, she wrote that it "was great fun to help with the men's afternoon lunch" even though the preparation work had been heavy (Myer, 1978, p. 3).

Washing Clothes and Making Beds

As with baking and cooking, the job of washing clothes and other items required specialized skills. The person performing the task had to decide the best means of washing particular items, determine whether bleach should be used, and choose an appropriate stain-removal technique when necessary (Johnston, 1973). Strength and endurance were also required since buckets of water might have to be hauled, washing was generally done by rubbing the items against a washboard immersed in soapy water, and the water was wrung out of the clean items by hand before drying (Doolittle, 1978). Further, there was some danger of injury since boiling water was used in the process of cleaning most items (Jordison, 1979) and the heavy cast-metal irons heated on the family stove to remove wrinkles could leave burns on those who were careless (Alice Lyons, 1902).

The basic washing process is described by Sylvia Mitchell (1976) in her memoir of life as a child on a farm near Regina, Saskatchewan. The first step was to ensure the availability of a supply of water sufficient for washing and rinsing the laundry. This could be done in several ways, depending on the situation on the particular farm. For Sylvia's family, it meant arranging for her father to haul barrels of water from a nearby slough on a stoneboat, but for those with wells, such as Kenneth Doolittle (1978) from Maymont, Saskatchewan, buckets were carried from the well to the house by the children or their mother.[2] The portion of the water to be used for washing was heated in a boiler on the wood stove; depending on how dirty the items were, they might also be boiled in the pot before being moved to a washtub filled with hot water and soap[3] to be scrubbed against a washboard until clean.

This work was particularly strenuous in large families. For example, attempting to wash the dirty clothes of "six men, a boy, two girls and a woman, [along with] bedding, table linen, towels," and other miscellaneous items translated into an all-day process (Holmes, n.d., p. 7). Even after washing, the work was not finished since the clean items had to have the excess water wrung out, and then had to be hung from a clothesline to dry. Sylvia Mitchell's wash was hung on a line that "stretched between the house and the little house (re. outhouse)." (Mitchell, 1976, p. 1). In the winter, the process became more cumbersome because the wash had to be "peeled off the line and [taken] in crackling, stiff as boards, to be set up or draped over chairs beside the stove to thaw out" and finish drying (Mitchell, 1976, p. 1).

Despite, or possibly because of, the amount of work needed to maintain the cleanliness of the family and the home, most of the girls who wrote of their work on the farm mention some involvement with the wash or the labour that followed, such as remaking beds with the fresh sheets and blankets. For example, in 1902, dozens of girls describe contributing their labour to these tasks, including fifteen-year-old Annie Penhall from Bear Creek, Manitoba, twelve-year-old Mary Lightbourn from Brandon, Manitoba, and eleven-year-old Lavinia Gaudin from Melita, Manitoba—all of whom report that they did the washing and helped with everything else around the house. Another five girls from Manitoba—Katherine Wightman from La Rivicre, Ann Davidson from Carberry, Laura Brander from Nebitt, Jane Chesney from Innerkip, and Blanche Keeping from Austin (all between the ages of eleven and thirteen)—report making beds in addition to having other household responsibilities. However, twelve-year-old Gracie Currie (1902) of Edrans, Manitoba, may have been the busiest of all of these girls; in a letter, she notes that she made the beds for her entire family, which included her parents and six other children.

Among farm boys, only two mentioned involvement with washing clothes and making beds. Robert Northey (1902), a nine-year-old from Holland, Manitoba, says that he helped to make the beds when the washing was complete, while ten-year-old Bertie Winter (1902) of Orange Ridge, Manitoba, took part only in the washing process. However, other boys were drafted into washing duty when the job was too large for the mother and daughters to handle. In these cases, an entire family could have a role to play in completing the task. For instance, Agnes Walker (1979) of Tullisville, Saskatchewan, describes one such job that her family performed as a group each spring when they could work outside and collect sufficient soft water (derived from melted snow)[4] for their laundry needs. Soft water was required to wash all of their pure woolen blankets and clothing because hard water matted the wool fibres and destroyed the cloth. The job began with Agnes and her brother hauling pails of snow and clean meltwater to the house to be boiled in large containers. The boiled water was mixed with cold water in the washing tubs until a moderate temperature was reached (care had to be taken since hot water would mat the wool and cold water would not dissolve the soap used to clean the fabric). The soap jelly prepared the night before formed suds when put into the warm-water tubs.[5] The blankets went into the tubs, and at that point, the children took over the process once again. Boots and stockings came off and bare feet went into the tubs. The blankets were then thoroughly stomped to circulate the warm soapy water through the fabric[6] (Walker, 1979, p. 3). Each blanket was turned over when Agnes's mother deemed one side done, and the stomping began again; once this process was complete, the blankets had to be held above the tub and twisted tightly to wring out the soapy water before being dumped into the rinse water for a bit more stomping to get the last soap particles out of the material.

Since the blankets were fairly large and quite heavy when saturated with water, the wringing process was generally a job for her mother and father. However, Agnes indicates that if her father was busy, the children helped the mother to twist out the soapy water, and later the rinse water, before the blankets were hung to dry. Whenever possible, their father was called upon for this task because he had the strength to hold the wet blankets off the ground and to twist out more water and thus reduce the drying time required. In the final step of the operation, the blankets were taken off the drying line and stretched out to restore their shape. Once again, the children helped by each taking a corner while their mother held two ends; however, they found that they did not have the strength to do the best job of it and the father was called upon for his assistance. Given that this was such a strenuous job involving all members of the family, the day became special to the Walkers as it came to represent a traditional celebration of the end of winter. In fact, they turned the job into a family festival complete with a special meal of "stovies" that the family loved to eat when all of the work was done.[7]

Cleaning the Home and its Contents

In addition to helping out with some of the more strenuous tasks around the home, four Manitoba boys also report assisting with basic cleaning duties in 1902. For example, nine-year-old Walter Brown from Portage la Prairie indicates that he washed dishes, while thirteen-year-old W.E. McIntyre from Oak River states that he both washed and dried the dishes. Nine-year-old Otto Miller of Carberry was somewhat more flexible in that he swept the floor in addition to cleaning up the dishes, while ten-year-old Bertie Winter of Orange Ridge was quite helpful around the house: he handled the dishwashing chores and swept floors but also scrubbed the floors, washed clothes, and dusted the house.

Although girls tended to handle more home-related tasks than did boys, some were responsible for only the same basic tasks as boys. For example, Violet Ness (1902), a nine-year-old girl from St. Charles, Manitoba, did nothing but wash dishes, sweep, and dust, while eight-year-old Annie Miller (1902) of Pierson, Manitoba, reports washing dishes and sweeping floors. Similarly, Mary Tudhope (1902), an eleven-year-old girl from Arcola, Saskatchewan, indicates that her duties involved washing dishes, scrubbing floors, sweeping, dusting, and peeling potatoes.

However, the cases in which girls took on more responsibility for domestic labour than their male counterparts were more numerous and their contributions more apparent. A case in point is that of Ethel Rand (1901, p. 598), an eleven-year-old from Crystal City, Manitoba. This girl performed the usual jobs of washing, scrubbing, sweeping, and ironing, but was also required to take care of her six younger siblings since her mother was "not very strong." The same spirit was shown by a nine-year-old girl from Calgary, Alberta, named Beatrice Moss (1901). She wrote that she was able to wash the dishes, set the table, sweep, and scrub the floor. Her desire to help even further is clear since she mentions that she hoped that her mother would eventually let her handle all of the washing for the family.

Other specialized cleaning assignments existed on the prairies, and girls were involved with these tasks as well. For example, six-year-old Evelyn McLeod's (1977) duties included all tasks associated with maintaining the home, performing the usual sorts of cleaning and tidying, but she also had to deal with the "rag carpet" that covered the floor in the main room of the house. This carpet, made up of three-foot-wide strips of woven material, had to be swept each day but on occasion required greater maintenance. At those times the tacks holding the carpet to the floor were removed and

> It was taken out to the clothes line and beaten to remove some of the dust, then the strips ripped apart and washed. It took several days to complete the task, as all these strips had to be sewn together again by hand before the carpet was relaid. (McLeod, 1977, p. 7)

As dirty as dealing with rag rugs could be, that chore did not compare to the task of cleaning lamp chimneys and cleaning and blacking[8] the stove. These tasks generated filth because the black carbon that coated lamp chimneys, the ash, burnt foods, and stove-blacking paste stuck to glass, metal, clothing, and skin alike. The girls who volunteered for or were assigned to this work—such as thirteen-year-old Gertie Slater (1902) of Portage la Prairie, Manitoba, eleven-year-old Bessie Robinson (1902) from Leduc, Alberta, and twelve-year-old Blanche Keeping (1902) from Austin, Manitoba—performed some of the worst tasks possible in the domestic sphere. As described by Ollie Bell (1976, p. 4), a girl who immigrated with her family from Oregon to High River, Alberta, blacking the stove was the worst job she had because at times she "looked more like the stove than the stove did!"

Sewing, Knitting, Crocheting, and Other Practical Skills

While labour directed at maintaining the cleanliness of the family home was necessary, it was work that could be performed by the least skilled girls and boys in the family. However, other tasks, such as sewing, knitting, darning, and crocheting, required either a natural aptitude for the work or training and practice to develop the necessary skills. When children were encouraged to perform such labour, they were able to contribute in a more advanced way and to reduce the workload for each adult individual. Such skills could also be of great benefit to the operation since money otherwise destined for spending on manufactured products could be redirected or saved. For example, one particularly inventive woman, Evelyn McLeod (1977), solved what could have been a major problem for her family. Her children faced the prospect of a winter with no shoes because the family had no money to spend due to the low purchase price offered for their crop. Mrs. McLeod borrowed the idea of moccasins, something she could sew by hand, from the Native tribes and managed to improvise functional winter footwear for the family out of binder canvas that they had on hand.

Of course, reserving all of the sewing duties for adult members of the household would not accord with the social duty to pass skills on to children so that they might become smoothly functioning members of the community. Thus, making or repairing clothing and other items was taught to the children of the family, mainly the girls, and many of them became quite competent.[9] Jean Murray (1902), for example, was taught to sew on her family homestead near Lyleton, Manitoba, and eventually became capable of the detailed work needed to create her own aprons and printwaists by the time she was fifteen years old. Mamie Coxe (1902) of Brandon, Manitoba, was also a quick study and was turning out decent sewn items and fancy work (stitching or embroidery) at age thirteen, while other girls, including thirteen-year-old Katherine Wightman (1902) and twelve-year-old Montana Barber (1902) of Moose Jaw, Saskatchewan, worked on projects that required knitting or crocheting. It should be noted that Montana Barber also used her skills for more practical purposes such as darning her stockings and making repairs to torn clothing, as did Elsie Brown (1902) of Winlaw, Saskatchewan. Elsie even repaired holes in her brother's stockings, saving her mother from having to spend her time on that project. Others, such as Annie Gilliland (1902), worked on homemade quilts, which were often used as blankets to cover beds or as throws over other furnishings.

Not all boys avoided such instruction and not all men had wives or domestic servants to handle the tasks for them, so learning the sewing arts could also be invaluable for males. For example, a young man using the pen name "Youth of Sixteen" writing to *The Nor'-West Farmer* in 1898 made the usefulness of his sewing abilities clear. In his letter, he indicates that rather than wasting away all of the hours on winter evenings when no work was being done on the farm, he learned from his mother that it was just as important for boys as for girls to learn the skills of sewing, knitting, and darning. Hours for playing, reading, or taking part in indoor games were thus cut back in favour of lessons that might help him be more comfortable than his peers when he left to take on paying work or when he obtained his own farm. Rather than having "the finger sticking out of a mitt, the toe sticking out of a sock or a hole in the heel," he could use his skills to regain warmth and comfort (Youth of Sixteen, 1898, p. 528). Youth of Sixteen finishes his letter to the newspaper by advising readers that he had been sewing since he was eleven (as had his brother, who was also taught these skills) and found this ability "very useful."

Other practical skills that contributed to the well-being of the family included the ability to build furniture out of available materials. For example, L.J.W. Montgomery of the Assiniboia district wrote to *The Nor'-West Farmer* about the nature of the furnishings used in his family's home. When he was a boy he helped to build handcrafted furniture for his family home out of articles available to most farmers or readily located in the wild. Such items were plentiful in the Montgomery home and the writer notes that

> a comfortable lounge has been made of a long, narrow dry
> goods box, and is well stuffed and covered with a pretty cover

made of the brightest pieces her [his mother's] patch-bag
contained. Several chairs (all of home manufacture) are
around and each has a bright cushion....One easy chair is
made out of a barrel...[and] neat home-made rugs cover the
floor. (Montgomery, 1898, p. 129)

While the use of old boxes and barrels could lead to the creation of useful
furnishings, the goal of Kathleen Smith's mother was to use her imagination and creativity to design unique furnishings that could be built out of
locally available materials. Her designs were so simple to use that a child
could (and did) follow them to create functional furniture for the home:

Mother would plan a chair, a cot, or a crib and show my
brother just how to go about building it. She would have him
peel the poplar bark off poles and dry them well, then give him
a plan and show him how to bolt the corners together by burning a fine hole through with a red hot poker. (Smith, n.d. p. 7)

Her mother's inventiveness and her brother's labour thus provided the
family with comfortable surroundings without the expenditure of their
hard-earned money, a valuable exercise in self-sufficiency.

Maryanne Caswell (1968) also reports her family's attempt to create
their own furniture, but she says that it was one of the more difficult jobs
they had been assigned. Attempting to construct a baby bed from freshly
chopped green willow branches required both co-ordination and some
technical skill, abilities that Maryanne lacked, but she did help with the
making of mattresses for use by all family members. These mattresses
were made from "cotton ticks" (mattress-sized bags made of cotton with
three sides sewn shut and one left open for insertion of stuffing material).
These ticks were often filled with "prairie hay" (Caswell, 1968, p. 61), but
since the wild hay cut on the prairies could contain a variety of plants
from grass to grain to thistles or nettles, individual beds could be full of
unpleasant surprises or quite comfortable. Elizabeth Woychyk also used
this mattress-making technique. She helped to stuff cotton ticks when
she was eight years old, and the only distinction was that in her family,
straw from harvested wheat was used for stuffing rather than hay. This
meant fewer prickly weeds but, as Elizabeth noted, "I remember the straw
coming through the ticking, kind of scratchy," so notions of comfort were
relative (Silverman, 1984, p. 21).

Caring for younger siblings, n.d. [PAA,B.240]

Caring for Children

While boys did not typically take part in domestic tasks such as food production, clothes washing, and sewing, they were relatively active as caregivers for younger children. Three of them, sixteen-year-old Percy Florence (1901) of Balmoral, Alberta, and two Manitoba boys, thirteen-year-old W.E. McIntyre (1902) of Oak River and eleven-year-old Harvey Brown (1902) of Portage la Prairie, describe their involvement in this type of work. They did not seem to mind looking after their siblings: Percy Florence (1901, p. 569) indicates that he wanted to "help mother with her work in the house by minding baby for her"; W.E. McIntyre (1902, p. 506) states, "in the house I churn, mind [the] baby, wash and dry dishes and many other things"; Harvey Brown (1902) churned butter, washed dishes, swept the floor, and set the table in addition to "minding" the baby. However, the enthusiastic participation of these three boys was a rarity since this work generally went to the girls in the family whether or not they were actually suited to the duty.

For example, as discussed earlier, the McNaught sisters, Isabel and Betty (1976), believed that their primary responsibilities lay in the productive sphere rather than in subsistence or domestic labour, yet they made it clear that they also had substantial responsibilities in the home. The girls cared for chickens, hauled water on a stoneboat for a mile from the river to the house, herded the cattle to the river for water, helped with the food, worked in the garden, and assisted in the cleanup by washing dishes. They also took care of a neighbour's two-year-old son so that their mother had some time to socialize with the baby's mother, but this turned into a minor disaster. They had never looked after a baby before and looked away after sitting the child on the second level of their bunk bed. As Betty describes the situation,

> I guess I didn't watch him very carefully because he fell off and hit his head, an awful bang. And for years I worried whenever anybody said anything about Jess [the two-year-old] for fear he was stupid. I felt terrible about that. (Mc-Naught, 1976, p. 13)

Of course, not all children who cared for younger siblings or family friends were incompetent. Twelve-year-old Mabel Brown (1902) of Portage la Prairie, Manitoba, for example, handled every type of household job including baking, cooking meals, washing, cleaning, and caring for her younger siblings when they were babies. As they grew, her job continued but changed into watching out for them and driving them to places they were supposed to be. Similarly, Florence Keeping (1902) was assigned to care for her baby brother when she was only nine years old, but she had some help because her sister Blanche (1902) was three years older and shared the duty. Between the two girls, the chore could be performed competently.

One of the youngest girls to be given the task of caring for other children was Mary Hiemstra (1997). In her published memoirs, Mary speaks of a fall day on which she reached the milestone of being asked to care for her siblings while her mother used the time to dig potatoes and haul them to the cellar the family had dug under their house. The work had to be completed before freezing weather arrived if they were to have food for the winter, and Mary's father was working off-farm. The potato patch was over half a mile from the house, so it would have been too exhausting to carry both the youngest child and the potatoes. Thus, there was little choice but to assign the child care to Mary even though she was only six years old at the time. On the first day, Mary ran out of patience before her mother finished working, and by the time her mother got home, all three children were tearing the house apart and banging on enamel bowls as if they were drums. The next day, her mother (Sarah) was not going to trust Mary to care for the younger children, but Mary assured her that they would be better behaved that day, so, stifling her misgivings, Sarah headed for the potato patch to finish up the necessary fall harvest.

Mary took the youngsters outside to play, made a playhouse with four pieces of wood and built a miniature fireplace with stones. Intending to make up for her lack of care the day before, Mary determined that her mother would like a cup of tea when she got home and headed for the matches to light a fire after getting her charges toys to play with. Knocking the matches to the floor from a shelf she could not reach proved easy when she used a piece of wood to extend her reach, but the heavy stove covers and iron boiling pot proved more difficult. Muscling the covers open and filling the pot cup by cup on the stove put her in position to begin making the tea. Wood was obtained by a trip to the chopping block to gather up chips, and by striking "quite a few matches" that "flared green and yellow" from the sulphur tips, Mary got her fire going (Hiemstra, 1997, p. 191). After clearing some plants out of her baby brother's mouth to stop his choking, she returned to setting the scene for her mother's supper.

Laying out a white tablecloth over the box the family used for a table, Mary set up a tea service, carved some bread, spread jam on the slightly misshapen pieces (the knife had been dull), and added wood to the fire to keep the water hot. As soon as her mother appeared with two pails of potatoes, she ran inside and poured water into the teapot and prepared to receive her mother's surprised gratitude:

> "Tea!" Mother dropped the pails of potatoes and her face turned pale. "You lit the fire?" Her voice was sharp. "Yes. I had to light it to boil the kettle. I—I thought you'd like some tea." I couldn't understand why she seemed upset when I thought she'd be pleased, and tears of disappointment came to my eyes. "Yes," Mother said quickly, "of course I would. I was just thinking when I came around the grove how nice some tea would be." She moved toward the stove, but slowly as if she was rather limp.... To my horror a stream of clear water came out of the curving spout. I had forgotten to put tea in the pot. (Hiemstra, 1997, p. 192)

Being a perceptive mother, Sarah drank three cups of the "weak tea" and, over the next several days, provided the children with instruction on how to put out fires by rolling a person on the ground or in a blanket. Much to the disappointment of the children, they were not allowed to roll each other on the ground for practice.

Given that domestic labour generally required less physical strength than chopping down trees, moving rocks, or harvesting crops, children were ideal workers, or would be, once they were old enough to follow basic directions properly. Further, as this work was likely to be carried out in or near the home, it was thought appropriate that it be performed by the women and their daughters rather than by the males in the family. This short-sighted application of accepted gender roles left many of the young men raised on farms deprived of basic domestic training. They would eventually strike out on their own, but without the assistance of a properly raised wife would be incapable of feeding themselves anything but the most basic of foods and would not have the ability to fix even small holes in their coats or replace lost buttons. Even child care might prove necessary for men. This may seem a strange assertion given the division of labour between genders noted earlier, but maternal deaths were not uncommon (Langford, 1995) and a man could be left to care for one or more children. Missing skills could have serious consequences for their strength, stamina, and health, and that of their families.

Of course, despite training, many were not competent to handle extreme cases. For instance, in her memoir Delia Woolf explains that she was born prematurely on the family homestead during the bitter winter of 1906–1907. Had her care been delegated to siblings, it is unlikely that she would have survived since she was quite underdeveloped. She had no hair, her fingernails had not yet formed, and she weighed only three pounds at birth. In Delia's words,

> I was so small and it was necessary to keep me alive. Baby incubators were something long in the future. So I was kept in a shoebox wrapped in cotton and a baby blanket, or I suppose just a small piece of cloth, and placed in the oven of a coal stove....When I was old enough and able to breathe properly then Grandmother said that I could come out of the oven. (Woolf, 1974, p. 7)

Given the nature of the care that was required, and the skills needed to keep the oven temperature moderate, only experienced adults could be trusted with her life.

Summary

Domestic labour was one of the most essential services provided by children on family farms. The tasks were generally less labour-intensive, involved less danger, and required fewer skills than most other activities and thus required less adult supervision. By performing this labour, children freed up adult time for other tasks and helped to ensure that all family members were fed and rested, and lived as comfortable an existence as possible. Girls, as expected given the attitudes of the time, contributed the most labour to the performance of these domestic functions.

SEVEN

Conclusion

CANADA'S PRAIRIES PRESENTED A VARIETY of obstacles that blocked or slowed the progress of those settlers seeking to take advantage of the opportunities in the region. Only those individuals and families with strength, determination, and persistence could overcome these impediments, survive the harsh conditions, and establish ongoing farming operations in a non-technological system founded on the use of human and animal muscle power. In such conditions, the labour of children was a valuable asset.

However, even if all of the natural barriers could be surmounted, settlers were also faced with the prospect of trying to achieve financial security in a monopolized marketplace. Under these adverse economic circumstances, only three possible paths to family survival and security existed. First, the production of wheat, livestock, or other cash crops could be increased each year in the hope that doing so would generate a higher cash flow instead of simply reducing produce prices by creating an oversupply situation. Second, settlers could work outside of the production cycle to obtain funds with no connection to their farm operation, such as paid employment, trapping furs, or selling products other than grain and livestock. Third, settlers and their families could intensify their efforts to supply as many of their own needs as possible and restrict the acquisition of outside goods and services to what was absolutely necessary. Cash reserves could thus be built up, or, at the very least, expenditures could be reduced, thereby helping the farming operation to survive. Each of these alternatives required the expenditure of labour, and as indicated by Lewis (1996, p. 5), children "were a cheap and readily accessible source of labour" for farm families.

As revealed by the stories of the children studied here, child labour assisted the family effort no matter which of these paths was followed. Children contributed to production,[1] took part in paid employment or other money-raising activities, worked at domestic and subsistence tasks, and thereby increased the supply of cash, food, and other necessary commodities

Croatians in Kenaston, Saskatchewan, 1910. [SAB, R-B10104]

to the family. This had the effect of freeing up some or all of the time
an adult would otherwise have expended on such tasks, improving the
comfort and morale of the family, and replenishing the labour power of all
family members. Labour cannot continue indefinitely without rest, water,
food, clothing, and health care, and the work of children contributed to
providing these necessities. These were no small contributions, as even if
a total cash crop failure occurred, sufficient effort applied to subsistence
could keep the family alive until the next crop was harvested (Neth, 1995;
Fontaine and Schlumbohm, 2000; Humphries, 1982).

Despite the hardships to be endured, the statistics set out earlier indicate that many hundreds of thousands of individuals, some in family
groupings and some on their own, did manage to establish ongoing farming operations in the region and achieve their dream of land ownership,
either through homesteading or purchase. The growing number of farms
in the prairie region during the study period, the expanding population,
and increased agricultural production all made this apparent. However,
looking at the statistics alone does not provide any sense of how settlers
managed to persevere despite the hardships they faced.

Based on the reports of the children and those researchers who have
considered the matter, the amount of labour that had to be poured into the

operations to convert undeveloped territory into grain, livestock, income, shelter, subsistence, and domestic arrangements for the settlers and their families was immense (Warren, 1917). Settlers had to work day after day, week after week, year after year with no guarantee of success or survival, yet they carried on despite the problems. The memoir of Mabel Hawthorne provides at least a partial explanation for their actions. When she, her mother, and her father migrated to live near Saskatoon, Saskatchewan, in 1905, they faced numerous problems. The washed-out bridges, heat, cold, dust, rain, windstorms, prairie fires, economic deprivation, and the hard work associated with breaking the land, building a sod house, and growing wheat for an export market that paid back barely enough for the family to survive all blocked their path. But to Mabel, it was the belief in and hope for a better future that

> gave us strength to overcome the unsurmountable barriers
> in making a home which called forth every oz. of physical
> strength we had to give. How did we do it? Baking dozens of
> loaves of bread, making our own butter, caring for chickens
> and turkeys, and gardens, milking cows, making our own
> soap, pickling our own pork for smoking and canning and
> preserving under almost primitive conditions, doing our
> own sewing for our family didn't leave much time for dream-
> ing, and yet dreams were there engrossed in our homes, we
> accepted all that went with it. But always dreaming of better
> days to come. (Hawthorne, n.d., p. 4)

While faith or hope for the future may have been the spirit driving the push into the prairie region and the fight to succeed, this study has revealed that one of the assets that made the fight against nature and greed possible in this region was the labour power of the children. The social attitudes that prevailed among at least the British settlers, and the fact that in such conditions many could not afford the luxury of feeding and clothing children who did not contribute to the family welfare, led to the acceptance of child labour as a family resource. Letters, newspaper articles, and the behaviour of farm parents in putting their children to work all reveal that both farmers and the general public supported this attitude.[2] Work served to initiate children into farming as a potential career, provided them with skills, and readied them to take over the family farm or establish their own operation when they came of age to apply for their own quarter section of homestead land.

Based on the patterns of work data revealed in the documents, it appears that children gained experience by assisting their parents with day-to-day chores and simple tasks that they could perform without unnecessary risk, and assumed more responsibility as they grew more competent. Children were not thrown haphazardly into any task that happened to present itself. Their lack of size and skills meant that periods for learning and gaining both physical and mental prowess had to be allowed before children could handle difficult and physically challenging jobs. For example, peeling potatoes was a rather common chore for younger girls, as were cleaning dishes, sweeping, and milking. For boys, washing dishes or performing other types of housework were uncommon activities, but milking cows, gardening, obtaining fuel, and hunting gophers were equivalent junior-level tasks. These jobs developed the children's confidence, built co-ordination and strength, encouraged them to recognize the necessity of work from an early age, and prepared them for the work to come. Graduation from simple work to involvement in a greater variety of more difficult jobs occurred once children reached the nine-to-eleven year age grouping and increased again for those between twelve and fourteen years of age, and again for those over fourteen.

While the amount of work performed by children increased with age, the data are inconclusive with respect to particular subcategories of work. For example, within the child care task, girls appeared to have become more active as they aged but there is no way to determine from the data whether this was a result of training needs, or simply an increase in the number of siblings needing care as settler children grew older.

The situation was less ambiguous in other work subcategories; for example, the participation of girls in all other domestic tasks appeared to increase with age, as was also the case with working on animal products, gardening, and collecting wild produce for family subsistence. Involvement in raising their own animals for sale and in family livestock production also increased with age for girls. The situation for boys was quite similar since, although very few boys worked in domestic areas, participation increased substantially for boys over eight years old (thus suggesting that training or physical development was needed for this work). Similarly, male involvement in raising animals for sale in the entrepreneurship category climbed with age.

In addition to receiving training for particular jobs, children were also influenced by parental behaviour and attitudes about work and the farming lifestyle. The clearest example of this acquisition of knowledge and behaviours between generations is the fact that it could extend even into the games that children made up to play. For example, one child indicated

> One of our favorite games that first winter was "filing on land."
> The house was not insulated, and our fuel was poor. There was
> very little wood, and lignite coal in those days left much to be
> desired for heat....We would eat our breakfasts, then pop back
> into bed to await more heat. On the bed were mother's patch-
> work quilts. They were made of bright print pieces. We took
> turns in choosing our favorite patch. We said we "filed" on it,
> as we had heard our parents talk of choosing land. If we saw
> one that we liked better, we had to "throw up" the first choice,
> and someone else could claim it....Hour after hour we played
> that game, and it seemed ever new. (Carr, n.d., p. 2)

Alternatively, more formal lessons could also prove useful for developing skills that required more knowledge than could be passed on by obser-
vation and play. Sewing, for instance, was a very practical skill, particularly
if a girl could be taught to make clothing, since a great deal of money
could be saved on store-bought items (Colinette, 1898).

While girls were expected to remain in a home setting (whether with
their families or husbands or as paid servants) and were thus directed into
work related to domestic tasks and subsistence labour, the type of male
child envisioned as best for the prairie settlement process was quite different. Boys required just as many skills as girls (although in different areas
of endeavour) and also had to be strong, hard-working, and honest. Just
as the qualities thought appropriate to girls are highlighted in the poem
"The Farmer's Daughter" (Anonymous, 1899a), quoted in Chapter 5, the
corresponding male attributes are captured in a poem printed in *The Nor'-
West Farmer* entitled "The Boys We Need":

> Here's to the boy who's not afraid
> To do his share of the work;
> Who never is by toil dismayed,
> And never tries to shirk.
>
> The boy who's [*sic*] heart is brave to meet
> All lions in his way;
> Who's not discouraged by defeat,
> But tries another day.
>
> The boy who always means to do
> The very best he can;

Who always keeps the right in view,
And aims to be a man.

Such boys as these will grow to be
The men who's [*sic*] hands will guide
The future land: and we
Shall speak their names with pride.
(Anonymous, 1898, p. 528)

Based on such social beliefs and the work patterns discerned in the data on children's work behaviour, a double standard existed with respect to social attitudes toward farm children as a result of their gender. The same social attitudes that encouraged a division of labour between adults thus carried over to the distribution of children's work, although the stringent split with men handling production and financial matters while women looked after domestic duties and subsistence production (assisting with men's work on request) does not appear to have been as absolute for children. The data indicate that once they outgrew the basic tasks that all youngsters of both genders performed, a tendency toward some specialized labour for each sex existed so that girls dominated domestic work and were strong in subsistence, while boys were more involved in entrepreneurial labour and dominated production.

Given the levels of participation in the various forms of work revealed in the children's documents, girls appear to have been more flexible as workers than boys. For example, in the two cases of obvious gender dominance, girls were more likely to cross the gender line to take up productive labour than boys, who less frequently assisted with domestic tasks. However, it would have been the children capable of taking on labour in any field of endeavour (whether or not they were acting within their gendered role) who would have been of the greatest assistance and thus contributed the most to ensuring the continuance of the family farm. Each area of work was vital in and of itself, but for the greatest effectiveness in the family response to harsh conditions, those children capable of filling many roles would have been most valued as workers. From the data gathered, this would have included a large number of the study children since many listed at least two tasks, and some three or four, as being within their capabilities.

In terms of the specific tasks undertaken by boys and girls in support of family efforts to farm in the prairie region, the most confusing, from a gender perspective, is participation in the construction of the family home and other infrastructure. Whether the family built using logs, sod, lumber, or clay/hay mixtures to form adobe structures, the work was physically demanding. Felling, hauling, notching, and lifting logs; digging, hauling, and lifting thousands of sod bricks; lifting, positioning, and nailing boards; or excavating, mixing, and applying clay all took strength and endurance. Some jobs (such as chinking cracks) were less tiring, but both boys and girls noted taking part in all phases of the process. It could be that parents were humouring their children by letting them think they were truly helping or that the jobs they helped with were actually less demanding than the children described. However, stories of digging cellars, dragging heavy sod bricks, felling trees in freezing weather, dragging logs out of the forest, and lifting and balancing logs while they were notched with an axe all ring true. These children of both sexes certainly contributed to family labour needs and earned their keep after being brought to the prairies.

Given the information set out above, it is clear that the children in the study could, and did in fact, contribute their labour to family efforts to farm in the prairie region, but the reason they did so was not as simple to determine. Certainly, societal pressure to work would have been of some influence, as might a feeling of obligation to parents for their support, or threats of punishment for those not performing up to the standards of the family patriarch. However, no threats or actual instances of punishment are recorded, and no indications suggesting that children might feel an obligation to work (beyond the existence of the family bond) are noted. These missing indicators could be explained as instances of selective memory recollection or an idealization of childhood, but there is no way to be certain. Of course, socialization was also an influence on child behaviour, as shown by the transmission to the children of the gendered division of labour that affected adults and the training of children in necessary skills. Each factor may thus have had some effect on children's work behaviour, but no single explanation for why children—apparently voluntarily—worked on all aspects of farm development and operation is revealed in the documents.

Rather, the information gathered suggests that virtually all children in the study worked in some fashion, their family farms benefited financially, and family members benefited emotionally from these efforts. The most likely explanation for child labour may well have been a pragmatic choice rather than an idealistic belief in duty, fear of authority, or parental and social influence. Food, water, shelter, and security would exist only if the necessary labour was performed—as noted by Lucy Johnson, "can't milk means no milk"—so children learned to help (Johnson, n.d., p. 36). Listening to parental conversations, observing other settlers, and experiencing prairie conditions all provided children with sufficient information to realize how difficult life was and thus motivation to work hard to improve their lives and those of the rest of the family. Self-interest, if not an organized family survival strategy, would push most children old enough to understand the situation to work, and others would follow.

The need for every possible survival tool, including the labour of children, is made clear in a report prepared for the Canadian Council of Agriculture by its secretary, R. McKenzie, in 1914. He analyzes the financial effects of the forces arrayed against settlers and reaches a conclusion concerning the prairie pioneer period similar to that of Fontaine and Schlumbohm (2000), who deal with the survival of farm families during historical periods of severe economic downturn in Europe.[3] Family survival was maintained through the efforts of every member capable of any type of work, and it was being accomplished outside of the market system.

McKenzie (1914) had access to better records than Fontaine and Schlumbohm had and also had the benefit of living during the period he studied, so he could trace the economic situation more closely. Even so, he found nothing except family sacrifice and hard work to account for survival under what should have been disastrous financial conditions. Surprisingly, the apparent success of prairie farming in terms of the growth in the number of farms, farmers, and output came without financial benefits for farmers when the relative profit margins and rates of return on investment for manufacturers and farmers were considered. His research indicated that the decade of fast-rising population between 1901 and 1911 was extremely beneficial for Canadian businesses but was at best neutral for the average farmer. Based on census information, McKenzie calculated that business net earnings (gross income less all raw material costs, power charges, wages paid, and all other expenses of operation) on capitalization (the dollar value of all outstanding company shares at the issue price) for manufacturers grew from 19.82 per cent in 1901 to 25.75 per cent in 1911. On average, businesses had achieved a growth rate of 30 per cent over the decade. For farmers, however, the situation was much different. Gross earnings (the total income generated by farming operations without considering the cost of inputs) dropped from 18.55 per cent to 17.5 per cent of the total capital investment made by farmers. The difference was actually larger than apparent from the numbers because comparatively low per-farm capital investment levels made for a smaller denominator when the earnings ratios were calculated.[4] As McKenzie (1914, p. 32) notes,

> manufacturers' net earnings increased in the decade, while
> the farmer's gross earnings decreased, notwithstanding the
> cost of production to the farmer had vastly increased during
> that period. The farmer's raw material consisting of seeds,
> manure, and other fertilizers, feed of animals fed in excess

of maintenance to produce flesh, milk, eggs and wool and to perform labour, is not taken into account, though the value of food raised on the farm and fed on the farm is included in gross revenue. The farmer's own labour and that of his family, like his raw material, is not counted. Were the value of the farmer's raw material, together with wages for himself and members of his family, deducted from the ascertained gross revenue, there would be nothing left for interest on his investment.

Given these figures, farmers had a choice of earning no profit at all on the farming side of the ledger, or reducing or eliminating the "wages" for all family members and leaving no income to support the family's lifestyle. This was equivalent to saying that farms could not have survived during the first decade of the century because either the families or the farms would have been without the wherewithal to continue. "Wages" for the family translated into food, clothing, footwear, bedding, coal for heat, lumber or other materials to build improved homes, and other necessities, thereby quite literally being the difference between life and death. However, profits were also required for a variety of purposes in the farming operation. The purchase of new seed and stock, buying improved tools or equipment to enhance the efficiency and size of the operation, and, most importantly, building up a reserve for the repair or replacement of worn equipment, without which a farm could not survive and prosper, could not be done without profits.

Unfortunately, and as was the case with the periods of economic disaster studied by Fontaine and Schlumbohm (2000), no comprehensive official or unofficial records were kept of children's hours of work (or for that matter of time devoted to play, school, or personal matters), or of the division of their time among tasks. Thus, no exact measurement of the amount of children's labour devoted to farm and family needs is feasible, and it is therefore impossible to prove the exact degree to which children's labour assisted family survival. The diaries, memoirs, letters, and other documents reviewed in this study do provide anecdotal evidence of the types of work children performed, but they are not specific enough to make possible an accurate evaluation of the actual amount of labour performed. The few references to how difficult a task might be or to the number of hours or days it might take to accomplish a particular goal (for example, cutting, stacking, and hauling sufficient hay for a family's animals) provide some of the information needed but seldom specify the exact work done by each person. Further, the effort put into each endeavour by the children and the level of skill they possessed for their different jobs would also have to be known to develop a measure of the contribution children made. Finally, since children were not paid a wage for family work, no convenient, socially accepted artificial measure of the value of their labour exists.

However, while it may be impossible to locate detailed information on the exact size of the labour contribution made by children, it has not been difficult to establish the fact that many children did indeed make contributions to family efforts and that these contributions were of value or importance to the families involved. It is also possible to show logically that these contributions were of monetary value and thus assisted family farms in achieving their goal of overcoming the hostile economic climate they faced.

With respect to the first point, little more need be said about the fact of the contributions made by the study children. Participation in farm labour was such that at least one child, and most often several, had performed or assisted with the performance of virtually every job required on pioneer farms. This broad statement, that the study proves that almost every child could make some valued contribution, may be challenged on the basis that the sample of children is too small or that the children may have been exaggerating, embellishing, idealizing, hiding, or forgetting the truth of their experiences. The limitation placed on the study by the fragmentary nature of the data available through historical documentation may also be a concern. However, each such critique, at least with respect to conclusions reached relating to the work these children performed, falters in the face of the consistency of the stories. The documents provide an interconnected web of support that speaks to the essential validity and reliability of the writings of the children studied.

These children had no reason to exaggerate or hide anything except, perhaps, some of the more unpleasant memories of their childhood. Aside from what might be childish exaggeration by the one four-year-old who suggested that he had handled almost every farm task on his own, it is more logical to suggest that children reported less work than they actually performed. Forgetting or repressing the memory of tasks that were boring, disagreeable, or repulsive is to be expected (not one child refers to changing or washing diapers, no reports of digging or refilling holes for outhouses are made, and few children note cleaning stables). In short, deliberate distortions respecting the work of children are unlikely, but minor exaggerations and withholdings of information are to be expected. These are unlikely to have distorted the overall picture developed in the study, and attempting to compensate for such concerns or to revise the idealistic or self-congratulatory tone of some of the documents would do more harm than good.

With the fact of children's performing necessary work established, logic leads to the conclusion that in addition to being of importance to the farm families themselves, the labour contributions must also have been of monetary value to the family. This is evident, since without children's labour, work would have been either abandoned, left incomplete, or dealt with by an adult. At the worst, the absence of child labour would have cost the family several acres of crop or a hired hand's wages. The value may be unrecorded and now unmeasurable, but it did exist and may be conservatively projected by using an estimate of the minimum hours a child would have worked each day, a wage rate typical for farm workers at the turn of the century, and the population statistics noted earlier.

By 1911, there were almost 300,000 children living in the Prairie provinces,[5] the equivalent of approximately one child per family. If each child worked only one hour per day (once again a bare minimum figure given references to the types of work done each day by most children), a family would obtain the equivalent of forty-six (eight-hour) days per year from each child. On a regional basis, this would translate to 13.5 million (eight-hour) days of work per year. Using the actual number of children in the region would increase the figures substantially, as would using a more realistic estimate of the actual hours per day spent working, but the point to be made is that even by conservative approximations, children's labour was more than a convenience to farm families. With the amount of work to be done on a non-mechanized farm, even ignoring the economic concerns they faced, adults would have been hard-pressed to make up for the loss of that amount of labour. The monetary value of one day's work might be only one dollar, but for the times, $46 would have been a large sum of money for a family to replace each year (being one-sixth of the cost of a one-year supply of food for a family in 1912). On a regional basis, the loss would have been immense since if even one-half of the 300,000 children on the prairies under the age of fourteen worked, the loss in productivity would have been almost seven million dollars per year, a sum equivalent to the amount needed to pay for essential food supplies for 115,000 families.

Given the information generated in this study, the fact that children worked on pioneer farms is beyond question. The work they performed contributed to satisfying a need for labour and provided a perceptible, if not precisely measurable, financial benefit for settler families. However, as with women, children's labour was unvalued, unpaid, subsumed within the family's total productive output, and thus invisible in the economy (Sachs,

1983). Children received no monetary compensation for their efforts, possessed only assets given to them, had no right to control their own money, and could even be sent to relatives (rather than remain with their mother) if the father died, as at law it was the father's right to determine the fate of the family offspring.[6] The effect of these social and legal restrictions was such that children were in an even worse position than their mothers in terms of being seen to have made an economic contribution to farming. They were almost literally the property of their fathers and completely powerless, while their mothers at least had some limited protection of their property and status as independent beings.

Because of the historical, legal, and social authority he commanded, the employer/father was able to utilize the labour power of his children to provide subsistence, domestic comfort, cash, and marketable commodities for the farm. Since children were also contributing to their own subsistence needs, a smaller portion of the farm output than would otherwise have been the case was used to support the members of the farm family. The excess value of the saleable commodities produced with child labour power over the cost of the children's subsistence needs, plus any cost savings generated by the effectively free labour of children, was appropriated by the father. This provided an asset that could be invested in the operation or disposed of by him. The fact that family bonds of affection and obligation existed, and that fathers were simply exercising the acceptable financial control granted them, does not mean that exploitation did not exist, just as a belief that work was enjoyable or being performed voluntarily did not change the fact that women's labour was also appropriated by their husbands under similar circumstances (Folbre, 1982; Ursel, 1992). Thus, just as farm women were relegated to the position of being economically invisible workers whose contributions were hidden within the family (Stansell, 1976; Wilson, 1982; Sachs, 1983; Whatmore, 1991), so too were children.

The actual extent of the economic contribution made by children will never be known given the scarcity of records other than anecdotal reports such as those used in this study. Even so, the veil that has hidden the economic importance of children behind a screen of standard accounting practices, legal ownership of assets, and a devaluing of children's efforts to the status of secondary chores has been drawn aside. Children were outnumbered by adults in the prairie region, out-muscled while performing physically demanding work, out-skilled by their parents when learning new jobs, and overlooked by record keepers, economists, and, to a large degree, historians. But the documents that form the subject of this study show that children could develop new abilities and contribute in the new environment just as adults did. They may not have played as large a role as adults, but they were a factor and thus deserve to be part of the record of this historical period. Their efforts should not remain relegated to the level of the meaningless or the trivial, since children were contributing members of the families that together built an agricultural society in the West.

Notes

One

1. The phrase "the last best West" was likely derived from the fact that the farmlands of Canada West (western Ontario) and the western United States were effectively filled by the 1890s, so the "last West" to be settled was the prairies. The "best" was presumably a matter of opinion and public relations.
2. Depending on the characteristics of their land and the area of the prairies they were located in, water might also have to be hauled from a nearby stream or loaded into barrels from an insect- or algae-infested slough miles away (Rodwell, 1965).
3. While a single man could potentially accomplish all of the necessary tasks on his own, albeit with no guarantee of success, it would be easier, and the chances of success greater, if the settler had a family (Warren, 1917; Stansell, 1976).
4. The listing of tasks to which the time of pioneer children could be devoted does not include any reference to attending school, studying, or participating in educational activities. Schooling is beyond the scope of this study. However, research indicates that few children attended school in the early years. This may be a result of the fact that for many years the population was too low to support the construction of schools (Cameron; Duesterbeck, 1950–56). Even when schools were being built, the region was so large that distance was a major factor restricting attendance (Dixon, 1950–56), and the danger of winter storms made closure during the harshest months, from Christmas until April, a prudent choice (Cooper; Wilkie, 1950–56).
5. Since the letters sent to the newspaper were not spontaneous revelations and may have been carefully drafted (with the assistance of parents or older siblings in the case of young writers) to meet the standards of the publisher, they do not contain details of abuse, overwork, punishment, or other negative perspectives of life on a family farm during the pioneering period. For these reasons, the letters may not provide a full disclosure of the lives and working conditions of the writers, but they do provide a glimpse into the details of children's work during the settlement process. As such, these letters are meaningful artifacts of the period and valuable sources of necessary information.
6. Of course, using historical documents as a source of data places a burden on the researcher to ensure that the limitations of the available record are made clear. As such, it is noted that the historical record of children's work is likely to be incomplete due to the passage of time, loss of materials, a failure of many settlers to record their experiences, the inaccuracy of memory in recording events after the fact, tendencies to recall childhood events in a romanticized or idealized fashion, and the fact that not all existing material is open to public scrutiny. Additional limitations exist as it is unlikely that a child under the age of seven or eight years could write without assistance (and interpretation) by someone older, making the story an edited version of reality. While such concerns exist, I sug-

gest that such critiques are muted in this case. The majority of the documents used in this study were written at or near the time that the work was performed, the data tends to be consistent and repetitive, and the materials are thus inter-supportive. Further, the stories of these children cannot be given voice without adopting their tone and accepting their reality. To fail to do so would be to re-draft their histories from a foreign perspective with no guarantee that the results would be accurate.

7. The term "productive labour" suggests a Marxist approach but does not rely on the Marxist definition. Settlers both held capital (land and machinery) and performed labour. However, the basic meaning, labour that produces commodities for sale in a marketplace, is retained.

8. Entrepreneurship is used in this context to identify alternate ways of using personal labour to generate funds not associated with the family enterprise, rather than to designate new approaches to performing the same work so as to enhance profits.

Two

1. Powered machinery such as self-propelled tractors was not readily available in the West during the pioneer period and played little role in establishing or operating settler farms (Warren, 1917).

2. In his self-published book about his family's homestead, W. Roland Murray (1982, p. 19c) provides descriptions of a number of implements used by the early farmers. For example, the stoneboat was a sled with (removable) walls generally "used on ploughed land for the removal of stone that was turned up by the plow while breaking new land." A walking plough had a single curved blade that cut through the sod and turned the soil over to destroy roots and bring a fresh nutrient-rich layer to the surface of the field. The walking plough, unlike other models, was made for small-scale operations since it was designed to be pulled by "one horse" and was "steered by one person." Unlike a plough, harrows were used for shallow tilling of land that had already been broken. Made up of a number of steel spikes mounted on a frame so that the spikes could be pulled through the upper layer of the soil "for breaking up lumps…and for leveling and seed bed preparation," the harrow was a versatile tool but did not turn the soil. Finally, cultivators were also in use and were, in effect, large harrows. The larger spikes on a cultivator and the ability to add additional sets of spikes to the unit to broaden its coverage ensured that it covered more ground than a harrow but did not dig as deep or turn the soil over like a plough.

3. As stated by Warren (1917, p. 8), "a single man or woman finds it difficult to manage a farm successfully. One may succeed in a city whether he has a family or not, but on a farm the chances are much better for married persons."

4. This phenomenon is also noted by Ellenor Merriken (1999) in her memoir about being an eleven-year-old immigrant in 1910. Her family's visits to nearby bachelors were marked by clouds of dust, dirty dishes, and messy homes since they did not have the time to handle both household chores and work in the fields efficiently.

5. See Kohl's (1976) discussion of the distribution of labour between all members, adult and child, of farm families. Her study examines farms in southern Saskatchewan in the 1960s, but aside from the changes in nature of the equipment

used, she discovered that work continued to be distributed in the same expected patterns. Heavy labour and market activities fell to the men, domestic matters to the women, with children assisting with all activities that they could physically manage. This point is also reviewed by Voisey (1988, p. 91) in terms of the ability of individual settlers to expand their operations by shifting to a mixed farming program based on growing wheat and raising animals for sale or personal consumption. He notes that the "willingness of settlers to stock their own pantries through mixed-farming activity also depended on one social condition more than any other: marriage." Further, children could be assigned the livestock tasks since this work would raise some extra money, feed the family, keep them busy, and train them to the "steady work habits" they would need as future wives or farmers (p. 94).

6. While work was healthy for children, overwork was not. As noted by Nancy Morrow (1898, p. 131), children were not to be driven to hurt themselves, but "every little helps, and by and by they will have done quite a bit of work."

7. The Fertile Crescent is marked by the Manitoba Escarpment, a plateau that runs from southeast to northwest, from the American border through Brandon, Manitoba, to the Precambrian Shield area in the north. The more eastern and northern portions of the escarpment lie between Brandon and the Qu'Appelle Valley of Saskatchewan in the south; it then arches to the northwest slightly above Saskatoon, Saskatchewan, and runs west to Edmonton, Alberta, and southwest to the level of Red Deer, Alberta. The area contains deeply trenched rivers and rich black-park soils, receives extra rainfall, and is marked by a belt of heavy brush and tree growth (Dawson and Younge, 1940). Those portions located farther to the north have less of an advantage due to the reduced length of the safe growing season.

8. Soddies could be much warmer than houses built with lumber but, even so, the warmth would disappear unless the necessary labour was expended to ensure that the stove kept burning. As stated by Evelyn McLeod (1977, p. 8), "when the thermometer registered 40 to 60 degrees below zero and the fire burned out, the household water pail would contain solid ice by morning."

9. While a well-built home could provide safety from most weather, some events could not be averted. For example, Lucy Johnson (n.d., p. 16) reports on two storms she had been through on her family homestead near Saskatoon, Saskatchewan, one a dust storm with a whirlwind that they held at bay by leaning "two ninety-eight pound sacks of flour" against the door, the other a tornado "that blew [their] chickens and turkeys away, never to be seen again."

10. "Chinook" was the name given to the dry southwesterly winds that frequently blew across the southern prairies. These winds scoured the moisture out of the area, eroded the land in the summer, and could change the weather from freezing to melting temperatures (or vice versa) in hours (Jones, 1987). An example of this weather phenomenon is provided by Eliza Wilson (1901), who describes a series of warm days caused by chinook winds in February 1901. For three days, she noted in her diary, there had been no frost overnight, snow was melting, and "water [is] running down the creeks and over the prairie in small streams, the dam is full and running over, quite a rush of water coming out of the outlet" (1901, p. 59). This changed on the fourth day, when the temperature plunged thirty-eight degrees in a few hours. A heavy blizzard with thick snow and gusting winds developed the same day. The blowing snow was dense enough to block vision

across the farmyard, and it took only a few minutes to go from having virtually no snow on the ground to a situation in which "the cattle were all covered with snow" (Wilson, 1901, p. 61).

11. Building with sod, logs, or other materials often left cracks or gaps where wind, rain, and snow could enter the interior. "Chinking the walls" by filling the cracks with moss or grass and then sealing the repair with mud solved the problem; the children of the family were often assigned this task since it was relatively safe and easy work.

12. A similar technique was used by the Miles family, who settled near Innisfree, Alberta, in 1904. The house used a natural knoll as its rear wall but relied on log walls for the remaining three sides. It was extremely small, particularly once the family furniture (or as much as would fit) was brought indoors. Movement from one end of the house to the other required a "careful winding around what was in the middle of the room" (Miles, 1905, p. 2).

13. According to Kennedy (1970), the grass continued to live after being severed from the soil. In fact the grass had to be mowed during the summer so that the sparks from the stovepipe would not set the roof grasses on fire.

14. It is interesting to note that Viola's grandmother, as the head of their small household and being fifty-four years old, qualified to acquire a free homestead parcel in her own right under the *Dominion Lands Act* (1872).

15. Laura Matz (1978, p. 1) and her family adopted a different approach to the problem of water dripping through their sod roof. Rather than take the oilcloth off the table and nail it to the roof, they "slept under the long table because it was always dry there" thanks to the oilcloth cover.

16. An alternative to the sod roof was recommended in a self-help column in a 1902 edition of *The Nor'-West Farmer* (Major, 1902, p. 139). A product referred to as "Mica Roofing" was sold in hardware stores in three-foot-wide rolls for $3 per hundred square feet. This product, once installed over one-inch by four-inch support boards with overlapping edges, was said to be both waterproof and fireproof (a combination of felt cloth, ground mica rock, and tar formed the primary ingredients of this wonder product). However, this precursor of the modern asphalt shingle cost money, a commodity in generally short supply among settlers and, unlike sod or straw, was not immediately available for use.

17. Stories about "THE winter" were researched by Jones (1987, p. 46), who refers to the period as the "season of execution." He reports that two snowfalls, each followed by a brief warm spell that melted a layer of snow and created an ice crust, were followed by January temperatures plunging to minus thirty degrees Fahrenheit with constant winds. Cattle, their food buried, and pushed by the winds, drifted toward the rivers for water but "left a trail of blood, their legs slashed to shreds by the sharp ice crusts." Thousands of animals, half the herds on the prairies, froze or drowned when the weight of animals seeking water broke the ice cover on rivers and streams, and the smell of rotting carcasses hung over the region for months once the weather broke that spring.

18. For most families, obtaining logs was a dangerous process; however, luck played a role for some, as is made evident by Leddie Wilson. She describes a heavy rainstorm that hit the area in which they were homesteading. The amount of rain was so great that the Red Deer River rose into flood stage and undercut hundreds, possibly thousands, of trees that then floated downstream past their farm. The male members of her family "were all wading up to their tummys in

the water" and managed to catch sixty-four trees and haul them to shore, enough to "build a stable, bunk room and an addition to the house" (Wilson, 1902, p. 1).

Three

1. Maria Adamowska (1978, pp. 60–61) recounts the story of her mother and herself when she was a small child in the early 1900s on their homestead near Yorkton, Saskatchewan. They were left to clear their fully treed land while her father worked off-farm. She states that "Mother and I began to clear our land. But since I was hardly strong enough for the job, I helped by grabbing hold of the top of each bush and pulling on it while mother cut the roots with the ax. Next we dug the ground with spades. How well did I do? At best, I had barely enough strength to thrust half the depth of the blade into the ground, no deeper…. [The] two of us cleared and dug close to four acres of land."

2. For those with the necessary skills, ploughshares could be sharpened and repaired on the farm. Ellenor Merriken (1999) notes that she and two brothers helped their father in his homemade "blacksmith shop" by putting fuel in the fire and working the bellows made from a pipe, the lining from an old coat, and a wood frame built from a packing box. They heated the dull or damaged metal until it glowed, and their father then beat it back into shape and sharpened the edge using a scavenged piece of rail as an anvil.

3. The gang plough was more efficient since it possessed a number of blades rather than the single blade of a walking plough and thus could plough a wider swath on each pass through the fields.

4. It is interesting to note that no girls report participating in the crop-seeding process, particularly as logic would dictate that anyone who could handle a plough or harrow was also likely to be capable of assisting with seeding.

5. Silverman's research on farm families also recounts the more detailed story of a twelve-year-old girl named Wilma Post who stooked grain with her father and sister and how the process of threshing became easier with the advent of advanced technology. The girl describes how "My dad threw the bundles into the rack, and my sister and I would take turns at cutting them with a sickle blade, which is a sharp blade but on both sides. We'd cut the twine and then feed it into the threshing machine by hand. Then Dad would go for another load and we could have a little rest till he'd come back. That first threshing machine was fed by hand. The next one that I remember was the old steam machine, and boy, you didn't have to cut bundles for that: you could feed them in. So this was progress" (1984, p. 20).

6. A binder was used to cut grain, bundle it together, and mechanically tie the bundle with twine, eliminating a portion of the labour previously required before stooking the grain bundles.

7. In terms of getting the crops to market, only one girl refers to involvement with transporting wheat to the grain elevator. Jean Murray (1902), a fifteen-year-old girl from Lyleton, Manitoba, indicates that her job had been to drive wagonloads of wheat twelve miles to the nearest railroad station. However, her workload had been recently decreased since the rail line had been extended and her driving distance reduced to two miles.

8. Some children were responsible for warning off predators that might harm the farm animals. John Watson (1975), for example, worked as a shepherd when he

was only ten years old. He had approximately five hundred sheep under his care and used his dogs to scare off coyotes. However, the job proved to be beyond his capabilities when packs of the predators started attacking the sheep. It was decided that the herd would be sold off since too many animals were being lost.

Four

1. Rollings-Magnusson (2000) recounts several examples of women active in the marketplace to raise funds for household or other farm needs. These women sold eggs, butter, preserves, doughnuts, and products that they had knitted or crocheted. Turner (1955) notes that some women even took in laundry for bachelors who had no one to help them and acquired capital in that fashion.

2. Robert Hogg was sent out to work at age eleven so that the family could buy a cow (Rowles, 1952). Since wages in 1883 were only 50¢ per day, he worked many weeks to raise the purchase price, but once acquired, the cow provided milk for over two years before being butchered. Unlike Roy, Robert was able to quit working once he attained a specific goal.

3. Children's labour could also be used to solidify relations between families in the area. For example, Nellie Hislop (Nuffield, 1987) was asked when she was eleven years old to leave her family over the Christmas season and spend two weeks assisting the local Presbyterian minister's wife with household tasks. The minister had a two-year-old daughter and did not expect to be available to help his wife due to his religious duties. While Nellie was surprised by the request, given her lack of domestic skills, she agreed to take on this work at no cost.

4. Not all children were happy with the prospect that their hard work would go unrewarded. For example, Ben Kroening (1913, p. 10) rebelled over his father's decision to rent him out to do field work for a neighbour. Given that the wages would be going directly to the father, Ben decided to sit under a tree, using the logic that "if he wasn't going to get paid, he was not going to do the work." Ben does not mention the result of his protest.

5. While grains were the primary source of earnings for farmers on the prairies, various types of livestock were also of importance. Urquhart and Buckley (1965, series L167–232) note that animal husbandry grew quite rapidly on the plains, with prairie residents owning 20,000 milk cows, 40,000 other cattle, 28,000 horses, 17,000 hogs, and 6,000 sheep in 1881. By 1891, the number of each type of animal had at least tripled and some had quadrupled or more. Thus, there were 83,000 milk cows, 148,000 cattle, 148,000 horses, 54,000 hogs, and 36,000 sheep reported that year, and the expansion continued as the century changed. Between 1901 and 1911, livestock herds (and flocks) continued to grow in size, with the number of milk cows increasing from 134,000 to 447,000, cattle from 216,000 to 1,362,000, and horses from 340,000 to 1,195,000. The number of hogs also rose, hitting 712,000 in 1911 (from 126,000 in 1901), as did sheep (285,000 from 183,000) and chickens (8,033,000 from 1,623,000).

6. Whether Ralph loved his cow and wanted to name it after royalty or hated the King and wanted to name a future steak after him, his plan with his sister was to "crown him with roses on Coronation Day" and make the name official (Ralph Clench, 1902, p. 333).

7. For a more detailed discussion of the rabbit population, see Chapter 5 respecting the trapping of rabbits for consumption.

8. Municipal governments on the prairies also became involved in efforts to eradicate these rodents. For example, the Municipality of Excelsior near Medicine Hat, Alberta, sponsored a gopher hunt lasting from spring to mid-July, 1915. Approximately 15,000 tails were turned in to the municipality, with the top five catchers having 6,984 kills recorded to their credit (Jones, 1987, p. 109).

9. As noted by Murray (1982, p. 45) in a privately published family history, not all children hunted gophers for profit. Murray had received a young gopher as a pet from his father. When it was killed accidentally, his mother located a new gopher pet for him, but after being bitten by the new pet, "she picked it up and took it to the door where she threw it just as far as she could. That was the end of the pet gopher era."

Five

1. For those who did not have streams and had to haul water in barrels on a wagon or stoneboat, a settler named Larson gave wise advice. He indicated that people with oxen to pull their wagons should stop watering them before the trek was made. The thirsty oxen would then drink while the barrels were being filled, delaying the animals' need for water for a few days. In effect, "this would be like taking two loads of water back, one load in the oxen and the other in the barrels" (Larson, n.d., p. 3).

2. Jones (1987) relates the story of Nels and Nikolai Sokvitne, a pair of professional well diggers on the prairies. Wells had to be deep to reach the water table in many areas and fouled air was a constant danger. The Sokvitnes solved this problem by lowering a candle down the well to see if it would stay alight, but in the absence of a candle, they would send captured cats or roosters down the shaft before resuming digging.

3. Merriken (1999) notes that her father dug the family well, but it was the children's job to haul the dirt and clay away for disposal. Even though they used a rope-and-pulley system hung from a wooden tripod over the well to make the lifting easier, it took the strength of three children to pull a bucket of dirt up from the hole to be dumped.

4. Ensuring a sufficient supply of fuel was literally a matter of life and death on the prairies, where temperature extremes could exceed safe levels for months at a time and many houses were poorly constructed. As noted by Amy Braithwaite (n.d., p. 2), the temperature could reach "50 or more below" zero degrees Fahrenheit and "the houses were so cold a pail of water would freeze on the back of the stove in the night."

5. The CPR brochure entitled *The North West Farmer* (CPR, 1891, p. 28) extols the virtues of coal deposits on the prairies, making it seem that fuel would never be a problem. Listing the several areas in which coal seams had been discovered, the advertisement notes that the coal had "been found at many points so conveniently situated as to appear almost as though specially designed by nature for distributing centers," but fails to mention that with the lack of suitable transportation in the West, the coal would be of benefit only to those who could access the mining areas lying near the American border.

6. Gladys Holmes (n.d.) notes that in her home, the stove was likely to be fuelled with "prairie chips" since they burned hot and clean.

7. It should be noted that any type of herbivore "chip" could be used to fuel a fire.

The key was that a high concentration of undigested foliage be contained in the chip. Buffalo had been effectively extinct for decades, so children like Dorthea were actually hunting for chips left primarily by cattle as they foraged across the prairie. However, Minifie (1972, p. 96) notes that "dry horse-droppings, weathered silvery grey over the winter," could also be used to feed a fire.

8. A different pattern seems to have been followed by fifteen-year-old E.O. Wright (September 1901, p. 568) of Rose Hill, Manitoba, since he reports that he would "chop the house wood" as needed during the summer. He did not mention when he began to chop wood for a winter stockpile, but presumably a wood supply was built up before winter for safety's sake.

9. Woodcutting duties were shared by the three youngest siblings in the Merriken family. Two would pull a crosscut saw back and forth across a log while the third sat on the log to steady it. Duties were traded when the non-cutting child got cold. Ellenor Merriken indicates that they would work at cutting for several days in a row to build up a stockpile for use (Merriken, 1999).

10. Milking was also assigned to Eva Clyde (1901), a young girl from Miniota, Manitoba. She had two cows to milk, Star and Beauty, and both were good-natured. However, Eva expressed some impatience: while she "thought it [was] cruel to hit a cow with the stool or a stick whenever she moves...[Eva] was provoked when she sometimes puts her foot in the pail or upsets it" (Clyde, 1901, p. 569).

11. B.A. Moss (1902) had two other sisters and one brother who also worked with the chickens. As all four siblings were trained to feed the flock, gather the eggs, and clean out the coop, there was always at least one child available to handle this work if the others were busy with different tasks.

12. As noted by Harrigan (1980), even with freezing to preserve the meat, cattle were too large for some families to consume over a single season. Thus, some families established co-operative food systems in which several families would receive meat from a single slaughtered animal. One family would provide the meat for the "beef ring" and, in this way, the meat would not be wasted even though "no one had a refrigerator and freezers were unheard of" (Thompson, 1979, p. 2).

13. Large game was quite rare since the Native peoples in the area tended to rely on elk, moose, and deer after their previous mainstay, the buffalo, was hunted almost to extinction by those seeking hides (Doolittle, 1978).

14. Although there is some indication that prairie residents frowned on the eating of prairie chickens, Roy DeVore discusses the fact that prairie chickens, partridges, and fool hens provided "plenty of fresh meat for a few days" (DeVore, 1970, p. 30).

15. Those who could not protect their gardens from insects such as cutworms had little chance of harvesting a decent crop. An anonymous young girl discussed this topic in a letter submitted to *The Nor'-West Farmer* (1901, p. 597); even though she had planted a very large garden, "the grub seemed to play 'havoc' with it" and little was produced for consumption over the winter.

16. Hailstorms were not always seen as a disaster. Caswell (1968) describes one, for example, that caused a few bruises and soaked some clothing and bedding, but was somewhat of a blessing as their water had been running low. By gathering the hailstones, the family was able to extend its supply.

17. Smudge pots were sources of thick smoke laid inside a metal or clay pot that held the hot embers. Portability could be achieved by varying the size and weight of the pot (Turner, 1955).

18. In a moment of humour in his memoirs, Roy DeVore (1970, p. 36) suggests that the advertisers who promised that settlers would not find a single mosquito on the prairies had not been lying at all. All the mosquitoes Roy had seen in his time in the region "seemed married and with very large families."

19. As described by Harrigan (1980, p. 8), "[a] prairie fire can travel much faster than a horse. It is a terrifying sight and yet it is fascinating."

Six

1. At the same time that borax was used as a preservative for food, it was also seen as a miracle product since it had many other applications including use as an effective bug deterrent, water softener, and dish soap (Exchange, 1900).

2. Mitchell (1976, p. 1) also notes that in the winter, buckets of snow might be gathered and melted in their large copper boiler, although "it took an awful lot of snow to fill."

3. As described by Jennie Johnston (1973) in her memoir of life on her family's Lake Manitou, Saskatchewan, homestead, the water in her area came from sloughs; after boiling and bleaching, items were dropped into the yellow water to be scrubbed against a washboard with homemade lye soap that did not lather because of the hard water. She does not mention whether a yellow tinge was left on their clothes after the washing process was complete.

4. As noted by Jennie Johnston (1973), it was impossible to gather soft water in the summer months unless a house had wooden shingles, since a sod roof would either absorb the soft rainwater or contaminate it.

5. The only available soap was hard yellow bars of Royal Crown, and it had to be prepared for use with the cloth. The soap was "shaved into an empty syrup pail" and water was added so that "in the morning it had become soft jelly" (Walker, 1979, pp. 2–3).

6. Stomping through the fabric seems to have been the children's favourite part of the washing process. As Agnes put it, "Back and forth and round and round. What fun!" (Walker, 1979, p. 3).

7. "Stovies" is described as a potato dish in which sliced potatoes, onions, and oatmeal were slowly boiled in milk and served with fried herring. The cooking continued while the blanket cleaning was underway and the meal was eaten after the work was complete.

8. "Blacking" the stove refers to applying a coat of black-coloured paste to the stove to hide blemishes and discoloration. The paste (prepared with turpentine, not water) was applied to a cold stove. The stove was then lit to "burn in" the blacking and could then be polished with a brush (Exchange, 1900).

9. Although not clothing in a strict sense, hats were practical items useful to farmers working in the hot prairie sunshine. Thus, the straw-weaving skills that Jessie McDonald (1902) of Morinville, Alberta, used to make hats for her father also proved beneficial.

Seven

1. Even if production could not be increased, child labour could reduce the cost of production and thus improve profits. For example, William Rand, a twelve-year-old from Crystal City, Manitoba, wrote that he was "a great help to [his]

father on the farm...[as he saved the cost of] hired help" (1901, p. 598). Similarly, twelve-year-old Amelia Johnson (1902, p. 506) reported that her "father was short on a man at stacking the grain so I built the loads on the wagons and brother pitched them." These children thus both provided productive labour and eliminated the expense of the hired hand whose wages would have been a drain on the revenue obtainable from the crop.

2. Children were meant to toil for the good of their families, yet overworking a child, making their days seem like "[a] thousand chores from house to barn, like... [an] endless chain" (Mitchell, 1900, p. 69), was also looked down on by many. A balance of work and other activity was the key to benefiting the family and children without driving them away from the occupation. Only a few, such as Doris Thompson (1979, p. 1), indicated that they might be overworked and, in her case, mentioning that "the continuous repetition of such jobs became a chore" seems a complaint more of boredom than of stress.

3. Fontaine and Schlumbohm (2000) found that the economic value of production fell below the level necessary to provide minimal subsistence for the population in a number of years, but death rates did not escalate to the degree that they anticipated given the economic upheaval they were studying. No welfare system existed, so families had to have been working outside of the market system, the only unrecorded source of subsistence available.

4. It is important to note that for many farmers, the capital invested in farming was much smaller than would have been required to establish a manufacturing company of equivalent size. Farmers could obtain their land, the most valuable portion of their investment, from the government at low or no cost. This would have increased the apparent profitability of a farm as, for example, earnings of $850 against an investment of $500 would show a better result than the same earnings against a total investment of $820 ($500 plus a land cost of $2 per acre for a 160-acre homestead).

5. Only those between four and fourteen are considered children for the purpose of this calculation since the population information set out in the census records placed fifteen- and sixteen-year-old individuals in the adult group for reporting purposes. Further, the intent is to determine the minimum effect that children had. Opening the category to include those up to sixteen would increase the number of children substantially.

6. See Ursel (1992) and Rollings-Magnusson (1999) for particulars on the actions of the federal and provincial governments that supported the patriarchal family system that kept both women and children under the control of the male head of the household. See also *An Ordinance Respecting the Administration of Civil Justice* (North-West Territories, 1886). Mothers did not begin to have control over the lives of their children until 1918, when *The Infants Act* (Saskatchewan, 1918–19) was passed, and other jurisdictions began to loosen restrictions on women.

Reference List

Abbreviations:

LAC Library and Archives Canada, Ottawa, Ontario
PAA Provincial Archives of Alberta, Edmonton, Alberta
SAB Saskatchewan Archives Board, Regina and Saskatoon, Saskatchewan

Books and Journal Articles:

Adamowska, Maria. (1978). Beginnings in Canada. In Harry Piniuta (Ed.), *Land of pain, land of promise: First-person accounts by Ukrainian pioneers, 1891–1914* (pp. 53–78). Saskatoon, SK: Western Producer Prairie Books.

Amey, Edward. (1885). *Farm life as it should be.* Toronto: Ellis & Moore.

Aries, Philippe. (1970). *Centuries of childhood: A social history of family life.* New York: Alfred A. Knopf.

Barber, Marilyn. (1991). *Immigrant domestic servants in Canada.* Ottawa, ON: Canadian Historical Association.

Bennett, John, Kohl, Seena, & Binion, Geraldine. (1982). *Of time and enterprise: North American family farm management in a context of resource marginality.* Minneapolis: University of Minnesota Press.

Broadfoot, Barry. (1976). *The pioneer years, 1895–1914: Memories of settlers who opened the West.* Toronto: Doubleday Canada.

Broadfoot, Barry. (1988). *Next-year country: Voices of prairie people.* Toronto: McClelland & Stewart.

Canada. Dept. of the Interior. (1905). *Prosperity follows settlement in western Canada.* Ottawa, ON: Canadian Government Print.

Canada. Dept. of the Interior. (1906). *The last and best West.* Ottawa, ON: Dept. of the Interior.

Canada. Dept. of the Interior. (1909). *Prosperity follows settlement in any part of Canada: Letters from satisfied settlers.* Ottawa, ON: Minister of the Interior.

Canada. Minister of Immigration and Colonization. (1894). *Canada West.* Ottawa, ON: Department of Immigration and Colonization.

Caswell, Maryanne. (1968). *Pioneer girl.* Toronto: McGraw-Hill of Canada.

Cherwinski, W.J.C. (1985). In search of Jake Trumper: The farm hand and the prairie farm family. In David C. Jones & Ian MacPherson (Eds.), *Building beyond the homestead: Rural history on the prairies* (pp. 111–134). Calgary, AB: University of Calgary Press.

Cohen, Marjorie. (1988). *Women's work, markets, and economic development in nineteenth-century Ontario.* Toronto: University of Toronto Press.

Conway, John. (1984). *The West: The history of a region in Confederation.* Toronto: James Lorimer.

CPR [Canadian Pacific Railway]. (1884). *Free facts, farms and sleepers*. Montreal, QC: CPR.

CPR. (1891). *The North West Farmer*. Montreal, QC: CPR.

Creighton, Donald Grant. (1963). *British North America at Confederation: A study prepared for the Royal Commission on Dominion-Provincial Relations*. Ottawa, ON: Queen's Printer.

Cunningham, Hugh. (1995). *Children and childhood in Western society since 1500*. London: Longman.

Davisson, Walter P. (1927). *Pooling wheat in Canada*. Ottawa, ON: Graphic Publishers.

Dawson, C.A., & Younge, Eva. (1940). *Pioneering in the prairie provinces: The social side of the settlement process*. Toronto: Macmillan of Canada.

Eager, Evelyn. (1953). Our Pioneers Say:—. *Saskatchewan History*, 6(1), 1–12.

Easterbrook, W.T., & Aitken, Hugh G.J. (1963). *Canadian Economic History*. Toronto: Macmillan of Canada.

Easterlin, Richard. (1976). Population change and farm settlement in the northern United States. *The Journal of Economic History*, 36, 45–75.

Engelmeyer, Mary. (1995). A farm under a class lens. In Antonio Callari, Stephen Cullenberg, and Carole Biewener (Eds.), *Marxism in the postmodern age: Confronting the New World Order* (pp. 365–374). New York: Guilford Press.

Espenshade, Thomas J. (1977). The value and cost of children. *Population Bulletin*, 32(1), 3–47.

Fairbairn, Garry Lawrence. (1984). *From prairie roots: The remarkable story of the Saskatchewan Wheat Pool*. Saskatoon, SK: Western Producer Prairie Books.

Farion, Anna. (1978). Homestead girl. In Harry Piniuta (Ed.), *Land of pain, land of promise: First-person accounts by Ukrainian pioneers, 1891–1914* (pp. 85–96). Saskatoon, SK: Western Producer Prairie Books.

Finch, Janet. (1989). *Family obligations and social change*. Cambridge, England: Polity Press.

Folbre, Nancy. (1982). Exploitation comes home: A critique of the Marxian theory of family labour. *Cambridge Journal of Economics*, 6, 317–330.

Fontaine, Laurence, & Schlumbohm, Jürgen. (2000). Household strategies for survival: An introduction. *International Review of Social History* 45 (Suppl. 8: *Household strategies for survival 1600–2000: Fission, faction and cooperation*), 1–17.

Fowke, Vernon. (1957). *The national policy and the wheat economy*. Toronto: University of Toronto Press.

Fox, Bonnie. (1991). Women's role in development. In Gordon Laxer (Ed.), *Perspectives on Canadian economic development: Class, staples, gender, and elites* (pp. 333–352). Toronto: Oxford University Press.

Fraad, Harriet. (1995). Children as an exploited class. In Antonio Callari, Stephen Cullenberg, & Carole Biewener (Eds.), *Marxism in the postmodern age: Confronting the New World Order* (pp. 375–384). New York: Guilford Press.

Friesen, Gerald. (1987). *The Canadian prairies: A history*. Toronto: University of Toronto Press.

Ghorayshi, Parvin. (1989). The indispensable nature of wives' work for the farm family enterprise. *The Canadian Review of Sociology and Anthropology*, 26, 571–595.

Gjerde, Jon, & McCants, Anne. (1995). Fertility, marriage, and culture: Demographic processes among Norwegian immigrants to the rural Middle West. *The Journal of Economic History*, 55, 860–888.

Gleave, Alfred P. (1991). *United we stand: Prairie farmers 1901–1975*. Toronto: Lugus Publications.

Hendrick, Harry. (1997). *Children, childhood and English society, 1880–1990*. Cambridge: Cambridge University Press.

Hiemstra, Mary. (1997). *Gully farm: A story of homesteading on the Canadian prairies*. Calgary, AB: Fifth House.

Hind, Henry Youle. (1883). *Manitoba and the North-West frauds: Correspondence with the Department of Agriculture &c, &c, &c, respecting the impostures of Professor John Macoun and others*. Windsor, ON: Author.

Horn, Pamela. (1994). *Children's work and welfare, 1780–1890*. Cambridge: Press Syndicate of the University of Cambridge.

Humphries, Jane. (1982). Class struggle and the persistence of the working-class family. In Anthony Giddens and David Held (Eds.), *Classes, power and conflict: Classical and contemporary debates* (pp. 425–445). Los Angeles: University of California Press. First published: (1977). *Cambridge Journal of Economics*, 1, 241–258.

Innis, Harold. (1954). *The cod fisheries*. Toronto: University of Toronto Press.

Jones, David C. (1987). *Empire of dust: Settling and abandoning the prairie dry belt*. Edmonton, AB: University of Alberta Press.

Knuttila, [Kenneth] Murray. (1994). *"That man Partridge": E.A. Partridge, his thoughts and times*. Regina, SK: Canadian Plains Research Center, University of Regina.

Kohl, Seena B. (1976). *Working together: Women and family in southwestern Saskatchewan*. Toronto: Holt, Rinehart & Winston of Canada.

Kohl, Seena B. (1977). Women's participation in the North American family farm. *Women's Studies International Quarterly*, 1, 47–54.

Langford, Nanci. (1995). Childbirth on the Canadian prairies, 1880–1930. *Journal of Historical Sociology*, 8, 278–302.

Lehr, John. (1996). One family's frontier: Life history and the process of Ukrainian settlement in the Stuartburn district of southeastern Manitoba. *The Canadian Geographer*, 40, 98–108.

Levy, Victor. (1985). Cropping pattern, mechanization, child labor, and fertility behavior in a farming economy: Rural Egypt. *Economic Development and Cultural Change*, 33, 777–791.

Lewis, Norah L. (Ed.). (1996). *"I want to join your club": Letters from rural children, 1900–1920*. Waterloo, ON: Wilfrid Laurier University Press.

Light, Harriett K., Hertsgaard, Doris, and Martin, Ruth E. (1985). Farm children's work in the family. *Adolescence*, 20, 425–432.

Mackintosh, W[illiam] A. (1939). *The economic background of dominion provincial relations: A study prepared for the Royal Commission on Dominion-Provincial Relations*. Ottawa, ON: King's Printer, 1939.

Marquis of Lorne. (1886). *Canadian life and scenery: With hints to intending immigrants and settlers*. London: Religious Tract Society.

Martin, Chester. (1938). *History of prairie settlement: "Dominion Lands" policy*. Toronto: MacMillan Company of Canada Limited.

McKenzie, R. (1914). Proposed solutions: C—Bigger profits[,] the economic situation. In J[ames] S[haver] Woodsworth (Ed.), *Studies in rural citizenship: Designed for the use of grain growers' associations, women's institutes, community clubs, young peoples' [sic] societies and similar organizations and groups desirous of obtaining an intelligent view of rural life in Canada, with its various needs and possibilities* (pp. 31–35). Winnipeg, MB: n.p.

Mendelievich, Elías. (1979). Introduction. In Elías Mendelievich (Ed.), *Children at work* (pp. 3–11). Geneva: International Labour Office.

Merriken, Ellenor Ranghild. (1999). *Looking for country: A Norwegian immigrant's Alberta memoir.* Calgary, AB: University of Calgary Press.

Minifie, James M. (1972). *Homesteader: A prairie boyhood recalled.* Toronto: Macmillan of Canada.

Morgan, E.C. (1965). Pioneer recreation and social life. *Saskatchewan History,* 28, 41–54.

Morton, Arthur S. (1938). History of prairie settlement. Vol. 2, pt. 1 of W.A. Mackintosh & W.L.G. Joerg (Eds.), *Canadian frontiers of settlement* (9 volumes). Toronto: Macmillan of Canada.

Murray, W. Roland. (1982). *The Murray-Hurlbert homesteads.* Los Angeles: Author.

Naylor, R.T. (1975). *The history of Canadian business 1867–1914.* Vol. 1: *The banks and finance capital.* Toronto: James Lorimer.

Neth, Mary. (1995). *Preserving the family farm: Women, community and the foundations of agribusiness in the Midwest, 1900–1940.* Baltimore: Johns Hopkins University Press.

Nett, Emily M. (1988). *Canadian families: Past and present.* Toronto: Butterworths.

North-West Canada Company, Limited. (1880). *Farms in Manitoba and the new North West.* Edinburgh: T. and A. Constable.

Nuffield, E.W. (1987). *With the West in her eyes: Nellie Hislop's story.* Winnipeg, MB: Hyperion Press.

Owram, Doug. (1980). *Promise of Eden: The Canadian expansionist movement and the idea of the West, 1856–1900.* Toronto: University of Toronto Press.

Place, Ethel. (1996). [Letter to the editor, n.d.]. In Nora L. Lewis (Ed.), *"I want to join your club": Letters from rural children, 1900–1920* (p. 139). Waterloo, ON: Wilfrid Laurier University Press.

Pollock, Linda. (1983). *Forgotten children: Parent-child relations from 1500 to 1900.* Cambridge: Cambridge University Press.

Potyondi, Barry. (1995). *In Palliser's Triangle: Living in the grasslands, 1850–1930.* Saskatoon, SK: Purich.

Pratt, Marjorie Barr. (1996). *Recollections of a homesteader's daughter.* Cobble Hill, BC: Author.

Rasmussen, Linda, Rasmussen, Lorna, Savage, Candace, & Wheeler, Anne (Comps.). (1976). *A harvest yet to reap: A history of prairie women.* Toronto: Canadian Women's Educational Press.

Reimer, Bill. (1986). Women as farm labour. *Rural Sociology,* 51, 143–155.

Roberts, Sarah Ellen. (1971). *Alberta homestead: Chronicle of a pioneer family.* Austin: University of Texas Press.

Rodwell, Lloyd. (1965). Saskatchewan homestead records. *Saskatchewan History,* 17(1), 10–29.

Rollings-Magnusson, Sandra. (1999). Hidden homesteaders: Women, the state and patriarchy in the Saskatchewan wheat economy, 1870–1930. *Prairie Forum,* 24, 171–183.

Rollings-Magnusson, Sandra. (2000). Canada's most wanted: Pioneer women on the Western Prairies. *The Canadian Review of Sociology and Anthropology,* 37, 223–238.

Rowles, Edith. (1952). Bannock, beans and bacon: An investigation of pioneer diet. *Saskatchewan History,* 5(1), 1–16.

Ruthig, Elizabeth. (1954). Recollections and reminiscences: Homestead days in the McCord district. *Saskatchewan History,* 7(1), 22–27.

St. John, S.T. (1949). Recollections and reminiscences: Homesteading at Wilcox. *Saskatchewan History,* 2(1), 23–27.

Sachs, Carolyn E. (1983). *The invisible farmers: Women in agricultural production.*

Totowa, NJ: Rowman & Allanheld.

Saskatchewan Land and Homestead Company, Limited. (1884). *The settler's guide to homesteads in the Canadian North-West.* Toronto: John T. Moore.

Scott, J.W., & Tilly, Louise. (1980). Women's work and the family in 19th-century Europe. In Alice Amsden (Ed.), *The economics of women and work.* Bungay, Suffolk: Chaucer Press.

Sharif, Mohammed. (1993). Child participation, nature of work, and fertility demand: A theoretical analysis. *The Indian Economic Journal,* 40(4), 30–48.

Silverman, Eliane L. (1984). *The last best West: Women on the Alberta frontier 1880–1930.* Montreal, QC: Eden Press.

Sommerville, C[harles] John. (1982). *The rise and fall of childhood.* Beverly Hills, CA: Sage.

Stansell, Christine. (1976). Women on the Great Plains, 1865–1890. *Women's Studies,* 4, 87–98.

Stewart, Norman. (1962). *Children of the pioneers.* Edmonton, AB: Author.

Still, George. (1996). [Letter to the editor, July 22, 1908]. In Nora L. Lewis (Ed.), *"I want to join your club": Letters from rural children, 1900–1920* (p. 128). Waterloo, ON: Wilfrid Laurier University Press.

Strong-Boag, Veronica. (1985). Discovering the home: The last 150 years of domestic work in Canada. In Paula Bourne (Ed.), *Women's paid and unpaid work: Historical and contemporary perspectives* (pp. 35–60). Toronto: New Hogtown Press.

Sutherland, Neil. (2000). *Children in English-Canadian society: Framing the twentieth-century consensus.* Waterloo, ON: Wilfrid Laurier University Press.

Symes, David, & Appleton, John. (1986). Family goals and survival strategies. *Sociologia Ruralis,* 26, 345–363.

Taggart, Kathleen. (1958). The first shelter of early pioneers. *Saskatchewan History,* 11(3), 81–93.

Thomas, Lewis (Ed.). (1975). *The Prairie West to 1905: A Canadian sourcebook.* Toronto: Oxford University Press.

Tilly, Louise, & Scott, Joan. (1987). *Women, work and family.* New York: Methuen.

Turner, Allan. (1955). Pioneer farming experiences. *Saskatchewan History,* 7(2), 41–55.

Urquhart, M.C., & Buckley, K.A.H. (Eds.). (1965). *Historical statistics of Canada.* Toronto: Macmillan of Canada.

Ursel, Jane. (1992). *Private lives, public policy.* Toronto: Women's Press.

Voisey, Paul. (1988). *Vulcan: The making of a prairie community.* Toronto: University of Toronto Press.

Wallace, Claire, Dunkerley, David, Cheal, Brian, & Warren, Martyn. (1994). Young people and the division of labour in farming families. *The Sociological Review,* 42, 501–530.

Warren, G[eorge] F. (1917). *Farm management.* New York: Macmillan.

Webb, Anne. (1989). Minnesota women homesteaders: 1863–1889. *Journal of Social History,* 23(1), 115–136.

Whatmore, Sarah. (1991). *Farming women: Gender, work and family enterprise.* Basingstoke, England: Macmillan.

Wilson, C.F. (1978). *A century of Canadian grain: Government policy to 1951.* Saskatoon, SK: Western Producer Prairie Books.

Wilson, S.J. (1982). *Women, the family and the economy.* Toronto: McGraw-Hill Ryerson.

Sources Used in Data Analysis:

Althouse, Archie. (n.d.) Autobiography. Accession No. R-E2930. SAB.

Anderson, Aquina. (n.d.). Autobiography. Accession No. R-E3249. SAB.

Anderson, Gertie. (1902, November 20). Letter. *The Nor'-West Farmer*, p. 1020.

Anderson, H.B. (n.d.). Autobiography. Accession No. R-E3253. SAB.

Anonymous. (1897, June). Agricultural education. *The Nor'-West Farmer*, p. 196.

Anonymous. (1898, November). The boys we need. *The Nor'-West Farmer*, p. 528.

Anonymous. (1898, December 10). A farmer's life. *The Nor'-West Farmer*, p. 577.

Anonymous. (1899a, May 20). The farmer's daughter. *The Nor'-West Farmer*, p. 341.

Anonymous. (1899b, August 21). The girl who makes a home. *The Nor'-West Farmer*, pp. 622–23.

Anonymous. (1899c, November 6). The farmer girl's allowance. *The Nor'-West Farmer*, p. 817.

Anonymous. (1900, August 6). The girl not to marry. *The Nor'-West Farmer*, p. 635.

Anonymous. (1901, September 20). Letter. *The Nor'-West Farmer*, p. 597.

Anonymous. (1902, June 20). Bob's calf but Pa's steer. *The Nor'-West Farmer*, p. 508.

Anonymous. (1908, June). Miscellany. *The Grain Growers' Guide*, pp. 43–45.

Anonymous. (1909, October 6). Community in the home. *The Grain Growers' Guide*, p. 24.

Arnold, Charlie. (1901, September 20). Letter. *The Nor'-West Farmer*, p. 598.

Arnott, Frederick. (1902, August 5). Letter. *The Nor'-West Farmer*, p. 697.

Barber, Montana. (1902, August 20). Letter. *The Nor'-West Farmer*, p. 740.

Barr, Welsey. (1902, August 20). Letter. *The Nor'-West Farmer*, p. 740.

Bassett, Vernon. (1902, November 20). Letter. *The Nor'-West Farmer*, p. 1020.

Bell, Ollie. (1976). Interview. Accession No. 81.279. PAA.

Biehn, Aaron. (n.d.) Autobiography. Accession No. R-E514. SAB.

Black, Florence. (1902, October 20). Letter. *The Nor'-West Farmer*, p. 917.

Braithwaite, Amy. (n.d.). Autobiography. Accession No. R-E514#2. SAB.

Brander, James. (1902, April 21). Letter. *The Nor'-West Farmer*, p. 333.

Brander, Laura. (1902, April 21). Letter. *The Nor'-West Farmer*, p. 333.

Brown, Elsie. (1902, June 20). Letter. *The Nor'-West Farmer*, p. 507.

Brown, Harvey (1902, May 20). Letter. *The Nor'-West Farmer*, p. 420.

Brown, Mabel. (1902, June 20). Letter. *The Nor'-West Farmer*, p. 506.

Brown, Walter. (1902, November 20). Letter. *The Nor'-West Farmer*, p. 1020.

Brownridge, Thomas Roy. (1950–56). Pioneer questionnaires. Accession No. SX2 1299. SAB.

Calverly, Dorthea. (1985). Autobiography. Accession No. R85–269. SAB.

Cameron, Margaret. (1950–56). Pioneer questionnaires. Accession No. SX2 1247. SAB.

Cameron, Viola. (1975). Interview. Accession No. 81.270 #17. PAA.

Campbell, Alice. (1902, April 21). Letter. *The Nor'-West Farmer*, p. 333.

Campbell, Alice. (1902, August 20). Letter. *The Nor'-West Farmer*, p. 740.

Card, Arthur. (1902, May 20). Letter. *The Nor'-West Farmer*, p. 420.

Carr, Grace Broad. (n.d.). Autobiography. Accession No. R-E2849. SAB.

Cheavins, Bertha. (1902, August 20). Letter. *The Nor'-West Farmer*, p. 740.

Chesney, Jane. (1902, November 20). Letter. *The Nor'-West Farmer*, p. 1020.

Chipman, G.F. (1969). G.F. Chipman papers. Accession No. 69.162/1–100. PAA.

Christensen, Christen. (1976). Autobiography. Accession No. 76.63. PAA.

Clench, Elsie. (1901, September 20). Letter. *The Nor'-West Farmer*, p. 598.

Clench, Ralph. (1901, September 20). Letter. *The Nor'-West Farmer*, p. 598.

Clench, Ralph. (1902, April 21). Letter. *The Nor'-West Farmer*, p. 333.

Clyde, Charles. (1902, April 21). Letter. *The Nor'-West Farmer*, p. 332.

Clyde, Eva. (1901, September 5). Letter. *The Nor'-West Farmer*, p. 568–569.

Colinette. (1898, April). Article. *The Nor'-West Farmer*, p. 180.

Cook, L. (1902, October 20). Letter. *The Nor'-West Farmer*, p. 917.

Cooper, James. (1950–56). Pioneer questionnaires. Accession No. sx2 1353. sab.

Corbett, Albert. (1902, October 6). Letter. *The Nor'-West Farmer*, p. 873.

Cotton, Sidney. (n.d.). Autobiography. Accession No. r-e3106. sab.

Cox, Eva. (1902, December 5). Letter. *The Nor'-West Farmer*, p. 1072.

Cox, George. (1902, December 5). Letter. *The Nor'-West Farmer*, p. 1072.

Coxe, Mamie. (1902, October 20). Letter. *The Nor'-West Farmer*, p. 917.

Crawford, Delia. (1976). Interview. Accession No. 81–279. paa.

Cummins, Mary. (1975). Autobiography. Accession No. r-e2552. sab.

Currie, Gracie. (1902, November 20). Letter. *The Nor'-West Farmer*, p. 1020.

Darwood, Dora. (1902, June 20). Letter. *The Nor'-West Farmer*, p. 507.

Darwood, Willie. (1902, June 20). Letter. *The Nor'-West Farmer*, p. 507.

Davidson, Ann. (1902, June 20). Letter. *The Nor'-West Farmer*, p. 507.

Dennison, Hazel. (n.d.). Autobiography. Accession No. r-e695. sab.

Desgagnie, Marie. (1902, August 5). Letter. *The Nor'-West Farmer*, p. 697.

DeVore, Roy. (1970). Autobiography. Accession No. 70.73 se. paa.

Dinsmore, Leola. (1901, September 20). Letter. *The Nor'-West Farmer*, p. 598.

Dixon, Alfred Lyman. (1950–56). Pioneer questionnaires. Accession No. sx2 1260. sab.

Doolittle, Kenneth. (1978). Autobiography. Accession No. r-e321#36. sab.

Dowkes, Ambrose. (1902, August 20). Letter. *The Nor'-West Farmer*, p. 740.

Duesterbeck, Martin. (1950–56). Pioneer questionnaires. Accession No. sx2 1300. sab.

Dunn, Henry. (1902, November 20). Letter. *The Nor'-West Farmer*, p. 1021.

Dunn, John. (1902, November 20). Letter. *The Nor'-West Farmer*, p. 1021.

Earl, Clifford. (1902, April 21). Letter. *The Nor'-West Farmer*, p. 332.

Ebbern, Elizabeth. (1901, September 20). Letter. *The Nor'-West Farmer*, p. 597.

Editor. (1898, March). Opportunities for country boys. *The Judd Farmer*, p. 116.

Erickson, Jennie. (1902, June 20). Letter. *The Nor'-West Farmer*, p. 507.

Evans, S.J. (1898, November). Child training. *The Nor'-West Farmer*, p. 521.

Exchange. (1900, August 20). Eleven things every housekeeper should know. *The Nor'-West Farmer*, p. 677.

Fardoe, John. (1902, June 20). Letter. *The Nor'-West Farmer*, p. 506.

A Father. (1902, July 5). To keep the boys and girls on the farm. *The Nor'-West Farmer*, p. 587.

Florence. (1901, March 20). What girls should know. *The Nor'-West Farmer*, p. 182.

Florence, Percy. (1901, September 5). Letter. *The Nor'-West Farmer*, p. 569.

Frew, Wilbert. (1902, November 20). Letter. *The Nor'-West Farmer*, p. 1020.

Frook, Gordon. (1901, September 20). Letter. *The Nor'-West Farmer*, p. 598.

Gaudin, Lavinia. (1902, November 20). Letter. *The Nor'-West Farmer*, p. 1021.

Gilliland, Annie. (1902, August 5). Letter. *The Nor'-West Farmer*, p. 697.

Graham, Bill. (1974). Interview. Accession No. 74–507/7. paa.

Graham, Mrs. M.E. (1909, October 13). Diseased persons should not marry. *The Grain Growers' Guide*, p. 24.

Griffiths, Florence. (1902, August 20). Letter. *The Nor'-West Farmer*, p. 740.

Hamlen, Arthur. (1902, May 20). Letter. *The Nor'-West Farmer*, p. 420.

Hamlen, Gordon. (1902, May 20). Letter. *The Nor'-West Farmer*, p. 420.

Hardy, Edwin. (1901, September 5). Letter. *The Nor'-West Farmer*, p. 568.

Harrigan, Sue. (1980). Autobiography. Accession No. 80–253. PAA.

Hawthorne, Mabel. (n.d.). Autobiography. Accession No. R-E2991. SAB.

Hayn-Stephans, Frederick. (1901, September 20). Letter. *The Nor'-West Farmer*, p. 598.

Henderson, Martin. (1902, June 20). Letter. *The Nor'-West Farmer*, pp. 506–507.

History of the Phillips family. (1908–1910). Accession No. 67.99 SE. PAA.

Hobson, Oliver. (1950–56). Pioneer questionnaires. Accession No. SX2 1290. SAB.

Holmes, Gladys. (n.d.). Autobiography. Accession No. R-E2148. SAB.

Household hints. (1897, January). *The Nor'-West Farmer*, p. 30.

Hunt, Verne. (1902, June 20). Letter. *The Nor'-West Farmer*, p. 507.

Hunt, Winnifred. (1902, June 20). Letter. *The Nor'-West Farmer*, p. 507.

Hyatt, A.X. (1901, March 20). An accomplished girl. *The Nor'-West Farmer*, p. 100.

Hyndman, Mildred. (1979). Autobiography. Accession No. R-E514 #10. SAB.

Interesting the children in livestock. (1901, June 5). *The Nor'-West Farmer*, p. 46.

Johnson, Amelia. (1902, June 20). Letter. *The Nor'-West Farmer*, p. 506.

Johnson, Bill. (1897, August). Bill Johnson's opinions. *The Nor'-West Farmer*, p. 289.

Johnson, Lucy. (n.d.). Autobiography. Accession No. R-E2878. SAB.

Johnston, Jennie. (1973). Autobiography. Accession No. R-E3144. SAB.

Jones, Alfred. (1902, August 20). Letter. *The Nor'-West Farmer*, p. 740–741.

Jones, H. (1901, September 20). Letter. *The Nor'-West Farmer*, p. 597.

Jordison, Bessie. (1979). Autobiography. Accession No. RE514 #17. SAB.

Keeping, Blanche. (1902, June 20). Letter. *The Nor'-West Farmer*, p. 506.

Keeping, Florence. (1902, June 20). Letter. *The Nor'-West Farmer*, p. 506.

Kennedy, Gladys Marie. (1970). Autobiography. Accession No. 86.459. PAA.

Kent, Lottie. (1902). Letter. *The Nor'-West Farmer*, p. 873.

Kirk, A. (1902, June 20). Letter. *The Nor'-West Farmer*, p. 506.

Koett, Augustine. (n.d.). Autobiography. Accession No. R-E157. SAB.

Kroening, Ben. (1913). Original diary. Owned by S. Rollings-Magnusson.

Lambert, Annie. (1902, May 20). Letter. *The Nor'-West Farmer*, p. 420.

Larson, Lars. (n.d.). Autobiography. Accession No. 80–558. SAB.

Leece, E. May. (1902, October 20). Letter. *The Nor'-West Farmer*, p. 917.

Lightbourn, Mary. (1902, October 20). Letter. *The Nor'-West Farmer*, p. 917.

Lippert, Leopold. (1981). Autobiography. Accession No. 81.342 SE. PAA.

Lockhart, Elmer. (1902, April 21). Letter. *The Nor'-West Farmer*, p. 333.

Lockhart, Elmer. (1902, August 20). Letter. *The Nor'-West Farmer*, p. 740.

Lockhart, Olive. (1978). Autobiography. Accession No. 82–372. SAB.

Lyons, Alice. (1902, September 20). Letter. *The Nor'-West Farmer*, p. 829.

Lyons, Noble. (1902, June 20). Letter. *The Nor'-West Farmer*, p. 506.

MacDonald, J. (1901, September 20). Letter. *The Nor'-West Farmer*, p. 598.

MacPhail, Bert. (1902, April 21). Letter. *The Nor'-West Farmer*, p. 332.

MacPhail, Edna. (1902, April 21). Letter. *The Nor'-West Farmer*, p. 333.

MacPhail, Edna. (1902, August 5). Letter. *The Nor'-West Farmer*, p. 697.

Macpherson, Bas. (1910). Letter—personal correspondence. Accession No. 8.79/6. PAA.

Major, M. (1902, February 20). A cheap roof for granaries. *The Nor'-West Farmer*, p. 139.

Marsh, Annie. (1902, April 21). Letter. *The Nor'-West Farmer*, p. 332.

Matz, Laura. (1978). Autobiography. Accession No. R-E321 #15. SAB.

McConnell, Ida. (1902, June 20). Letter. *The Nor'-West Farmer*, p. 506.

McDonald, Jessie. (1902, April 21). Letter. *The Nor'-West Farmer*, p. 333.

McDonald, Mabel. (1902, December 5). Letter. *The Nor'-West Farmer*, p. 1072.

McElhone, W.E. (1975). Interview. Accession No. 75–539. PAA.

McIntyre, W.E. (1902, June 20). Letter. *The Nor'-West Farmer*, p. 506.

McIver, Hugh. (1902, June 20). Letter. *The Nor'-West Farmer*, p. 506.

McLay, Alex. (1901, April 20). How to keep boys on the farm. *The Nor'-West Farmer*, p. 245.

McLean, Jas. (1901, September 5). Letter. *The Nor'-West Farmer*, p. 569.

McLeod, Charlie. (1902, October 6) Letter. *The Nor'-West Farmer*, p. 873.

McLeod, Evelyn. (1977). Autobiography. Accession No. 77.39. PAA.

McMahon, Wellington. (1902, June 20). Letter. *The Nor'-West Farmer*, p. 507.

McNaught, Isabel and Betty. (1976). Interview. Accession No. 81–279. PAA.

Middleton, Jessie. (1902, November 20). Letter. *The Nor'-West Farmer*, p. 1020.

Miles, Jim and Sophie. (1905). Letter—personal correspondence. Accession No. M843. PAA.

Miller, Annie. (1902, October 20). Letter. *The Nor'-West Farmer*, p. 917.

Miller, Otto. (1902, April 21). Letter. *The Nor'-West Farmer*, p. 333.

Mitchell, Agnes. (1900, January 20). Poem. *The Nor'-West Farmer*, p. 69.

Mitchell, Sylvia. (1976). Autobiography. Accession No. E-94. SAB.

Montgomery, L.J.W. (1898, March). The pioneer farm house. *The Nor'-West Farmer*, p. 129.

Montjoy, Cora. (1901). Autobiography. Accession No. R-E514 #12. SAB.

Montreal Herald (1886). What women say of the Canadian North West.

Moore, Willie. (1902, June 20). Letter. *The Nor'-West Farmer*, p. 506.

Morrow, Nancy. (1898, March). Letter. *The Nor'-West Farmer*, p. 131.

Moss, B.A. (1902, April 21). Letter. *The Nor'-West Farmer*, p. 332.

Moss, Beatrice. (1901, September 20). Letter. *The Nor'-West Farmer*, p. 598.

Moss, Norman. (1902, August 20). Letter. *The Nor'-West Farmer*, p. 740–741.

Mumby, Ina. (1902, November 20). Letter. *The Nor'-West Farmer*, p. 1020.

Murray, Jean. (1902, December 5). Letter. *The Nor'-West Farmer*, p. 1072.

Myer, Bertha. (1978). Biography. Accession No. R-E321 #19. SAB.

Ness, Violet. (1902, September 20). Letter. *The Nor'-West Farmer*, p. 829.

Northey, Eddie. (1902, August 5). Letter. *The Nor'-West Farmer*, p. 697.

Northey, Robert. (1902, August 5). Letter. *The Nor'-West Farmer*, p. 697.

Parkinson, Harriette. (1978). Autobiography. Accession No. R-E205. SAB.

Penhall, Annie. (1902, September 20). Letter. *The Nor'-West Farmer*, p. 829.

Phillips, Charles. (1967). Accession No. 67.99. PAA.

Potter, Harvey. (1901, September 20). Letter. *The Nor'-West Farmer*, p. 597.

Prout, Lena. (1902, November 20). Letter. *The Nor'-West Farmer*, p. 1021.

Pue, Pansey. (1975). Interview. Accession No. 75.27/4. PAA.

Rand, Ethel. (1901, September 20). Letter. *The Nor'-West Farmer*, p. 598.

Rand, William. (1901, September 20). Letter. *The Nor'-West Farmer*, p. 598.

Rayner, Florence. (1902, November 20). Letter. *The Nor'-West Farmer*, p. 1021.

Redfern, Alan. (1902, April 21). Letter. *The Nor'-West Farmer*, p. 333.

Rees, Anna. (1901, March 5). Our little ones. *The Nor'-West Farmer*, p. 148.

Reesor, William Colby. (1977). Autobiography. Accession No. 77.57. PAA.

Ririe, Horace. (1974). Interview. Accession No. 74.508/3. PAA.

Robinson, Bessie. (1902, November 5). Letter. *The Nor'-West Farmer*, p. 697.
Roff, Raymond. (1902, August 5). Letter. *The Nor'-West Farmer*, p. 697.
Roxburghshire Lad. (1902, August 5). Letter. *The Nor'-West Farmer*, p. 697.
Ruskin. (1900, June 5). Advice to young ladies. *The Nor'-West Farmer*, p. 435.
Russell, James. (1912). Diary. Accession No. M1087. PAA.
Sanford, F.A. (1898, April). The bright side of the farm. *The Nor'-West Farmer*, p. 178.
Shaver, Rose. (1902, October 20). Letter. *The Nor'-West Farmer*, p. 917.
Slater, Gertie. (1902, May 20). Letter. *The Nor'-West Farmer*, p. 420.
Smith, Amelia. (1975). Autobiography. Accession No. 81–279. PAA.
Smith, George. (1902, September 20). Letter. *The Nor'-West Farmer*, p. 829.
Smith, Kathleen. (n.d.). Autobiography. Accession No. R-E3289. SAB.
Spackman, Elmer. (1975). Interview. Accession No. 75–562. PAA.
Stewart, Ruby. (1902, November 20). Letter. *The Nor'-West Farmer*, p. 1020.
Stringer, Herbert. (1888). Letter—personal correspondence. Accession No. 85.2 SE. PAA.
Strong, Madge. (1968). Autobiography. Accession No. 68.93/1–5. PAA.
Taylor, Stanley. (1902, September 20). Letter. *The Nor'-West Farmer*, p. 829.
Thompson, Doris. (1979). Autobiography. Accession No. R-E514#26. SAB.
Tipping, J.L. (1900, July 5). Baching in the North-West. *The Nor'-West Farmer*, p. 563.
Tucker, Selena. (1902, May 20). Letter. *The Nor'-West Farmer*, p. 420.
Tudhope, Mary. (1902, December 5). Letter. *The Nor'-West Farmer*, p. 1072.
Turnbull, Elizabeth. (n.d.). Autobiography. Accession No. R-E321#30. SAB.
Turner, Marion. (1902, October 6). Letter. *The Nor'-West Farmer*, p. 873.
Useful hints. (1900, May 5). *The Nor'-West Farmer*, p. 354.
Vance, Clarence. (1902, August 5). Letter. *The Nor'-West Farmer*, p. 697.
Waddell, Mary. (n.d.). Autobiography. Accession No. R-E695. SAB.
Walker, Agnes. (1979). Autobiography. Accession No. R-E514#25. SAB.
Wathen, Harry. (1975). Interview. Accession No. 75–421. PAA.
Watson, John. (1975). Interview. Accession No. 75.317. PAA.
Weir, Anne. (1976). Interview. Accession No. 81.279. PAA.
What other women have found out. (1908, August). *The Nor'-West Farmer*, p. 52.
White, Agnes. (1902, June 20). Letter. *The Nor'-West Farmer*, p. 506.
White, Mabel. (1902, August 20). Letter. *The Nor'-West Farmer*, p. 740.
Whitehead, Aylmer. (1902, October 20). Letter. *The Nor'-West Farmer*, p. 917.
Wightman, Katherine. (1902, August 20). Letter. *The Nor'-West Farmer*, p. 740.
Wilkie, Mary Salina. (1950–56). Pioneer questionnaires. Accession No. SX2 1294. SAB.
Williamson, Lillian. (1902, August 20). Letter. *The Nor'-West Farmer*, p. 740.
Williamson, Meta. (1902, August 20). Letter. *The Nor'-West Farmer*, p. 740.
Wilson, Eliza. (1901). Diary. Accession No. A W749. PAA.
Wilson, Leddie. (1902). Letter—personal correspondence. Accession No. M1320. PAA.
Winstone, Gertrude. (1902, November 20). Letter. *The Nor'-West Farmer*, p. 1020.
Winter, Bertie. (1902, May 20). Letter. *The Nor'-West Farmer*, p. 420.
Wood, John Henry. (1976). Autobiography. Accession No. 76.45. PAA.
Woolf, Delia. (1974). Interview. Accession No. 74.474/4–6. PAA.
Wright, Albert. (1902, April 21). Letter. *The Nor'-West Farmer*, p. 332.
Wright, E.O. (1901, September 5). Letter. *The Nor'-West Farmer*, p. 568.
Wright, Fred. (1902, April 21). Letter. *The Nor'-West Farmer*, p. 332.
Wright, Oliver. (1902, April 21). Letter. *The Nor'-West Farmer*, p. 332.
Youth of Sixteen. (1898, November). Advice to boys. *The Nor'-West Farmer*, p. 528.

Census Material, Legislation, and Cases:

First Census of the Canadas 1870–71, Ottawa, Ontario
Second Census of Canada 1880–81, Ottawa, Ontario
Third Census of Canada 1890–91, Ottawa, Ontario
Fourth Census of Canada 1901, Ottawa, Ontario
Report on the Census of the Northwest Provinces, 1906
Fifth Census of Canada, 1911, Ottawa, Ontario
1916 Census of Prairie Provinces
Sixth Census of Canada, 1921, Ottawa, Ontario
Dominion Lands Act, 1872 (Canada)
The Infants Act, 1918–19 (Saskatchewan)
The North-West Territories Acts of 1875 and 1877, 1875 and 1877 (Canada)
An Ordinance Respecting the Administration of Civil Justice, 1886 (North-West
     Territories)
An Ordinance Respecting the Personal Property of Married Women, 1889, (North-West
     Territories)
An Ordinance to Facilitate the Conveyance of Real Estate by Married Women, 1886 (North-
     West Territories)
Murdoch v. Murdoch [1974], 13 RFL 185 (SCC)

Index

Names without a title (such as "Mrs.") refer to children.
Italic locator numbers refer to illustrations or figures.

and survival, 81
  See also boys; girls
Gilliland, Annie, 119, 125
girls
  appearance, 115–16
  and building, 38–39, 41–42
  and domestic labour, 16, 111, 112–17
  and entrepreneurial labour, 61–62
  junior-level tasks, 136
  and productive labour, 44, 48–49
  and subsistence labour, 81–82
  See also gender; marriage
goats, 93
gophers, 74–76, 95–96, 102, 153n8, 153n9
Graham, Bill, 56, 103
grain
  crop, 8, 50-51, 53, 151n7
  "prairie chewing gum", 75
  See also harvesting
Grain Growers' Guide, 24, 115
Griffiths, Florence, 72, 93
grubstakes, 101
guns. *See* firearms

Hamlen, Arthur, 50
Hamlen, Gordon, 54
handwriting, 64
Hanson, Mrs. J.D., 23
Hardy, Edwin, 71
Harrigan, Sue, 30, 48–49, 93, 104
harrowing, 48, 49, 50, 148n2
harvesting
  gardens, 78, 99
  grain, 151n5
  hay, 51–53
  labour diversion to, 45, 155n1(ch7)
  meals for, 51, 120
  wild fruits, 99–101
  women's role, 6
Hawthorne, Mabel, 34, 135
hay, 41, 51–53
Hayne-Stephenson, Frederick, 48
health. *See* danger; injuries; medical benefits
  of farm life
Henderson, Martin, 46, 73
hens. *See* chickens
herding. *See* cattle; pigs; sheep
Hickely, Mr. S.G., 45
Hiemstra, Mary, 37–38, 95, 104, 128–29
Hillson family, 26, 31–32
Hislop family, 67, 94, 95
Hislop, Johnnie, 41
Hislop, Nellie, 34–35, 41, 52, 94, 152n2

Hogg, Robert, 152n2
hogs. *See* pigs
Holmes, Gladys, 117, 153n6
home. *See* domestic labour; houses
homesteading, 14, 20, 26–32, 137, 150n14,
  156n4
horses
  caring for, 54, 67, 71, 91, 93
  driving, 58, 116, 151n7
  numbers of, 152n5
  owned by children, 71, 72, 116
  riding, 63
  runaways, 47
  working with, 43–44, 47, 51, 53, 56, 148n2
housecleaning, 104, 111–12, 114, 116–17, 122–24
housekeeping. *See* domestic labour
houses
  building, 4, 26–30, 37–40, 138–39, 153n4
  finishing, 30–31, 39, 114, 150n11, 150n16
  maintaining, 31–35, 150n13
  temporary, 37
  See also housecleaning
housework. *See* domestic labour
Houston, Ethel, 58–59
Houston, Pearl, 58–59
Houston, "Son," 58
Hunt, Verne, 71, 90
Hunt, Winnifred, 71, 90
hunting
  for bounties, 74–76
  for food, 77, 93–96, 154n13–14
  for furs, 76–77
  and gender, 95
Hyndman, Mildred, 30, 107, 117–18

implements, 47–51, 148n1–2, 151n2, 151n5–6
individual, family over, 24
The Infants Act, 156n6
injuries, 47, 49, 154n16. *See also* danger
insects, 32, 102–04, 154n15, 154n17–18,
  155n1(ch6)
investing, 71, 79
invisible workers, x, 8, 11

Johnson, Amelia, 155n1(ch7)
Johnson, Lucy, 84, 85–86, 91–92, 139, 149n9
Johnston, Jennie, 49, 120, 154n3
Jones, Alfred, 79

Keeping, Blanche, 121, 124, 128
Keeping, Florence, 128
Kennedy, Gladys, 32, 33, 107
Kent, Lottie, 118

survival
family, 89, 59, 60, 68–69, 81, 108–09, 126, 133–34, 138–42
and gender, 81
as motivation for work, 24

Taylor, Stanley, 92–93
teaching, 70, 113–15, 119, 124, 126, 137
tents, 37, 107
Thompson, Doris, 54, 156n2
Tipping, J.L., 20
training. *See* careers; teaching
trapping, 75–77, 96–97
tree felling, 37, 44–45, 151n1
Tucker, Selena, 92
Tudhope, Mary, 123
turkeys, 93, 104
Turnbull, Elizabeth, 52, 69
Turner, Marion, 92
typology of labour, 14–16

value of children's labour, 9, 60, 131, 133, 135, 137, 139–43, 155n1(ch7)
values, teaching through labour, 24
Vance, Clarence, 93
vegetables, 78–79, 97–101. *See also* gardening
voluntariness of work, 139, 144

Waddell, Mary, 26, 91, 119
wages
given to the family, 61, 66, 67, 68, 152n2, 152n4
in-family, 143–44
See also paid employment
Walker, Agnes, 121–22, 155n6
washing. *See* blankets; clothing; domestic labour
water
hauling, 120, 121–22, 127, 147n2
for livestock, 54, 150n17, 153n1
supplies, 82–87, 93, 121, 154n16, 155n2, 155n4
treatment and quality, 83–85, 147n2, 154n1(ch6)
Wathen, Harry, 75, 89
Watson, John, 26–27, 66–67, 89, 151n8
weasels, 104
weather
cold, 26–27, 37, 74, 98, 149n8, 150n17, 153n4
hail, 102, 154n16
rain, 33–34, 150n15
and school attendance, 147n4
snow, 147n4, 149n10, 150n17, 155n2

winds, 149n9–10
weeding, 50–51, 97, 98
Weir, Anne, 56, 68
wells, 84, 85–87, 153n2
wheat. *See* grain
White, Agnes, 118
White, Mabel, 100
Whitehead, Aylmer, 48
Wightman, Katherine, 121, 125
Williamson, Lillian, 93
Williamson, Meta, 119
Wilson, Eliza, 149n10
Wilson, Leddie, 27, 95, 150n18
Wilson, Mrs. Eliza, 59
Winstone, Gertrude, 51
winter. *See* weather
Winter, Bertie, 121, 123
wolves, 74, 76, 77, 104
women. *See* feminist theory; marriage; mothers
Women's Grain Growers Club, 119
Wood, Bill, 67–68
Wood, John, 67–68
Wood, John Henry, 94
Woolf, Delia, 97, 100, 130
work ethic, 10
Woychyk, Elizabeth, 126
Wright, Albert, 93
Wright, E.O., 154n8
Wright, Fred, 59
Wright, Oliver, 73

Yeomans, Mrs. G.M., 23
"Youth of Sixteen" (pseud.), 125

Zeller, Clarence, 96

CLEVERLY COMICAL ANIMAL JOKES

Animal Cracker Uppers

RICHARD LEDERER & JIM ERTNER

International Punsters of the Year

ILLUSTRATIONS BY JIM MCLEAN

Marion Street Press

Portland, Oregon

To my wife, Ruth, who has always encouraged me to write joke books for kids. —Jim Ertner

To the creators and supporters of the San Diego Zoo and Safari Park. —Richard Lederer

Published by Marion Street Press
4207 SE Woodstock Blvd # 168
Portland, OR 97206-6267
USA
http://www.marionstreetpress.com/

Orders and review copies: (800) 888-4741

Printed in the United States of America
ISBN 978-1-936863-15-0

Library of Congress Cataloging-in-Publication Data Pending

CONTENTS

PART 2
Even More Animal Jokes

INTRODUCTION

Animals
> leap and bound,
>> climb and swing,
>>> flap and flutter,
>>>> and scuttle and splash

through our everyday lives.

Animals live in our language:
> "gentle as a lamb,"
>> "sly as a fox,"
>>> "free as a bird,"
>>>> "loose as a goose,"
>>>>> and "mad as a hornet
>>>>> (or a wet hen)."

Animals become symbols of athletic excellence:
> the St. Louis Rams, the Anaheim Ducks,
>> the Florida Marlins,
>>> and the New Orleans Hornets.

And everybody loves animal jokes:

Dinosaur jokes are too old, and antelope jokes are gnu. Giraffe jokes tell tall tales. They may be over our heads, but we look up to them.

Chihuahua jokes are short and Dachshund jokes are long, but Retriever jokes are fetching, Dalmatian jokes hit the spot, and Boxer jokes have great punch lines.

Here are more than 500 animal jokes that are guaranteed to make you

honk,

hoot,

squawk,

and squeal

with lots of laughter.

PART 1
A DICTIONARY
OF ANIMAL JOKES

Aardvark

Aardvark and no play make Jack a dull boy.

What do aardvarks eat for breakfast?
Aard boiled eggs.

Alligator

Did you hear about the alligators that joined the FBI?
They were investigators.

What do you cook alligator meat in?
A croc pot.

Amoeba

Why did the amoeba cross the biology lab?
To get to the other slide.

Animals (in general)

Why can't some animals keep secrets?
Because parrots talk, pigs squeal, yaks yak, and someone always lets the cat out of the bag.

Did you hear about the allergic animals at the zoo?
They broke out.

Why isn't farming an easy life?
You go to sleep with the chickens, get up with the roosters, work like a horse, eat like a pig, and they treat you like a dog and pay you chicken feed.

Ant

Why was the young insect confused?
All his uncles were ants.

Where do insects go when they want to eat?
To a restaur-ant.

What's the opposite of a restaurant?
A worker-ant.

What kind of insect is good at math?
An account-ant.

What two insects come here from foreign countries?
Immigr-ant and import-ant.

What is an insect's favorite continent?
The Ant-arctic.

Ape

Where do monkeys get their gossip?

From the ape-vine.

What does the government use when it takes a census of all the monkeys in zoos?

An ape recorder.

What does a monkey do when he feels sorry for something he did?

He offers an ape-ology.

Baboon

A cowboy took his young son to the zoo for the first time. While they were standing in front of the baboon's cage, the boy asked what the animal was. The rancher replied, "It must be a cowboy judging by the way that the seat of its pants is worn off."

Basset Hound

What do you call a dog that plays a guitar?
A bassist hound.

Bat

What floats in the ocean, but only at night?
A bat buoy.

Beagle

Did you hear about the dog that was inducted into the Boy Scouts?

He was a beagle scout.

Did you hear about the woman who taught her dog to open safes?

It was a locks and beagle act.

Bear

Did you hear about the advertising executive's version of a fairy tale?

"Once upon a time, there were three bears: the small size, the regular size, and the giant economy size."

What cuddly little bear complains all the time?

Whine-y the Pooh.

What did the teddy bear say when he was done eating?

"I'm stuffed!"

Did you hear about the newspaper editor who wanted to cover the story about the birth of a baby bear at the zoo?

She sent a cub reporter.

Beaver

Why did the misbehaving pet beaver chew the furniture?

Because it was gnawty.

Bee

What is black and yellow on the outside and black and yellow on the inside and drives down the street like crazy?
> *A school bus full of bees.*

What's worse than being with a fool?
> *Fooling with a bee.*

What does a lumberjack bee use to cut down trees?
> *A buzz saw.*

What do you call an insect with a low buzz?
> *A mumble bee.*

What do you call a tenor bee?
> *An opera stinger.*

What do bees chew?
> *Bumble gum.*

What did the bees do after they finished building their hive?
> *They had a house swarming.*

Why did the farmer cross his bees with fireflies?
> *He wanted them to work at night.*

When does B come after U?
> *When you take some of its honey.*

Bird

What bird is chocolate on the outside and vanilla on the inside?
> *A Baltimore Oreo.*

What sign did the two birds place above their nest?
> *"Home Tweet Home."*

Did you hear about the two lovebirds that got married?
They were childhood tweethearts.

What do birds say on Halloween?
"Twick or tweet."

Bloodhound

Why do bloodhounds have a lot of money?
Because they're always picking up cents.

How is a bloodhound like a tall basketball player?
They're both centers.

Boa

What do snakes wear with a tuxedo?
A boa tie.

Boxer

Why did the dog go to the corner when the doorbell rang?
It was a Boxer.

Buck

Who was the first deer astronaut?
Buck Rogers.

Buffalo

Did you hear about the herd of 10,000 buffalo that Canada sold to the United States?
America received a buffalo bill.

Show us a home where the buffalo roam, and we'll show you a messy house.

Bug

Why was there a bug in the computer?
It was looking for a byte to eat.

Did you hear about the exterminator's slogan?
"As soon as you call, we step on it."

What keeps out bugs and shows movies?
Screens.

Bulldog

Dad: "Why are you making faces at that bulldog?"
Son: "He started it."

Burro

What's the most important donkey in New York City?
The burro of Manhattan.

Butterfly

Did you hear about the tailor who thought that a butterfly was a zipper on the front of a stick of margarine?

Camel

What do Arab soldiers use to hide from their enemies in the desert?

Camelflage.

What do you call a camel with three humps?

Humpthree Bogart.

Canary

A woman brought along her pet canary each day that she drove to work.

The little bird was her flying car pet.

What warning did the veterinarian give after hearing that a pet canary swallowed a gun?

"Beware of cheep shots."

What kind of canary does a bargain hunter shop for?

A cheaper cheeper.

Carp

Why do rug salesmen like to keep a certain type of fish in their home?

Because they love carp petting.

Cat

How can you tell that a cat likes inclement weather?

Because when it rains, it purrs.

What kind of feline likes bowling?

An alley cat.

When do cats and dogs get along together?

When you have hot dogs with catsup.

Did you hear about the cat who robbed McDonald's and Wendy's?

She was a cat burgerlar.

Did you hear about the cat who entertained himself with a piece of yarn?
After a while he had a ball.

What did the fast cat put in his litter box?
Quicksand.

Caterpillar

Did you hear about the new book titled *From Caterpillar to Butterfly*?
It's by Chris A. Liss.

Cattle

Is it easy to milk a cow?
Yes, any little jerk can do it.

When was beef the highest?
When the cow jumped over the moon.

Where did the cow go when it jumped over the moon?
It went to the Milky Way.

What do Alaskans call their cows?
Eskimoos.

Farmer No. 1: "I have 200 cows on my farm."
Farmer No. 2: "Yesterday you told me that you had 199 cows."
Farmer No. 1: "That was before I rounded them up."

Why do cows have bells around their necks?
Because their horns don't work.

Centipede

What goes 99-thump, 99-thump, 99-thump?
A centipede with a wooden leg.

What did the centipede say to the octopus?
"You're missing 92 feet."

What lies on the ground a hundred feet in the air?
A centipede on its back.

Did you hear about the speedy centipede that won a race by a hundred feet?

Chameleon

Why is a chameleon good in the kitchen?
It's a good blender.

Chicken

Why did the apple farmer's chicken cross the road?
To get to the other cider.

What did Barbie, the play director, do when the actor playing Chicken Little forgot his lines?
Barbie cued the chicken.

What noise does Rice Chickies cereal make?
"Snap, cackle, and peep."

What do you call a chicken boxer?
A bantamweight.

What illness did everyone on the *Enterprise* catch?
Chicken Spocks.

What do you say to a chicken before a performance?
>*"Break an egg!"*

If the chicken had used his noodle, then he wouldn't be in the soup.

Chihuahua

A Chihuahua is a Great Dane after taxes.

Chimpanzee

What is a chimp's favorite energy bar?
>*Monkey bars.*

What is a monkey's favorite dessert?
>*Chocolate chimp cookies.*

Chow Chow

A woman was showing off her recently purchased pet to a neighbor and said, "This is my new dog."
The neighbor asked, "A chow?"
And the woman replied, "Gesundheit."

Clam

Did you hear about the clever clam who owned a nightclub in San Francisco?
Samuel, the owner, featured a harpist who accompanied the dancing music. One morning, the musician realized he had forgotten his instrument and he began singing, "I left my harp in Sam Clam's disco."

Cockatoo

What is a cockatoo called after it's two years old?
>*A cockathree.*

Cockroach

Show us an arrogant insect, and we'll show you a cocky roach.

Cod

What fish wears spurs and a cowboy hat?
> *Billy the Cod.*

Collie

What are dog biscuits made from?
> *Collie flour.*

Crab

What is a fisherman's favorite fruit?
> *Crab apples.*

What is a crab's favorite newspaper column?
> *"Dear Crabby."*

Crane

What bird can lift the most?
> *A crane.*

Cricket

Who wore a coonskin cap and played a British game?
> *Davy Cricket.*

Crocodile

What reptiles prefer old-fashioned telephones?
> *Croco-dials.*

While on a safari in Africa, a man decided to take a refreshing swim in a river. He asked the guide if there were any sharks in the water and was assured that there were none.

After diving in, the man shouted to the guide, "Are you absolutely sure there are no sharks in here?"

"No sharks," came the reply. "Sharks are afraid of crocodiles."

Crow

What is a ghost's favorite kind of bird?

A scare crow.

Did you hear about the scarecrow?

It was so scary that the crows not only stopped stealing corn, but they also brought back the corn they stole the year before.

Dachshund

What do you give a dachshund with a fever?

Mustard. It's the best thing for a hot dog.

Why are dachshunds mean?

Because they're low-down dogs.

Did you hear about the mascot for the boating club?

It was a Dockshund.

Deer

What do you call a deer with no eyes?
No idea.

What do you call a deer with no eyes and no legs?
Still no idea.

If a female deer has antlers, then does a male deer have unclers?

Dinosaur

How do we know that dinosaurs raced?
Because archeologists have found dinosaur tracks.

What dinosaur roamed the Wild West?
Tyrannosaurus Tex, riding his Bronco-saurus.

Why did some dinosaurs opt to live on land and others in the water?
It was either slink or swim.

What was the scariest dinosaur?
The terror-dactyl.

What dinosaurs ate burritos and enchiladas?
Tyrannosaurus Mex.

Doe

How did the doe win the race?
By passing the buck.

Dog

Why did the dog keep running around in circles?
> *He's a watchdog, and he's winding himself up.*

Did you hear about the veterinarian who was so sick of treating dogs that he threw a distemper tantrum?

Two guys were talking about a dog with no nose.
"How does he smell?" asked one.
The other replied, "Awful."

Did you hear the story about the dog that ran after a stick for three miles?
> *OK, we admit that it's too far-fetched.*

Patient: "Doctor, doctor! I think I'm a dog."
Psychiatrist: "Lie down on the couch."
Patient: "I'm not allowed on the furniture."

What did Elvis teach his dog?
> *To rock 'n roll over.*

What does a dog do that a man steps into?
> *Pants.*

Dragon

Why do dragons sleep during the day?
> *So they can hunt knights.*

Why don't baby dragons like knights?
> *They hate canned food.*

Duck

What is a duck's favorite snack?
Cheese and quackers.

What do you call an unemployed duck?
A fired quacker.

Who's the most famous duck explorer?
Sir Francis Drake.

Why was the duck so smart?
Because it always made wisequacks.

There was a fowl special on TV that was a duckumentary. It had a ducky introducktion that showed ducks vacationing in both North and South Duckota.

Eagle

Those who hope that Congress will pass laws to ensure a safe environment for our national bird are lobbying for an Eagle Rights Amendment.

Why did the eagle sit atop the church steeple?
It was a bird of pray.

Eel

Did you hear the story about the slippery eel?
Never mind. You wouldn't be able to grasp it.

What do electric eels do after earthquakes?
They generate aftershocks.

Egret

Bird No. 1: "Are you sorry that you waded so far out into the lake?"

Bird No. 2: "No, I have no egrets."

Elephant

Why did the elephant wear dark sunglasses?
> *So he wouldn't be recognized.*

What did Tarzan say when the elephant came up over the hill?
> *Nothing. He didn't recognize the elephant because it was wearing dark sunglasses.*

Why do elephants paint their toenails red?
> *So they can hide in the cherry trees.*

But there aren't any elephants in cherry trees!
> *See, their camouflage is working.*

How did Tarzan die?
> *Picking cherries.*

What would you get if Batman and Robin were trampled by a herd of elephants?
> *Flatman and Ribbon.*

Ewe

Ad in a farmer newspaper: "Used ewes are cheap sheep."

Fawn

What do you call a good time among young deer?
Fawn and games.

Finch

What do you call a close race between two canaries?
A photo finch.

Firefly

What did the mother firefly say to her husband while looking at their son?

"He's bright for his age, isn't he?"

Why did the firefly cross the road?

Because the light was with her.

As the firefly said, "When you gotta glow, you gotta glow."

Fish

How do you communicate with a fish?

By dropping it a line.

Why are fish more intelligent than human beings?

They stay in schools their whole lives. And have you ever seen a fish spend a lot of money trying to hook a human?

Did you hear about the fight in the seafood restaurant?

Two fish got battered.

Sign at a seafood market: "Our fish come from the best schools."

Sign at another fish market: "If our fish were any fresher, they'd be insulting."

Flea

Did you hear about the mathematical flea?

It adds to your misery, subtracts from your pleasure, divides your attention, and multiplies like crazy.

How did the flea travel around the country?

By Greyhound.

A man was reading Bible stories to his young grandson, "The man named Lot was warned to take his wife and flee out of the city, but his wife looked back and was turned into a pillar of salt."

The young lad asked, "What happened to the flea?"

Here is the world's shortest poem (titled "Fleas"):

> *Adam*
> *Had 'em.*

And remember: The pest things in life are flea.

Flounder

Flounder Fisherman No. 1: "How's business?"
Fisherman No. 2: "Sales are floundering."

Fly

A mother fly and her daughter were walking across the head of a bald man, when the mother observed, "How quickly times change. When I was your age, this was just a footpath."

Did you hear about the guy who went fly-fishing?

He caught a two-pound fly.

Why do some insects have a knack for swarming around you when you start a picnic?

Because flies time when you're having fun.

Fowl

Why did the basketball player sit on the sideline and sketch pictures of chickens?

He was learning how to draw fowls.

Chickens use fowl language.

Frog

What did the frog say when he split his trousers?

"Rip it! Rip it!"

A frog went to a fortuneteller and was told that he'd soon meet an attractive young woman who would get very close to him and who would have an intense desire to learn more about him. "Where will I meet her?" the frog asked excitedly. "On a blind date?"

"No," replied the fortuneteller, "in Biology class."

Did you hear about the frog who hung a flag on a tadpole?

What happened when two frogs tried to catch the same fly?

They ended up tongue-tied.

What are a frog's favorite games?

Hopscotch and croquet.

Gander

Why did the chicken and the goose cross the road?

So the chicken could take a gander on the other side.

Gibbon

Did you hear about the man who rescued a drowning ape from frigid water?

The owner of the ape decided to give him the blue gibbon.

Giraffe

Giraffes are the highest form of life, and at school they have the highest marks.

Why do giraffes have such long necks?
Because their head is so far from their body.

Why are giraffes the snobbiest animals in the jungle?
Because they look down on everything.

A short poem on a tall subject:
Just think how long a tall giraffe
Would take to have a belly laugh.

Why do giraffes have such small appetites?
Because a little goes a long way.

Gnat

What kind of bugs bother spacemen and spacewomen?
Astro-gnats.

Gnu

Why are gnus more clever than dogs?
Because you can't teach an old dog gnu tricks.

What is it called when you feel as if you've seen a strange-looking animal before?
Déjà gnu.

There once was a gnu in a zoo
Who tired of the same daily view.
To seek a new site,
He stole out one night,
But where he went gnobody gnu.

Goat

Why did the goat eat some fluorescent tubes?
He wanted a light lunch.

Did you hear about the angry farmer?
Someone got his goat.

Goldfish

Did you hear about the bankrupt goldfish?
It became a bronzefish.

Why did the man surround his goldfish bowl with postcards?
So the fish would think they were getting somewhere.

Goose

What happened to the man who was charged with stealing geese from farms all over the county?
He was accused of leading police on a wild goose chase.

What kind of birds live in Lisbon?
Portugeese.

Gopher

What animal makes the best butler?
A gopher.

Gorilla

What do you call chest-thumping and limb-swinging?

Gorilla tactics.

Why did the female gorilla go on a diet?

To keep her gorillish figure.

Grasshopper

A biology student conducted a scientific experiment. He shouted, "Jump!" at a grasshopper, and the insect jumped. He then removed one of the grasshopper's legs and shouted, "Jump!" and the insect jumped. The results were identical with each of the ensuing four amputations. However, when he cut off the sixth leg and shouted, "Jump!" the insect lay motionless. The student concluded that when all six legs have been removed, a grasshopper becomes deaf.

Greyhound

One flea to another: "I'm taking a Greyhound to the city."

Groundhog

Did you hear about the swine who bought a thousand acres of farmland for development?

He was a real ground hog.

Haddock

Two guys were fishing when one of them caught a fairly large fish and exclaimed, "I think I got a haddock."

The other fellow replied from the opposite end of the boat, "Then why don't you take an aspirin?"

Hare

What do you call the tending of rabbits?
Hare care.

A rabbit owner was disappointed. She washed her hare and couldn't do a thing with it. She had a bad hare day.

A happily hopping hare suddenly collapsed in front of a barbershop. The barber grabbed one of his cans of spray and emptied it on the furry little animal. The hare rapidly recovered and, showing its gratitude, gestured with its paw as it hopped away.

This shows that the can has the right directions to deal with the problem: "Hair spray. Restores life in dead hair. Adds permanent wave."

Hawk

What kind of hawk has no wings?
A tomahawk.

Heifer

What did the bull groom say to his cow bride?
"I will love you for heifer and heifer."

Hen

Why did the soldiers throw eggs at the enemy?
Because they were hen grenades.

A beggar asked a farmer for an egg every day for a month. The farmer eventually inquired why the poor man didn't request a large number at one time. The man replied, "You shouldn't put all your begs in one ask it."

"It is not in my nature to fiddle,
And thumbs I am lacking to twiddle,"
Said the hen as with pride
She laid sunny-side
Two fried eggs on a piping hot griddle.

The lovesick hen was smitten by the metal rooster atop the barn. "You're so vane," she clucked.

It must be eggsasperating reading all these eggscentric and eggsotic puns on eggs. We could try to eggsplain that they are really eggscellent, eggsceptional, and eggsplosive eggsamples of eggsclusive, eggsquisite, eggsalted, eggstatic, and eggshiliarating literary genius! We just eggspress our hope that you don't become eggscessively eggshausted and eggspire!

Hippopotamus

What weighs over a ton and thinks it's always sick?
> *A hippochondriac.*

Hog

What did the carpenter exclaim after his pigsty was broken into?
> *"I don't have mahogany more."*

They've just discovered a long-lost Elvis Presley song about a pig swept away in a flood.
> *It's called "You Ain't Nothing but a Drowned Hog."*

Horse

A dumb guy couldn't tell the difference between his two horses. A friend suggested measuring the two, which is how the guy discovered that the brown horse was two inches taller than the white one.

Why do horses have six legs?
> *Because they have forelegs in front and two legs behind.*

Why is the old, decrepit horse named Flattery?
Because it gets you nowhere.

What is a jockey's motto?
Put your money where your mount is.

How did the horse avoid participating in a joust?
It got the knight off.

How do jockeys determine which racehorses are the favorites?
By taking a Gallop poll.

Owner: "Did you find my horse well-behaved?"
Guest: "Yes, indeed. In fact, whenever we came to a fence, he let me over first."

Hyena

What happened when the hyena swallowed a bouillon cube?
He made a laughing stock of himself.

Insect

A couple spread their blanket in the woods, when the lady commented, "What a lovely place for a picnic."

"It must be," replied the man. "Ten million insects can't be wrong."

Jackass

A couple was chatting one evening when the wife asked her husband what the differences were between a sigh, a car, and a jackass. When the husband couldn't guess, the wife said, "A sigh is 'Oh, dear!' and a car is 'too dear.'"

"Then what's a jackass?" he asked.

She replied, "You, dear."

Jellyfish

What does a jellyfish have on its tummy?

A jelly button.

Kangaroo

When does a kangaroo jump the highest?

In a leap year.

How can a zookeeper tell when a kangaroo is getting old and run down?

When it's often out of bounds.

> *When a sailor in Santa Fe's zoo*
> *Snatched a cute little baby kangaroo,*
> *Its mother said, "Jack,*
> *You can put it right back.*
> *You know picking my pocket's taboo."*

What do kangaroos like to read?
Pocketbooks.

What did the mother kangaroo say when the clerk in the supermarket line asked her if she wanted "paper or plastic"?
"Pouch."

Kid

Or, as one goat said to another, "I kid you not."

Kipper

A herring and a whale were fine friends, and they even traveled in the same school together. On a rare occasion, another fish noticed the herring swimming alone and asked where his friend was. "How should I know?" replied the herring. "Am I my blubber's kipper?"

Kitten

Why are kittens such good TV announcers?
They have wee paws for station identification.

Koala

What is a koala from outer space?
An Austr-alien.

Labrador

What dog is the most popular with scientists?
A laboratory retriever.

Lemming

Why was the lemming so hesitant?
He didn't want to jump to a conclusion.

Leopard

A leopard went to see an optometrist because he thought he needed an eye exam. "Every time I look at my wife," he worriedly told the optometrist, "I see spots before my eyes."

"So what's to worry about?" replied the doctor. "You're a leopard, aren't you?"

"What's that got to do with anything?" replied the patient. "My wife is a zebra."

Lion

Why do lions never eat leftovers?
Because they always have gnu meat to eat.

What happened to the man who tried to cross a lion with a goat?
He had to get a new goat.

What was the name of the film about a killer lion that swam underwater?
"Claws."

A mother lion scolded her child for chasing a hunter around a tree: "How many times must I tell you not to play with your food before you eat it?"

Why did the lion feel sick after he'd eaten the pastor?
Because it's hard to keep a good man down.

Or, as one lion said to another, "Let us prey."

Lizard

A cruise ship captain made an announcement: "I have some good news and some bad news. The bad news is that the refrigeration system failed, the food has spoiled, and we have nothing to eat except lizards. The good news is that there aren't enough lizards to go around."

Llama

Why are llamas easily frightened animals?
Because it's easy to a llama them.

Lobster

What lobster visits you on Christmas Eve?
Santa Claws.

Locust

How do insects save money?
They live in locust housing.

Lox

One salmon said to another salmon, "Lox of luck."

Lynx

A wildcat that has disappeared is a missing lynx.

Mole

Have you ever met a mole with a woman on its cheek?

Monkey

What were King Kong's last words?
"Don't monkey around with me."

The best way to make a monkey out of a man is to ape him.

How did the monkey go from the second floor to the first floor?
She slid down the banana-ster.

Mosquito

Why was the young mosquito actress so happy?
She passed her first screen test.

Moth

Why didn't the baby moth cry after being spanked?
Because it's hard to make a moth bawl.

Mouse

What has six eyes but can't see?
Three blind mice.

What is a cat's favorite foods?
Mice Krispies, Minute Mice, and Mice Cream.

A mouse in her room woke Miss Dowd,
She was frightened, almost screamed aloud;
But a happy thought hit her:
To scare off the critter,
She sat up in bed and meowed.

How are mousetraps like the measles?
Both are catching.

Did you hear about the new mousetrap that tempts mice with music?
It plays a catchy, snappy tune.

What city has the most mice and cattle?
Mousecow.

Mule

A mule is a stubborn animal that is backward about going forward.

Nag

Did you hear about the man who met his future wife at the racetrack?

He went there to bet on a nag, and he wound up saddled with one for life.

Newt

What do salamanders like to watch on TV at night?
>   *The evening newts.*

Boy No. 1: "Why do you call your pet salamander Tiny?"
Boy No. 2: "Because he's my newt."

Nightingale

What singing bird did King Arthur value highly?
>   *Knightingales, even though they made for many
>   sleepless knights.*

Ocelot

Who was King Arthur's favorite animal knight?
Sir Ocelot.

Octopus

An octopus is an eight-sided cat with only one life.

What did the octopus take with him on a camping trip?
Tentacles.

What does an octopus wear?
A coat of arms.

Orangutan

What do you call a monkey's answering machine?
A who-rang-utang.

Ostrich

An ostrich is the giraffe among birds.

Otter

Where do alien web-footed mammals live?
In otter space.

Owl

Many a woman tries to change her night owl into a homing pigeon.

As the sea captain announced to his bird passenger, "Owl aboard!"

Patient: "Doctor, doctor! I know a man who thinks he's an owl."
Doctor: "Who?"
Patient: "Now I know TWO people."

Ox

What university is also the favorite car of cattle?
Oxford.

Oyster

An oyster met an oyster, and they were oysters two;
Two oysters met two oysters, and they were oysters, too;
Four oysters met a cup of milk, and they were oyster stew.

There was a woman who was so polite that she wouldn't open an oyster without knocking on its shell first.

Parrot

A parrot is a mocking bird.

Why did the talking bird join the Air Force?
He wanted to be a parrot-trooper.

A man gave his wife a parrot for her birthday, complete with ribbons attached to the bird's legs. When the woman pulled one ribbon, the parrot said, "Happy Birthday." When she pulled the other ribbon, the parrot said, "I love you."

The woman then mused, "I wonder what would happen if I pulled both ribbons at once."

The parrot replied, "I'd fall off my perch."

Peacock

How many eggs can a peacock lay in a year?
None. Peacocks don't lay eggs. Peahens do.

Peacocks pay careful attention to de tail.

Pelican

What do you call a big-billed bird with a negative attitude?
A pelican't.

Why do pelicans carry fish in their beaks?
Because they don't have any pockets.

Penguin

What is a penguin's favorite vehicle?
An ice-cycle.

What do penguins wear to keep their heads warm?
Polar ice caps.

Pet

Sign in a veterinarian's waiting room: Back in 10 Minutes. Sit! Stay!

Pheasant

As one game bird said to another, "Pheasant greetings to you."

Pig

One pig said to another on a very hot day, "I never sausage heat."

The other pig replied, "Yeah, and I'm almost bacon."

What do you call a dancing pig?
Shakin' bacon.

What do you call someone who steals pigs?
A hamburglar.

What's the best move by a pig that knows karate?
A pork chop.

Did you hear about the pig who built himself a home?
He made a knot in his tail and called it a pig's tie.

Pigeon

Patient: "Doctor, doctor! My wife insists on keeping a goat in the bedroom, and the smell is terrible."
Doctor: "Why not open a window?"
Patient: "What? And let all the pigeons out?"

Polar Bear

What is an Arctic bear's favorite sport?
Polar vaulting.

Polliwog

Did you hear about the parrot that married a frog?
They had a pollywog.

Pony

How is a person coming down with a sore throat like buying a small pony?

In both cases, you're getting a little horse.

Poodle

Did you hear about the dog that enjoys having his hair washed every day?

He's a shampoodle.

Porcupine

What pine has the sharpest needles?

The porcupine.

As the baby porcupine said when it bumped into a cactus plant during the night, "Is that you, Mom?"

Did you hear about the two porcupines that fell in love?

They got stuck on each other.

Praying Mantis

Did you hear about the religious insect?

It was a praying mantis.

How do praying mantises gather?

In sects.

Puppy

What sounds does a baby dog's favorite breakfast make?

Snap, crackle, and pup.

Quail

Who's boss between a father and mother quail?
Neither. They're e-quail.

Rabbit

Where does the Easter Bunny get his eggs?
> *From an eggplant.*

What's a rabbit's favorite dance style?
> *Hip-hop.*

> *A bit of a pest is the rabbit.*
> *When she spies your lettuce, she'll grab it.*
> > *Then she'll sing a ballad*
> > *About eating a salad—*
> *A tasty and quite healthy habit.*

Did you hear about the egg-laden rabbit that jumps off bridges?

He's called the Easter Bungee.

Ram

What is a sheep's favorite football team?

The Rams.

Rat

What is a mouse's favorite dish?

Ratatouille.

Rattlesnake

Before going on his first camping trip, the cautious camper asked his doctor what he should do if a rattlesnake bit him in the arm.

"Have a friend cut open the wound and suck out the poison," advised the medical man.

"Suppose I get bitten in the leg?" asked the man.

"Follow the same procedure," added the doctor.

"What should I do," persisted the man, "if I happen to sit down on a rattlesnake?"

"In that case," responded the doctor, "you'll find out who your real friends are."

Reindeer

Among the reindeer who pull Santa Claus's sleigh, you surely know about Olive, the other reindeer.

Robin

Did you hear about the sheriff who named his pet robin Hood?

Rooster

What did the boss rooster tell his employee?
> *"Don't be a cluck watcher."*

What famous chicken once lived in the White House?
> *Teddy Roostervelt.*

Salmon

What is a young fish's favorite game?
   Salmon says.

Sand Dollar

How did the sea urchin pay for his meal?
   With a sand dollar.

Scallop

Why did the shell fisherman scratch his head?
His scallop itched.

Seagull

What bird enjoys soccer?
A gull keeper.

As one seagull said to another after easily deceiving him, "You're so gullible."

As another seagull said to another as they flew over a casino, "This one's on the house."

Seahorse

Did you hear about the performing seahorses?
They get wave reviews.

Seal

What is a seal's favorite subject in school?
ART-ART-ART.

What sea animals pose no hazards for kids?
Childproof seals.

Seeing-Eye Dog

Did you hear about the two seeing-eye dogs who went on a blind date?

I wanted to join the army, but they wouldn't take me. My seeing-eye dog had flat feet.

Shark

What is a shark's favorite hobby?
Anything he can sink his teeth into.

Two coworkers were talking when one commented, "I saw a man-eating shark at the aquarium."
"Big deal," replied the other. "I saw a man eating mahi-mahi in a restaurant."

Sheep

Little girl: "Baaa, baaa, black sheep, have you any wool?"
Black sheep: "What do you think this is? Nylon?"

Did you hear about the two sheep that were shorn identically?
It was shear and shear alike.

What is a ewe's second favorite football team (after the St. Louis Rams)?
Navy, since everything is kept sheep-shape.

Why did the sheep call the police?
Because he'd been fleeced.

A tourist asked a farmer how many sheep he had. "I don't know," was the reply. "Every time I try to count them, I fall asleep."

Sheepdog

What animal goes, "Baaa! Woof! Baaa! Arf!"?
A sheepdog.

Shellfish

Here's an old tongue twister (repeat five times rapidly): *selfish shellfish.*

Shrew

Did you hear about the astute mouse-like mammal?
He was very shrewd.

Skunk

The vicar of crowded Bombay
Met a skunk that was passing his way.
The skunk gave a squirt,
So the smell's on the shirt
Of the vicar, who said, "Let us spray."

How are skunks able to avoid danger?
By using their instincts and common scents.

Are skunks good at games?
No, they stink at everything.

Why did the mother skunk take her baby to see the doctor?
Because it was out of odor.

Skunk mother: "What do you want to be when you're older?"
Skunk kid: "A big stinker."

What is the feeling that you've smelled a certain skunk before?
Déjà phew.

Snail

Did you hear about the two snails that got into a fight?
They really slugged it out. (It was a real slugfest.)

How fast does a mollusk travel?
At a snail's pace.

Where can you find giant snails?
At the end of giants' fingers.

A snail was gradually crawling up an apple tree during the winter. A squirrel spied the slowly moving snail and said, "You're wasting your time. There aren't any apples up there."

The snail replied, "There will be when I get there."

Snake

Why don't snakes do well at school?
Because they can't raise their hands to answer the teacher's questions.

What is a snake's favorite subject in school?
Hisstory.

Did you hear about the nearsighted snake?
He fell in love with a rope.

What is a snake's favorite vegetable?
Coily-flower.

Spider

Why was the spider late for her date?
It took her so long to put in eight contact lenses.

Did you hear about the spiders that just got married?
>*They're newlywebs.*

When do spiders go on their honeymoon?
>*After their webbing day.*

Squid

Who was the infamous pirate octopus?
>*Captain Squid.*

Squirrel

What do you call a crazy squirrel in a spaceship?
>*An astronut.*

How do you catch a squirrel?
>*You climb a tree and act like a nut.*

Steer

What is the favorite movie of cattle?
>*Steer Wars.*

Stork

That boy is so nasty that his mother should have kept the stork and thrown him away.

Swine

What telephone number does a pig dial when it needs help?
>*Swine-One-One.*

Termite

Did you hear about the termites that invited themselves to dinner?

They ate a family out of house and home.

Or, as the termite comedian said, "This one will bring the house down."

Tick

Did you hear about the stupid guy who put bug spray on his watch to get rid of the ticks?

What do you call crazy arachnids?
  Loony ticks.

What do you call arachnids that crawl around your mouth?
  Lips ticks.

Tiger

What marching song do you get when you cross the ape man with a tiger?
  "Tarzan Stripes Forever."

What is a tiger's favorite book?
  Revenge of the Tiger, by Claude Ribbs.

Toad

Did you hear about the angry amphibian on the highway?
  He suffered from toad rage.

What kind of shoes do frogs wear?
  Open-toad sandals.

What goes "dot-dit-dit-dot-croak"?
  A Morse toad.

Tuna

How do you tuna fish?
Adjust its scales.

Why do some men prefer to go fishing alone?
Because they think tuna boat is one too many.

Turkey

Did you hear about the woman who ate so many leftovers after Thanksgiving that she decided to quit cold turkey?

Why couldn't the turkey eat any more?
Because it was stuffed.

Which side of the turkey has the most feathers?
The outside.

What shows that turkeys are good at arithmetic?
They count the number of chopping days until Thanksgiving.

As the mother turkey said to her misbehaving daughter, "If your father could see you, he'd turn over in his gravy."

Turtle

What do fashion-conscious turtles wear?
People-neck sweaters.

What was the turtle doing on the turnpike?
About four feet an hour.

Unicorn

As one mythical creature said to another, "Unicorniest guy I ever met."

Vampire

Did you hear about the unsuccessful vampire hunter?

He tried to kill a vampire by driving a porkchop through its heart because steaks were too expensive.

What do you get when you cross Long John Silver with a vampire?

You get a vampirate.

Knock, knock.
Who's there?
Ivan.
Ivan who?
Ivan to drink your blood.

Why are there so many vampires in Hollywood?
Somebody has to play the bit parts.

How did the race between two vampires end?
They finished neck and neck.

Vampire's are happy knowing that there's a sucker born every minute.

Vulture

What did one vulture say to another?
"I've got a bone to pick with you."

Weevil

What kind of insects are found in tenpin alleys?

Bowl weevils.

Werewolf

Why do werewolves love to eat sheep?

So they can dine and floss at the same time.

Whale

Who was the strongest man in the Bible?
> *Jonah, because even the whale couldn't keep him down.*

How did Jonah feel after the whale swallowed him?
> *Down in the mouth.*

Why did the whale release Jonah?
> *Because he couldn't stomach him.*

What does Jonah have in common with a fire siren?
> *They both have big wails.*

Wolf

Where do wolves stay on vacation?
> *At the Howliday Inn.*

Why are wolves like playing cards?
> *Because they belong to a pack.*

Woodpecker

Why did the homeowner get mad at the woodpecker?
> *He was sick and tired of saying, "Come in."*

Did you hear about the poor fellow who was a real blockhead?
> *Woodpeckers followed him everywhere.*

Worm

As one worm said to another, "You're late for our meeting. Where in earth have you been?"

What happened to the worm in a cornfield?
It went in one ear and out the other.

What's worse than biting into an apple and finding a worm?
Finding half a worm.

Did you hear about the bird that flew into a library?
It was looking for bookworms.

Yak

What is the favorite children's story in Tibet?
  "Yak the Giant Killer."

Or, as the Tibetan chef exclaimed when he smelled something burning in his oven, "Oh, my baking yak!"

Zebra

Why did the horse break into the jail?

> *He wanted to impersonate a zebra by standing behind bars.*

Did you hear about the dumb guy who bought a pet zebra?

> *He named it Spot.*

Zebu

As the Frenchwoman commented at the zoo, "Asian oxen are zebu-tiful animals."

PART 2
EVEN MORE
ANIMAL JOKES

50 Rhyming Animals

Have you ever seen a regal beagle, a free bee, a poor boar, a stuck buck, a funny bunny, an enamel camel, a sharp carp, an odd cod, a drab crab, a slow crow, a golfin' dolphin, a braggin' dragon, a lucky ducky, a steel eel, a silly filly, a rounder flounder, a grander gander, a fibbin' gibbon, a loose goose, a super-duper grouper, a deafer heifer, a coarse horse, a hipper kipper, an itty-bitty kitty, a stark lark, a cryin' lion, a mama llama, a fair mare, a white mite, a chunky monkey, a cloth moth, a cute newt, a hotter otter, a pleasant pheasant, a phony pony, a misbehavin' raven, a sobbin' robin, a real seal, a dark shark, a selfish shellfish, a punk skunk, a fake snake, a narrow sparrow, a dear steer, a fine swine, a stern tern, a jerky turkey, a shorn unicorn, a diesel weasel, and a pale whale?

20 Animals In Restaurants

A waiter was bringing food to the table of her customer, a moth. She tripped and then said to the moth, "I'm sorry. I made the butter fly."

Another waiter managed to spill an entire Thanksgiving dinner. He feared he had created an international incident and exclaimed, "This is the downfall of Turkey, the ruin of Greece, and the breaking up of China!"

A flounder was dining in a seafood restaurant when he started frantically waving his empty glass in the air. One waiter said to another, "I think there's a fish out of water over there."

A deli restaurant tried to lure new customers with the promise that they'd pay you $15 if you ordered a sandwich they couldn't make. A smart aleck ordered an elephant-ear sandwich. After several minutes, the waiter returned from the kitchen and gave the customer $15, saying they couldn't make that sandwich.

The customer said, "I didn't think you could find elephant ears."

"Oh, it's not the ears," replied the waiter. "We're out of those big buns."

Customer: "Waiter, I've changed my mind. I don't want chicken soup. I want pea soup."

Waiter [shouting to cook]: "Hold the chicken! Make it pea!"

Customer: "Is it OK to eat fried chicken with my fingers?"

Waiter: "No, you should eat your fingers separately."

Customer: "Waiter, the chicken you served me is nothing but skin and bones."

Waiter: "Just a minute. I'll get you some feathers."

Waiter: "Would you like a hero sandwich?"
Customer: "No, thanks. I'm the chicken type."

Customer: "I'd like some crocodile soup."
Waiter: "Yes, ma'am. I'll make it snappy!"

Customer: "I think there's something wrong with this hot dog."
Waiter: "How should I know? I'm not a veterinarian."

Waiter: "How is your duck dinner, sir?"
Customer: "It isn't all it was quacked up to be."

Customer: "I'd like a gnu steak."
Waiter: "How about something as good as gnu?"

Customer: "I'm hungry enough to eat a horse."
Waiter: "You came to the right place."

Customer: "I'd like a nice lobster tail."
Waiter: "Once upon a time, there was a nice lobster…"

Customer: "Waiter, this lobster has only one claw."
Waiter: "He was probably in a fight."
Customer: "Then bring me the winner."

Waiter: "Our special tonight is twin lobsters."
Customer: "How can they tell?"

Customer: "Waiter, are raw oysters healthy?"
Waiter: "I've never heard one complain."

Customer: "Waiter, does the chef have frog's legs or pig's feet?"

Waiter: "I don't know, ma'am. He has his trousers and shoes on."

Customer: "How do you serve shrimp in this restaurant?"

Waiter: "We bend down."

Customer: "Waiter, I've been waiting a half hour. Where are my snails?"

Waiter: "If you wanted fast food, you shouldn't have ordered snails."

10 Classroom Classics

Teacher: "This essay you wrote, 'My Dog,' is the same as your brother's paper."
Student: "It's the same dog."

Teacher: "How do you spell *farm*?"
Student: "E-I-E-I-O."

Teacher: "Did you know that a single fly has millions of offspring?"
Student: "How many offspring does a married fly have?"

Teacher: "What would Thanksgiving dinner be like if the Pilgrims had landed in Africa instead of America?"
Student: "I don't know, but I'd sure hate to try to stuff a hippopotamus."

Teacher: "I asked you to draw a horse and cart, but you only drew a horse."
Student: "The horse will draw the cart."

Teacher: "Name the sexes."
Student: "Male sex, female sex, and insects."

Teacher: "Name nine animals from Africa."
Student: "Eight lions and a giraffe."

Teacher: "What steps would you take if you saw a lion charging you?
Student: "The longest steps I could."

Teacher: "Taurus the bull, Pisces the fish, and Cancer the crab are all animal signs of the zodiac. What is another one?"
Student: "Mickey the mouse."

Teacher: "Swimming is an ideal exercise for losing weight."
Student: "Try telling that to a whale!"

15 Animal Crossings

What do you get when you cross two punsters with a hen?

Two comedians who lay eggs with a lot of bad yolks.

In these days of genetic miracles, you never can tell what you'll end up with when you combine one animal with another animal.

What do you get when you cross . . .

. . . a lion with a lamb?

Something that's wild and woolly.

. . . a camel with a cow?

Lumpy milkshakes.

. . . a mink with an octopus?

A fur coat with too many sleeves.

. . . a parrot with a shark?

An animal that talks your ear off.

. . . an ostrich with a turkey?

A bird that buries its head in the mashed potatoes.

. . . a bear with a dog?

Winnie the Poodle.

. . . a chicken with a centipede?

We don't know, but EVERYONE gets a leg.

. . . a parrot with a lion?

An animal that says, "Polly wants a cracker—NOW!"

. . . a penguin with a zebra?

An animal in a striped tuxedo.

. . . a woodpecker with a homing pigeon?
A bird that knocks on your door before delivering a message.

. . . a terrier with a bulldog?
A terribull.

. . . a deer with a hornet?
Bambee.

. . . a small parrot with a kangaroo?
Budgie jumping.

. . . a vampire with a duck?
Count Duckula or Count Drakeula.

. . . a vampire with a moose?
Vamoose!

15 Animal Contrasts

What's the difference between racing dogs on a hot day and the authors of this book?

> *The dogs run and pant, while the authors of this book pun and rant.*

And what's the difference between . . .

. . . a horse trainer and a tailor?

> *One tends a mare, and the other mends a tear.*

. . . grizzly embraces and lice?

> *The first are bear hugs, and the second are hair bugs.*

. . . a run-down hotel and a banner for a hive?

> *One is a fleabag, and the other is a bee flag.*

. . . a counterfeit coin and a crazy rabbit?

> *One is bad money, and the other is a mad bunny.*

. . . sacks of dough and rabbit periodicals?

> *One is money bags, and the other is bunny mags.*

. . . a miser and a canary?

> *One is a little cheap, and the other a little cheeper.*

. . . an Indian elephant and an African one?

> *About 3,000 miles.*

. . . muddy cows and a royal war?

> *One is brown cattle, and the other is a crown battle.*

. . . a coyote and a flea?

> *One howls on the prairie, and the other prowls on the hairy.*

. . . a deer and a small witch?

> *One is a hunted stag, and the other is a stunted hag.*

. . . St. George and Rudolph the red-nosed reindeer?

> *One slays the dragon, and the other's draggin' the sleigh.*

. . . a racehorse and a duck?

> *One goes quick on its legs, and the other goes quack on its eggs.*

. . . an elephant and a flea?

> *An elephant can have fleas, but a flea can't have elephants.*

. . . an aching vulpine and two pair of stockings?

> *The first is a sore fox, and the others are four socks.*

. . . a father gorilla, a bald-headed man, and a crown prince?

> *One is a hairy parent, one has no hair apparent, and one is an heir apparent.*

30 Daffynitions

Somebody once defined *buoyant* as "a male insect." Such "daffynitions" take a fresh approach to the sounds of familiar words, and some of the daffiest can be found in the animal kingdom:

Antelope: When an insect runs off to get married.

Aqueduct: A waterfowl.

Atom: A male cat.

Barstool: What Davy Crockett stepped in.

Behold: What bee wrestlers use in matches.

Braid: How the donkey made noise.

Buttress: A nanny goat.

Camelot: Where humped animals are parked.

Catacomb: An implement for grooming felines.

Catsup: Where the cat goes when the dog chases it.

Chinchilla: Aftershave skin bracer.

Cranium: That part of the zoo where cranes are kept.

Distinct: De smell a skunk makes.

Dreadlocks: Fear of smoked salmon

Extinct: A dead skunk.

Furlong: Yak hair.

Grammatical: Pertaining to the matriarch of the tick family

Isolate: The White Rabbit's exclamation in *Alice in Wonderland*.

Jaywalker: Somebody who takes birds for walks.

Mammoth: The mother of all butterflies.

Moon: What cows are always doin'.

Myth: A female moth.

Otter: What water becomes as you heat it.

Pigmy: A midget hog.

Polygon: A missing parrot.

Polynesia: Memory loss in parrots.

Questionable: What to do upon discovery of a dead matador.

Shampoo: A fake bear.

Wholesale: Where a gopher goes to buy a new home.

Wow!: Half a dog bark.

10 Knock-Knock Jokes

Knock, knock. *Who's there?* Yoda. *Yoda who?* Yoda best knock-knock jokester we've ever met!

Knock, knock.
Who's there?
Alpaca.
Alpaca who?
Alpaca trunk, and you pack a suitcase.

Knock, knock.
Who's there?
Badger.
Badger who?
Too badger got a chip on your shoulder.

Knock, knock.
Who's there?
Catgut.
Catgut who?
Catgut your tongue?

Knock, knock.
Who's there?
Gillette.
Gillette who?
Gillette the cat out?

Knock, knock.
Who's there?
Hence.
Hence who?
Hence lay eggs.

Knock, knock.
Who's there?
Jupiter.
Jupiter who?
Jupiter fly in my soup?

Knock, knock.
Who's there?
Llama.
Llama who?
Llama Yankee Doodle Dandy.

Knock, knock.
Who's there?
Ocelot.
Ocelot who?
You ocelot of questions.

Knock, knock.
Who's there?
Rhoda.
Rhoda who?
Rhoda horse and now I'm sore.

Knock, knock.
Who's there?
Yukon.
Yukon who?
Yukon lead a horse to water, but you can't make it drink.

Knock, knock. *Who's there?* Orange. *Orange who?* Now orange you glad that you read all these knock–knock jokes?

10 Worst Animal Maladies

- a centipede with athlete's foot, corns, and fallen arches
- a giraffe with a sore throat and a stiff neck
- a dragon with bad breath and hiccoughs
- a lion with laryngitis
- an elephant with a runny nose
- a turtle with claustrophobia
- a parrot with a stutter
- a hen with a hernia
- a mountain goat that's afraid of heights
- a Dalmatian with measles

40 Animal Anagrams

An anagram is a rearrangement of all the letters in a word or group of words to form another word or group of words. Thus, *wolf* and *fowl* are anagrams of each other because they both contain the same letters but each in a different order.

In the examples that follow, all the letters in each animal's name form all the letters in the word or words that come before or after that name:

Have you ever seen a low owl, a mall llama, a nut tuna, bare bear, calm clam, dog god, shore horse, tan ant, leaf flea, dread adder, tar rat, rat art, ram arm, wasp paws, asp spa, wee ewe, toga goat, raked drake, paroled leopard, seal sale, reed deer, ranged gander, garden gander, cabaret bearcat, gnat tang, snail nails, swine wines, grade-B badger, one-sail sea lion, salty pup platypus, taco cook cockatoo, cop-outs octopus, hornet throne, wine-lover wolverine, a count toucan, upper coin porcupine, flub oaf buffalo, any he hyena, lo a girl gorilla, and the Nepal elephant?

15 Dog Palindromes

A palindrome is a word, like *pup*; a compound, like *pooch coop*; or a sentence, like STEP ON NO PETS, that communicates the same message both forwards and backwards. Have fun reading each statement and then in reverse.

REX: I'M A MIXER.

SALT A PUP, ATLAS.

STARK RABID, I BARK, "RATS!"

A DOG? A PANIC IN A PAGODA!

GODS RIDICULE LUCID IRS DOG.

GOD! NATE BIT A TIBETAN DOG.

TEN ALPO DOGS GO DO PLANET.

DRAW PUPIL'S PUP'S LIP UPWARD.

FOOL A POOR DOG. GO DROOP ALOOF.

GODDESSES SO PAT A POSSESSED DOG.

RISE, SIR LAPDOG–GOD, PAL. RISE, SIR.

GOD! A RED NUGGET! A FAT EGG UNDER A DOG!

DID I STEP ON DOG DOO? GOOD GOD! NO PETS! I DID!

"WARDEN IN A CAP," MAC'S PUP, SCAMP, A CANINE DRAW.

ARE WE NOT DRAWN ONWARD, PUP, DRAWN ONWARD
TO NEW ERA?

Collect the Whole Series!

IN STORES NOW!